WARRIORS
OF THE RIO GRANDE:
THE HISTORY OF MAVERICK COUNTY IN WWII

WARRIORS
OF THE RIO GRANDE:
THE HISTORY OF MAVERICK COUNTY IN WWII

WILLIAM J. MUNTER • JUDY MUNTER • JOLENE GARCIA

COMPILED BY:
WILLIAM J. MUNTER
JUDY MUNTER

Harrison House Publishing

Warriors Of The Rio Grande: The History Of Maverick County in WWII
Copyright ©2015. All Rights Reserved

This book may not be reproduced, transmitted, or stored in whole or in part by any means, including graphic, electronic, or mechanical without the express written consent of the publisher except in the case of brief quotations embodied in critical articles and reviews. Any reproductions without written permission from the publisher is illegal and punishable by law. Please purchase only from authorized distributors to protect the author's rights.

PUBLISHER'S NOTE
The opinions expressed in this manuscript are solely the opinions of the author in addition, do not represent the opinions or thoughts of the Publisher. The author has represented and warranted full ownership and/or legal right to publish all the materials in this book.

The publisher does not have any control over and does not assume any responsibility for author or third party websites or their content.

Harrison House Publishing
www.theharrisonhousepublishing.com
info@theharrisonhousepublising.com

Harrison House Publishing and the "HH" logo are trademarks belonging to Harrison House Publishing.

ISBN: 978-09861285-4-7

Library of Congress Control Number: 2015955965

Editing by Judy Munter, Ellen Munter Schwabe, Lisa Munter, Jolene Garcia

Book and cover design by Fishead Design Studio • www.fisheadproductions.com

Cover Photo: John Staggs from Quemado serving in the US Army Airforce in front of his B-24. Courtesy of John Stockley and the Fort Duncan Museum.

PRINTED IN THE UNITED STATES OF AMERICA

DEDICATION

This book is dedicated to the men and women, and their families, of Maverick County who endured the hardships of World War II, both at home and abroad. Many made the ultimate sacrifice and many more continued their lives with the emotional and physical scars of war.

Thanks to you and your sacrifices, the path of freedom was paved for citizens of Maverick County and the United States of America. You will never be forgotten.

TABLE OF CONTENTS

Preface	viii
WORLD WAR II	1
Brief History of World War II	2
War in the Pacific	6
Map of War in the Pacific	7-8
War in Europe	10
Map of the War in Europe	12-13
THE ROLL OF HONOR	14
THE HOMEFRONT	166
History of Maverick County	167
Eagle Pass Army Air Force Base	170
Women in World War II	175
Cadets and Soldiers Killed During Training	183
Military Influence on Eagle Pass and Maverick County	192
Discrimination and Racism	196
HOLOCAUST AND MAVERICK COUNTY	205
END OF THE WAR AND BEYOND	217
APPENDIX	220
Acknowledgements	221
Glossary	223
Medals of WWII	227
Bibliography	230

PREFACE

The idea for this book all began with a letter. It was a solicitation letter requesting donations from the National World War II Museum in New Orleans. The museum was collecting names of veterans from World War II to be placed in the "Roll of Honor," a computer bank listing those who served in World War II. I sent the names of my father, Lloyd Munter, and my two uncles, J.M. and Arnold Schwartz, to the museum to be included in the "Roll of Honor." I then began thinking of other people who had served in the war from Eagle Pass, Texas, my hometown. So began a remarkable journey of discovery. I collected stories and information, both oral and written, from approximately 900 men and women from Maverick County who had served in World War II. In the end, I developed a reverential bond with these men and women, as if they were my own uncles and aunts.

It is my wish that this book will become a source of pride to the families of those who unselfishly gave of themselves and to the sacrifices made by its citizens during the war effort. Maverick County had experienced a transformation, not seen since the days of the Mexican Revolution of 1910. It is my hope that this book will convey those changes brought by WWII.

It is also my hope that this book will become a reference book for students and others interested in gathering knowledge of how Eagle Pass and Maverick County were affected during the war years.

My Uncle, 1st Lt. Joseph Mayer (JM) Schwartz, a 1940 graduate from The University of Texas at Austin, was one of the many soldiers from Maverick County that died in WWII. Because of this tragedy, his memory influenced my whole family's lives in different ways.

Every Friday night, my grandmother, Ellen K. Schwartz, lit a candle for her son until she died at the age of 95. She was a member of the American Gold Star Mothers, which was formed after World War I to provide support for mothers who lost sons or daughters during war. It was a custom for family members of service members to hang a banner called a Service Flag in the window of their homes. Each gold star on the banner symbolized the death of a son or daughter.

My grandfather, Sam Schwartz, never talked about the death of his son, although he kept JM's photo displayed in his office for his entire life inside of the Aztec Theater, his only lament would be, "Poor JM never had a chance."

My mother, Yolanda S. Munter, always adored her older brother. She was very proud that he was an officer, soon to be promoted to captain.

JM's brother, my mother's twin brother, Arnold Schwartz was also highly influenced by JM. Arnold joined the army at the same time as his brother in 1942. After the war, Arnold became a huge fan of the University of Texas football team, JM's alma mater. His nickname became

PREFACE

"The Horn" because of his unrelenting support. Arnold named his son Joseph Mayer (Pepe) Schwartz, in honor of his older brother. Pepe and I also graduated from The University of Texas at Austin, therefore continuing to honor our uncle.

I was also personally influenced by his memory. Before JM went into the army in 1942 he worked for the American Consulate in Piedras Negras, Mexico. My Grandmother would tell me stories about his work there, such as, visiting the Kickapoo Indian Tribe in Nacimiento, Mexico monthly to deliver government checks. Because of these stories, I developed an interest in the Kickapoo Indian Tribe and went to visit Nacimiento. When I was in college, I wanted to become a consular officer like my uncle JM. I never took the consular entrance exam, but I did continue to follow my interest and became an immigration lawyer.

My father, PFC Lloyd T. Munter, was also a WWII veteran. He was born and raised in Brooklyn, New York and was drafted into the U.S. Army in 1943. After training to become an airplane mechanic, he was stationed at Eagle Pass Army Air Force Base from 1944-1945. He then met my mother at a Hanukkah party, hosted by my grandfather and grandmother, for Jewish soldiers stationed at the base. After the war ended, my parents married on May 19, 1946 in Eagle Pass. My Father went to work for my grandfather, Sam Schwartz, and never returned to New York. My father used to tell me interesting stories about the time he served in the U.S. Army.

This book is not to glorify war, but to recognize the disastrous changes and sacrifices of families of Maverick County during the war. It has inspired me to tell the stories of many of these soldiers and to recognize the names of all the veterans from Maverick County that served during WWII. We must never forget the bravery displayed by each of them during the most catastrophic event in the history of the world.

It has been my attempt to list every military member from Maverick County that served during WWII. A problem arose when trying to define those who were actually from Maverick County. The criteria we used is the following:

- Those born or raised in Maverick County
- Those who spent their adult lives in Maverick County
- Airmen stationed at Eagle Pass Air Force Base who married Maverick County women
- Those whose military discharge documents showed Eagle Pass or Maverick County as their home of record
- Men who joined the US armed forces from Piedras Negras and Northern Mexico.

Every service member listed in this book was important to the United States and its Allies during World War II. The length of the biographies is only indicative of the amount of information we were able to obtain, not of their significance during the war. All members lent their expertise in the war efforts and are equally respected.

Billy Munter

PREFACE

When my husband, Bill, and I began to write this book in 2009, I had a faint interest in World War II. After our visit to the World War II Museum in New Orleans in 2011, I realized this was really a story of my parents' generation. An intense interest was sparked within me on that trip and I have spent the last four years, along with Bill, collecting stories and information to catalog the lives of hundreds of service members.

David and Ruth Hoff, my parents, died in 2006 and 2009, respectively. I consider this book a memorial to them and their generation. Although they never openly discussed the war, I became curious about it and how it affected both of my parents. While attending college, my father kept a diary, and in it he referenced events surrounding the war. I learned, that after Pearl Harbor, he was inspired to volunteer for the Army, but for medical reasons was denied entry twice. This denial was devastating to him because he had no choice but to sit back and watch all of his close friends ship off in support of the United States, some never to return.

On December 7, 1941, as a nineteen-year-old sophomore at Raleigh School of Mines in Missouri, my father made this entry in his diary:

"It doesn't seem right that because there are a few greedy men in this world that thousands of men and women should die, while millions of others must live on to suffer. I have been against entering a shooting war, but now we have been forced into it, and we must fight not to win in the sense of winning, but for Freedom and Humanity. School suddenly seems very unimportant_____! We are forever changed."

Now I am honored to have the opportunity to tell my parents' story.

Judy Munter

WORLD WAR II

Brief History of WWII

From 1914 to 1918, the devastation caused by the First World War (WWI), threw Europe into a state of instability. The Versailles Treaty was the peace treaty that ended the state of war between Germany and the Allied Powers on June 28, 1919. Borders between countries were redrawn across Europe. WWI left the world in an economic and political chaos which led to several revolutions and new political leaders. This state of unrest set the stage for another international conflict: World War II (WWII).

From 1939 to 1945, over 100 million people from more than 30 different countries were engaged in military service. These nations were divided into two opposing alliances: the Allies and the Axis. The Allies included The United States, Britain, France, Soviet Union, Australia, Belgium, Brazil, Canada, China, Denmark, Greece, Netherlands, New Zealand, Norway, Poland, South Africa, and Yugoslavia. The Axis powers were Germany, Italy, Japan, Hungary, Romania, and Bulgaria. WWII was marked by an estimated 60 million fatalities, mostly civilians, to include approximately 11 million people who were systematically murdered in Nazi concentration camps, later became known as The Holocaust.

UNITED STATES

Following WWI, The Versailles Treaty was debated for six months, then finalized at the Paris Peace Conference. At the conference, United States President Woodrow Wilson proposed an international organization comprising of representatives of all the world's nations known as the League of Nations. This organization would serve as a forum preventing the escalation of any future conflicts.

European Leaders were fearful of any future wars and decided to strip Germany of all of its war-making capabilities to prevent them from being able to wage another war. Although not invited to attend, Germany was forced to sign the treaty, restricting its military and to concede much of their territories to Belgium, Poland and France. All German overseas colonies became the mandate of the League of Nations. Germany was forced to accept all responsibility for starting World War I, therefore was required to pay large sum in reparations.

After the Paris Peace Conference, President Wilson explained the peace treaty and his proposal for the international organization to Congress. Unfortunately, the United States Congress rejected the Versailles Treaty and consequently, the League of Nations. The United States felt that the oceans that separated us from the war in Europe were adequate protection. Americans felt that European problems were not our concern which eventually lead to isolationism. Between

1850 and 1930, the United States saw a large influx of over 25 million European immigrants: approximately 5 million Germans, 3.5 million British, and 4.5 million Irish, along with Italians, Greeks, Hungarians, and Poles. Due to this diversity, the United States felt it should remain neutral to the troubles that were brewing overseas. The Neutrality Act of 1937 was enacted by Congress, making it unlawful for the United States to trade with countries at war.

However, the United States wanted to prepare for war, just in case. The National Defense Act of 1920 passed by the United States Congress, authorized the Army to expand to more than 280,000 men, the largest in peacetime history. Although authorized, Congress never appropriated funds to pay for much more than half of the manpower.

After the Stock Market crash of 1929, the United States entered into the greatest economic crisis in history, known as The Great Depression. The banking system collapsed, people lost their homes and savings, companies went bankrupt, and farmers lost their farms. Over one fourth of the work age population was unemployed; some cities such as Toledo, Ohio, reached 80% unemployment. The middle class became non-existent and depended on "soup lines" to provide meals and prevent starvation. Before WWII started, nearly 50% of all white families and 90% of black families still lived in poverty. Franklin Roosevelt was then elected President of the United States, ensuring more direct relief and assistance. Between 1932 and 1938, President Roosevelt organized the New Deal Programs, the WPA, Social Security, US Housing Authority, Securities and Exchange Commission, Civilian Conservation Corp and many other agencies for depression relief.

In early 1939, due to the fear of the establishment of air bases in the Western Hemisphere by hostile forces, President Roosevelt organized a readiness campaign. This limited campaign placed Army volunteers in small garrisons throughout the continental United States, Hawaii, the Philippines, and Panama. Army and Navy leaders' devised new war plans to deal with an increasingly threatening international situation. The Signal Corps developed vast improvements in radio communication and practiced artillery attacks with the most sophisticated fire-control techniques in the world. The Army developed an interest in amphibious warfare that was being pioneered by the U.S. Marine Corps. By the outbreak of WWII, the Signal Corps was a leader in improving radio communications. General George C. Marshall took over as Chief of Staff, the Army remained hard pressed simply to carry out its mission of defending the continental United States, and consequently found themselves unprepared for the war that broke out in Europe on September 1, 1939.

ENGLAND AND FRANCE
With the loss of nearly 700,000 British soldiers and 1.5 million French soldiers killed in WWI, England and France suffered the loss of almost an entire generation of its men, which was referred to as the "lost generation." Because of this, England and France would do almost anything to avoid going into another war, which led to the policy of "appeasement." The Nazi leader, Adolph Hitler had already annexed Austria into Germany and the conquest of

Czechoslovakia was his next step. The British and French prime ministers, Neville Chamberlain and Edouard Daladier, along with the Nazi leader, Adolph Hitler, signed the Munich Pact on September 30, 1938, allowing Germany to occupy Sudetenland, Czechoslovakia. Chamberlain announced to the British people that the Munich Pact brought "peace with honor in our time."

During the 1930's, with the looming fear of German invasion, the French constructed a line of defense called the Maginot Line along the country's borders. The Maginot Line was a series of fortifications stretching from La Ferte to the Rhine River. However on May 10, 1940, nine months after WWII began, the Germans outflanked the line and invaded France through Belgium and Holland.

RUSSIAN EMPIRE

During WWI, the Russian Empire was engaged in civil war between the aristocratic class, led by Czar Nicholas II, and the Communists (the Bolsheviks). Even though the communists murdered the Czar and his family, the aristocratic class (White Russians) continued the fight. The Communists gained power in Russian, emerging new leaders - Vladimir Lenin, Josef Stalin & Leon Trotsky. Lenin, as the leader of the Communist Party, signed a separate peace treaty with Germany in 1917. The treaty included a clause that Russian would surrender territory to Germany. The war between England, France, and the United States against Germany continued until Germany formally surrendered on November 11, 1918. The formal agreement called the Versailles Treaty was not signed until June 28, 1919.

In 1922, Stalin became the dictator of the Russian Empire, now called the Soviet Union, after purging his government of real and imagined enemies. Trotsky was murdered in Mexico City. Lenin later died in 1924 of natural causes.

On August 23, 1939, The Soviet Union and Nazi Germany formed a mutual non-aggression pact, in the process splitting up Poland between Germany and the Soviet Union. Germany invaded Poland from the west on September 1, 1939 and Soviet troops invaded Poland from the east on September 17, 1939. With this invasion of Poland, England and France declared war on Germany, sparking the start of WWII. The non-aggression pact ended when Germany later invaded the Soviet Union in 1941.

POLAND

In 1939, England and France signed a series of military agreements with Poland for military aid in the case of German invasion. The leaders of Poland knew they could only defend themselves against Germany for a couple of weeks. Upon attack by German forces, the agreements were violated when England and France failed to come to Poland's aid. Poland was conquered and in fact, England and France agreed to allow the Soviet Union to keep the Polish territory that was seized in that attack. Poland suffered one of the worst occupations is history, roughly 6 million Poles were murdered or deported. After WWII, Poland was reconstituted as a communist state and forced to integrate with the Soviet Union.

ITALY

During WWI, Italy declared war on Germany after signing a secret treaty with France and England. In the treaty, France and England agreed that Italy would be given the Adriatic Coast (territories along the eastern coast of the Adriatic Sea) at the end of the war, if the Allies won. In the Versailles Treaty, France and England did not give the Adriatic Coast to Italy. With much unrest, high unemployment, and the unfulfilled promise from the Allies of WWI, Benito Mussolini promised to solve the nation's economic problems by bringing Italy up to the level of its great Roman past with the Fascist Movement. In October 1922, Mussolini was elected the youngest Prime Minister in Italian history. After employing his secret police, destroying all political opposition, and outlawing labor strikes, Mussolini and his fascist followers combined their efforts and created a series of laws designed to transform Italy into a one-party dictatorship. Free elections, free speech, and free press were abolished. In 1935, Italy laid clams on Ethiopia and conquered the country. This invasion was condemned by The League of Nations through economic sanctions, however this tactic proved ineffective due to the lack of support among the nations.

GERMANY

Under the Versailles Treaty, Germany lost around 13 percent of its home territory and all of its overseas colonies. Limits were placed on the size and capability of the country's armed forces and reparations were imposed. Many Germans, including a young Austrian born Adolph Hitler felt the Versailles Treaty was unfair. In 1933, the National Socialist German Workers' (Nazi) Party, led by Hitler, came to power. This was a mass movement that was anti-democratic and anti-Semitic. Hitler demolished democracy and created a totalitarian single-party state led by the Nazis and was appointed Chancellor of Germany. Securing a place to live for the German "master race" in Eastern Europe, was Hitler's main goal.

Adolph Hitler began planning Germany's invasion of Europe to recover the German territories lost to the Versailles Treaty. Between 1932 and 1939, Germany increased their Navy from 30 to 95 warships, their Air Force from 36 to 8,250 planes, and their Army from 100,000 to almost a million soldiers. Hitler's plan was to take over Belgium, Austria, France, and Russia within a few months. He figured that Great Britain was weak and America would not be a factor. Meanwhile, Germany signed strategic treaties with Italy and Japan to further Hitler's ambitions of world domination.

JAPAN

The worldwide Depression affected Japan very harshly. Combined with its militaristic history and its lack of resources, Japan looked to build an empire to dominate the Asia-Pacific area. Japanese propaganda called this "The Greater East Asia Co-Prosperity Sphere" or "Asia for Asiatics," however; in reality this was a move to control other Asian countries. Because Japan did not have enough natural resources within its borders, the government believed a sure way to remedy its economic and social woes was by occupying neighboring territories. Japan seized Manchuria in 1931 and declared war on China in 1937. In 1940, when Japan decided to invade the oil-rich Dutch East Indies (now Indonesia), the U.S. government along with Australia and England boycotted Japan via a trade embargo, stopping access to 90% of their oil supply.

Because of this embargo, Japan felt they had to either withdraw from China or take preventative actions to keep the U.S. Pacific Fleet from interfering with military actions planned in Southeast Asia and the Dutch East Indies. Bases manned by American's in the Philippines were in the perfect location to intercept and destroy lines of communication between the Japanese home islands and the East Indies. Every oil tanker with courses marked for Japan, would pass through the American controlled, Luzon area of the Philippines. From these needs and constraints, the Japanese created their war plans. Japan planned to neutralize the American fleet by engaging in a surprise attack on Pearl Harbor, Hawaii. Japan went on to capture American bases in central Pacific bases at Guam and Wake Island and invaded the Philippines.

Germany had already invaded the Soviet Union. Japan's leaders thought that Germany would conquer the Soviet Union within months of their attack on Pearl Harbor. Japan was convinced that the United States would be willing to negotiate peace in the Pacific.

THE WAR IN THE PACIFIC

PEARL HARBOR

The war in the Pacific began on December 7, 1941, when carrier based warplanes from Japan launched a surprise attack on Pearl Harbor. The most famous words spoken in Pearl Harbor were "Don't worry about it." by 2nd Lieutenant Kermit Tyler in response to a telephone call from Private Joseph Lockhard, who reported a large blip on the radar screen that was rapidly approaching Pearl Harbor. Tyler believed they were B-17's flying from California. (Dan Martinez, chief historian of the National Park Service at Pearl Harbor Memorial).

The attack on Pearl Harbor led to the declaration of war by the Japanese against the United States. The day after the attack, December 8, 1941, United States declared war on Japan and Germany declared war on the United States.

PHILIPPINES

In the aftermath of the Pearl Harbor attack, Japan began a massive campaign of expansion throughout the Southeast Asia–Pacific region, including the invasion of Guam, Wake Island, the Philippines, Dutch East Indies, Hong Kong, Malaya, Singapore, and Burma, which formed a heavily protected barrier with the islands in the south and the central Pacific.

The day after the attack on Pearl Harbor, the Japanese invasion of the Philippines (comprised of more than 7,000 islands) began. Japanese forces invaded and seized Manila, the capital of the Philippines. American and Filipino troops defending the island of Luzon, where Manila was located, were forced to retreat to the Bataan Peninsula. Without air or sea support, U.S. and Filipino troops fought for the next three months. Plagued by starvation and disease and the lack of naval and air support, U.S. General Jonathan Wainwright surrendered approximately 75,000 American and Filipino troops at Bataan. This was largest surrender in U.S. military history.

The surrendered troops were rounded up by Japanese forces and were forced to march 65 miles from Mariveles on the southern end of the Bataan Peninsula to San Fernando, in groups of approximately 100 men. This 5-day trek became known as the Bataan Death March. The exact figures are unknown, but it is believed that thousands of troops died because of the brutality of their captors, who starved and beat them and killed those too weak to walk. Survivors were transported via train from San Fernando to POW camps, where thousands of men died from disease, mistreatment, and starvation.

It was not until March 3, 1945, that the Americans liberated the Island of Luzon and Manila, rescuing the surviving captives from imminent death.

BATTLE OF MIDWAY

In spring of 1942 provoked by the Doolittle Air Raid where 16 medium bombers attacked military targets in Japan from the aircraft carrier, the U.S.S. Hornet, the Japanese Empire wanted to expand their protective barrier of islands by invading the island of Midway. Through the American intelligence breakthrough of solving the Japanese fleet codes, Admiral Chester Nimitz from Fredericksburg, Texas was able to intercept a radio message from the Japanese commander to his fleet about the plan of invasion. Acting upon this information, Admiral Nimitz sent an aircraft carrier task force to ambush the approaching Japanese Fleet at Midway. The 3 aircraft carriers, U.S.S. Yorktown, U.S.S. Hornet and U.S.S. Enterprise sailed to northeast of Midway (known as "Point Luck"). The U.S. Navy won a decisive victory over the Japanese. The battle of Midway was considered the turning point of the Pacific war.

THE SOLOMON ISLANDS AND GUADALCANAL

Between August 1942 and February 1943, the United States engaged Japan in a battle for the Solomon Islands, located near Allied shipping routes in the south-western Pacific. Allied forces carried out an invasion at Guadalcanal, as British and Indian forces battled Japanese forces in Burma. This was the beginning of the Japanese retreat from the Solomon Islands.

THE APPROACH TO JAPAN

General Douglas McArthur and Admiral Chester Nimitz planned the ultimate defeat of Japan through the strategy of island hopping. Rather than attacking Japan's Navy, the goal was to control and capture strategic islands along the path toward Japan to prepare for a possible invasion. The largest battles took place on the Japanese held islands of Guadalcanal, Leyte, Iwo Jima, and Okinawa which is the largest island of Ryukyu.

By the late spring of 1945, the majority of the territories seized by Japan had been liberated. Allied forces closed in on Japanese home islands and began heavy bombardment against major Japanese cities, including Tokyo. The bombing continued through the summer of 1945 until finally, in early August, the United States dropped two atomic bombs on the cities of Hiroshima and Nagasaki. Overwhelmed by the immense devastation, Japan surrendered days later.

The occupation of Japan by the Allied Powers began on August 28, 1945. On September 2, 1945,

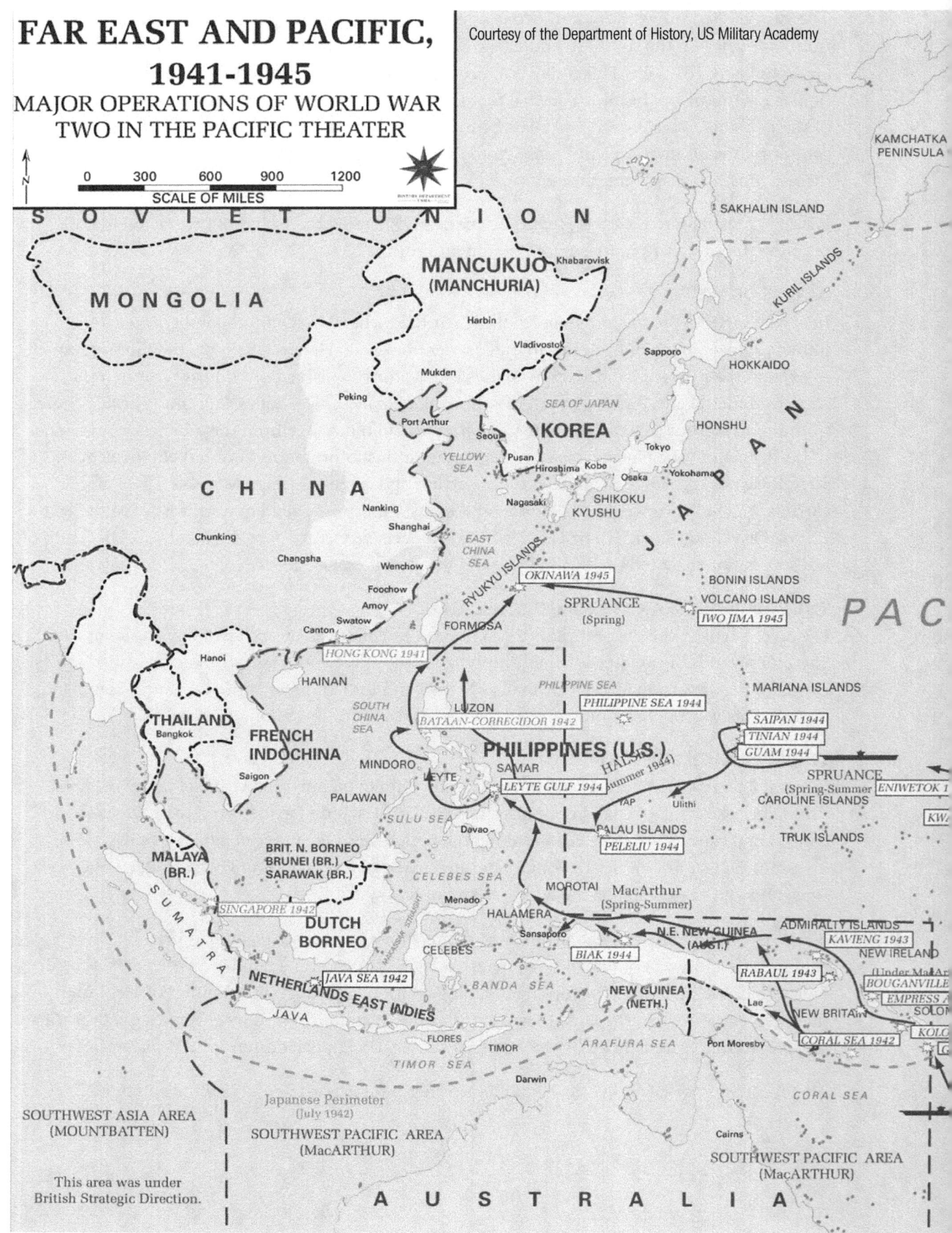

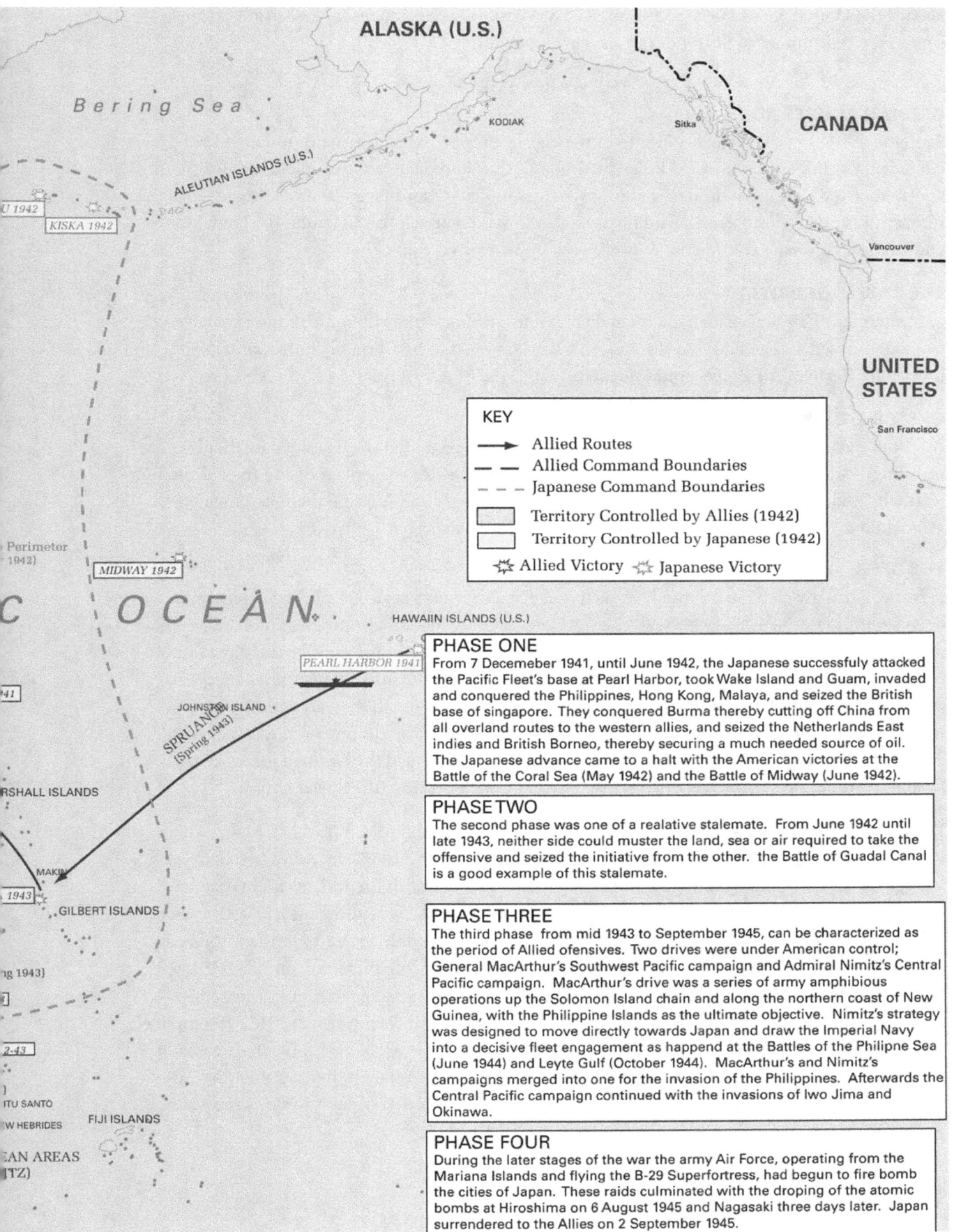

PHASE ONE
From 7 Decemeber 1941, until June 1942, the Japanese successfuly attacked the Pacific Fleet's base at Pearl Harbor, took Wake Island and Guam, invaded and conquered the Philippines, Hong Kong, Malaya, and seized the British base of singapore. They conquered Burma thereby cutting off China from all overland routes to the western allies, and seized the Netherlands East indies and British Borneo, thereby securing a much needed source of oil. The Japanese advance came to a halt with the American victories at the Battle of the Coral Sea (May 1942) and the Battle of Midway (June 1942).

PHASE TWO
The second phase was one of a realative stalemate. From June 1942 until late 1943, neither side could muster the land, sea or air required to take the offensive and seized the initiative from the other. the Battle of Guadal Canal is a good example of this stalemate.

PHASE THREE
The third phase from mid 1943 to September 1945, can be characterized as the period of Allied ofensives. Two drives were under American control; General MacArthur's Southwest Pacific campaign and Admiral Nimitz's Central Pacific campaign. MacArthur's drive was a series of army amphibious operations up the Solomon Island chain and along the northern coast of New Guinea, with the Philippine Islands as the ultimate objective. Nimitz's strategy was designed to move directly towards Japan and draw the Imperial Navy into a decisive fleet engagement as happend at the Battles of the Philipne Sea (June 1944) and Leyte Gulf (October 1944). MacArthur's and Nimitz's campaigns merged into one for the invasion of the Philippines. Afterwards the Central Pacific campaign continued with the invasions of Iwo Jima and Okinawa.

PHASE FOUR
During the later stages of the war the army Air Force, operating from the Mariana Islands and flying the B-29 Superfortress, had begun to fire bomb the cities of Japan. These raids culminated with the droping of the atomic bombs at Hiroshima on 6 August 1945 and Nagasaki three days later. Japan surrendered to the Allies on 2 September 1945.

aboard the United States Navy battleship, U.S.S. Missouri, government officials from Japan, signed the Instrument of Surrender in a special ceremony.

THE WAR IN EUROPE

GERMAN AGGRESSION

September 1939 marked the beginning of the war in Europe, when Germany, under rule of Chancellor Adolf Hitler, invaded Poland. Although they had declared war on Germany, Britain and France took minimal military action over the following months. In 1940, Germany engaged in relentless attacks on Denmark and Norway, followed by attacks on Belgium, the Netherlands, and France. Germany conquered all of these nations relatively quickly.

THE BATTLE OF BRITAIN

Late summer of 1940, Germany launched an extensive attack on Britain, this time exclusively from air, known as The Battle of Britain. This battle proved to be Germany's first failure. The Luftwaffe, German Air Force, could not stand up to the power of Britain's Royal Air Force.

GREECE AND NORTH AFRICA

As Hitler devised his strategies, Italy, an ally of Germany, expanded the war even further by invading North Africa and Greece. In early 1941, The British Army sent troops to the region, but Germany and Italy captured Greece, detaining 7,000 soldiers and holding them as Prisoners of War. United States joined the British in defending North Africa.

THE USSR

Because Germany came to aid the Italians in Greece, Germany's invasion of the Soviet Union was delayed until later in 1941. Although the Germans initially made swift progress and advanced deep into the Russian heartland, the invasion of the U.S.S.R would prove to be the downfall of Germany's war effort. The country was too big, and although the initial Soviet resistance was weak, the German army was no match for its brutal winters and national strength. In 1943, Germany had no choice but to start retreating from Soviet territory following the battles of Stalingrad and Kursk. In 1945, Soviet troops continued to advance the German forces across Eastern Europe, slowly but steadily forcing them completely out of the Soviet Union.

THE ITALIAN INVASION

After defeating the Italians and Germans in North Africa in June 1943, the Allies invaded Sicily, code name Operation Husky. Operation Husky was a success, with the Italians and Germans retreating from Sicily within 38 days. However one fatal mistake was allowing 100,000 soldiers to escape to Italy with all their equipment. The Allies invaded Italy to draw German troops away from the northwest coast of France, Normandy and Russia. During this time, on July 24, 1943 Prime Minister Benito Mussolini was arrested and a new provisional government was set up under Marshal Pietro Badoglio who opposed Italy's alliance with Nazi Germany. He contemplated about surrendering Italy to the Allies. Germany, not wanting the Allies to establish air bases in Italy that could threaten German cities, deployed 16 divisions in Italy to fight against the Allies. The Allies priority was not to take over Italy, but to keep as many German divisions busy as possible. There were many land battles in Italy, mostly through treacherous mountain terrain - Anzio, Salerno and Monte Cassino. The U.S. Army moved into Rome on June 4, 1944, however 6 Allied divisions were ordered to leave Rome and to help with the D-Day operation in Normandy, France. Allied soldiers pushed across Po Valley in northern Italy when Germany surrendered on May 2, 1945, 2 days after the collapse of Berlin.

THE NORMANDY INVASION
The D-Day operation of June 6, 1944, the largest military invasion in human history, brought together the land, air and sea forces of the Allied armies. This operation, given the codename Overlord, delivered assault forces to the beaches of Normandy, France-code named: Utah, Omaha, Gold, Juno and Sword. The invasion force included 7,000 ships and landing craft manned by over 195,000 naval personnel from eight allied countries. With almost 133,000 Allied forces landing on these beaches on D-Day, over 10,000 men became instant casualties. By June 30th, over 850,000 men, 148,000 vehicles, and 570,000 tons of supplies had landed on the Normandy shores. (Dwight D. Eisenhower Museum) By the time Normandy was fully liberated more than 20,000 French civilians had died, most of them victims of the Allied bombings that pummeled the cities and towns.

BATTLE OF THE BULGE
In mid-winter of December 1944, the German army launched a surprise massive counteroffensive from the Ardennes Forest toward the port of Antwerp, Belgium, with the intention of splitting the Allied forces in two. This was intended to cut off the supplies to the Allies coming through the port of Antwerp. Hitler believed the Allies would surrender and negotiate peace. German troops advanced some 50 miles into the Allied lines, creating a deadly "bulge" pushing into Allied defenses. Despite freezing weather conditions, Allied forces held their ground until airpower was able to provide relief.

After the war ended, this battle became known as The Battle of the Bulge. The Battle of the Bulge was the largest battle fought by the United States in World War II. By early 1945, after the weather cleared the Allied forces closed in on Germany from both east and west. The air strikes brought the line back to where it began. Over 600,000 American troops fought and approximately 75,000 to 80,000 Americans lost their lives. The Germans had approximately 80,000 to 100,000 fatalities.

On May 7, 1945, shortly after the suicide of Adolf Hitler, Germany surrendered.

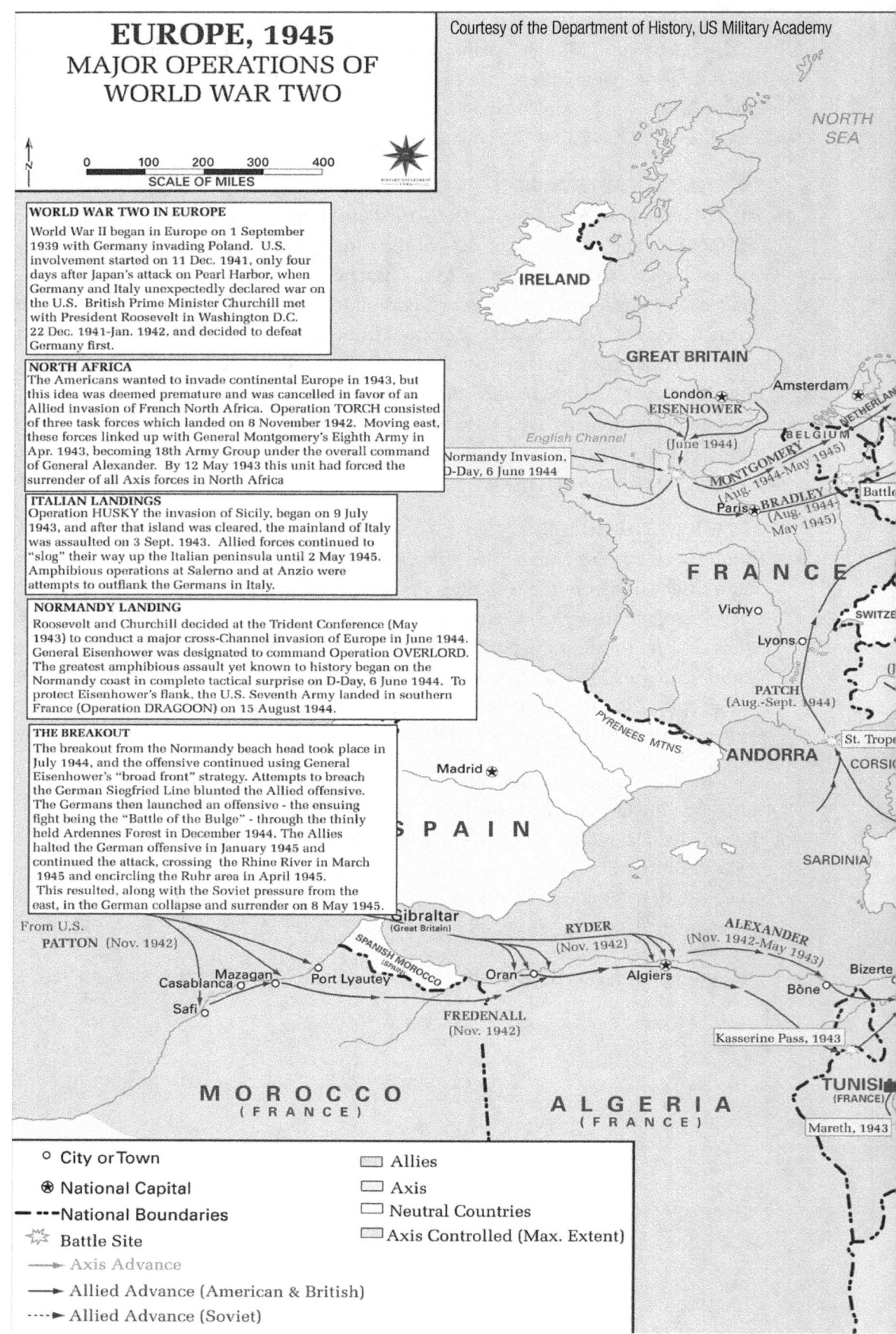

ROLL OF HONOR MAVERICK COUNTY

"All the real heroes are not storybook combat fighters. Every single man in the army plays a vital role. So don't ever let up. Don't ever think that your job is unimportant. What if every truck driver decided that he didn't like the whine of the shells and turned yellow and jumped headlong into a ditch? That cowardly bastard could say to himself, 'Hell, they won't miss me, just one man in thousands.' What if every man said that? Where in the hell would we be then? No, thank God, Americans don't say that. Every man does his job. Every man is important. The ordnance men are needed to supply the guns, the quartermaster is needed to bring up the food and clothes for us because where we are going there isn't a hell of a lot to steal. Every last damn man in the mess hall, even the one who boils the water to keep us from getting the GI shits, has a job to do."

General George Patton
speech to his troops in England in February 1944.

" I can imagine no more rewarding a career. And any man who may be asked in this century what he did to make his life worthwhile, I think I can respond with a good deal of pride and satisfaction: 'I served in the United States Navy."

John F. Kennedy

The Roll of Honor from Maverick County

We are honored to present this roll of honor who served our country to preserve the freedom for the future generations.

The Gold Star represents the soldiers who died during WWII. A service flag was given to every mother who lost a child in the WWII. The flag was displayed in the window in their home.

ABASCAL, MANUEL "MANOLO"
Corporal, U.S. Army, HQ Army; clerk typist.

Qualifications: Marksman

Battles: Rome, PO Valley, Northern Apennines

Honors: European-African-Middle Eastern Campaign Medal with 3 battle stars, Good Conduct Medal, Victory Medal, American Theatre Medal, Combat Infantry Badge (June 30, 1944)

ABERNETHY Jr., EUGENE HOLMES
U.S. Navy

ADAME, SAUL
Private First Class, U.S. Army, Company B 187th Combat Engineer Battalion; electrician

Qualifications: Sharpshooter

Battles: Rhineland, Central Europe

Honors: European-African-Middle Eastern with Campaign Medals with 2 battle stars, 4 Overseas Service Bars, Good Conduct Medal, Victory Medal

ADAMS, ALBERT V. "Johnny Q"
U.S. Army

Albert had 4 brothers in service: Harold Adams, Rex Arthur Adams, William Adams, Thomas Adams and younger brother, Carl Lee Adams served in Korea.

ADAMS, GEORGE FORBES

ADAMS, HAROLD

Machinists Mate First Class, U.S. Navy, Seabees

ADAMS, MILTON B.

Major General, U.S. Army Air Forces, 22nd Pursuit Squadron, (Commander) 328th Fighter Group, (Commander) 18th Fighter Group

Qualifications: Pilot wings, 1940

Duty Stations: Langley Field, VA; Puerto Rico, Trinidad, 1940-1943; Hamilton Field, CA, 1943; Southwest Pacific, 1943-1945

Major Gen Adams' father was in the Army stationed at Ft. Duncan, Eagle Pass, Texas, where he was born. He was a graduate of the US Military Academy in 1939. Upon the conclusion of Major Gen Adams' military service, he had flown over 275 combat missions.

ADAMS, REX A.

Corporal, U.S. Army Air Forces, 273rd Army Air Force; airplane armorer

Qualifications: Marksman

Honors: American Campaign Medal, Victory Medal with 1 Service Stripe

ADAMS, THOMAS LEO

U.S. Navy

Duty Station: U.S.S. Arizona, Pearl Harbor, Hawaii, 1941

Thomas Adams lost part of his hearing on December 7, 1941 in the attack on Pearl Harbor by Japanese forces.

ADAMS, WILLIAM E.

Sergeant, U.S. Army Air Forces, 422nd Bomb Squadron, 305th Bomb Group; airplane electric mechanic

Battles: Central Europe, Normandy, Air Offensive-Europe, Northern France, Ardennes, Rhineland

Honors: European-African-Middle Eastern Campaign Medal with 6 battle stars, Good Conduct Medal, Distinguished Unit Badge, American Defense Service Medal

ADAN, JOSE M.

Sergeant, U.S. Army, 3rd Battalion, 101st Airborne Division, 502nd Parachute Infantry Regiment

Qualifications: Sharpshooter

Battles: Normandy, Rhineland, Central Europe

Honors: American Campaign Medal, Good Conduct Medal, Victory Medal, Purple Heart

Medal with 3 Oak Leaf Clusters, European-African-Middle Eastern Campaign Medal, Distinguished Unit Citation, Orange Lanyard of the Netherlands Government Holland, the Fourragere Belgian Government Citation (Oct 1945), Combat Infantry Badge

On June 6, 1944 (D-Day) Sgt Adan made his first combat jump. The 101st Airborne had been assigned the threefold mission involving the capture of causeways leading inland from the invasion beaches and the destruction of bridges across vital German communication roads. According to an article from the July 7, 1994 Eagle Pass News Guide, Sgt Adan stated that their division missed their landing point and were scattered over a 15 mile area. "I remember that there was 4 or 5 of us landed together where there were a lot of cows and we did not know where we were or where the beach was. About 5AM, we heard all these church bells ringing and we asked the French underground what was going on. That was the invasion they said." It turned out that they had landed near St. Mere Eglise.

The Eagle Pass News Guide stated "All night long we were ordered fix bayonets: for the close-in stuff until noon June 7. A German aircraft strafed them, then a corporal, Sgt Adan was ordered to set up his 30-calibre machine gun position at a hedgerow and started firing it. When one German defender popped up unexpectedly close by, the lieutenant in charge reassured Adan, "Don't worry, Chief. He's mine. I don't know why everybody always called me "Chief," Adan tells you, "but it stuck with me throughout the war." "For some 45 days Adan and the 101st fought close to famed Carentan, it was the longest 45 days I've ever seen" he says. But eventually the beach was secured (Omaha) and we were sent back to England for a rest.

The Eagle Pass News Guide stated, "Of the men who flew across the English Channel over a month before, only a little more than half returned in July. The rest had been evacuated earlier to hospitals in England, or had been buried in graves in France." The second combat jump was in the unsuccessful Allied military operation, "Operation Market Garden" September 17-24, 1944, the largest airborne operation in history, fought in the Netherlands and Germany. Field Marshal Montgomery's goal was to force an entry into Germany and over the Rhine. He wanted to circumvent the northern end of the Siegfried Line and this required the operation to seize the bridges across the Meuse River and the two arms of the Rhine as well as several smaller canals and tributaries. Crossing the Lower Rhine would allow the Allies to encircle Germany's industrial heartland in the Ruhr from the north. It made large-scale use of airborne forces, whose tactical objectives were to secure the bridges and allow a rapid advance by armored units into Northern Germany."

Market Garden employed four of the six divisions of the first Allied Airborne Army. The 101st Airborne Division, under Major General Maxwell D. Taylor, would drop into two locations just north to take the bridges northwest of Eindhoven in Holland at the towns of Son and Veghel on September 17, 1944. "This was a big operation, "Adan recalls, "There were a helluva lotta planes and men." Indeed the fleet of planes was so large for the Holland operation that the lead elements were jumping out of their planes over Dutch soil, while the last ones of the flight were still taking off from the airfields in England."

A month later in Holland while his unit was on patrol, "by a big windmill" Adan recalls, a Nazi bullet grazed the left side of the 5'3" combat infantryman's head above the ear "and sat me on my butt." "When a bullet hits you, you don't keep going forward like in the movies, it throws you back with the impact."

"It was in the cold and ferocious winter of '44-'45 during the Battle of the Bulge near Bastogne that Adan was wounded the second and third time. The second time I got hit was January 1, 1945, a bullet in the right side of the chest. God, it was cold. We had to fight the cold, the Germans and hunger all at the same time." Since this was a scrape, he was not hospitalized. Thirteen days later, Adan caught a German bullet in the groin which ended his fighting career and his participation in the war.

In an interview with Jose in 2014, he said "In my dreams I see 50 people running and I didn't receive a scratch. This is what you think about when you get old"

AGUILERA, AMADO GUERRA

Private First Class, U.S. Army Air Forces, Company D 598th Signal Aircraft Warning Battalion; auto equipment operator

Qualifications: Sharpshooter

Honors: Asiatic-Pacific Campaign Medal, Victory Medal

AGUIRRE, JOSE V.

Tec5, U.S. Army, 132nd Signal Company; field lineman

Qualifications: Sharpshooter

Battles: Rhineland, Central Europe

Honors: American Campaign Medal, European-African-Middle Eastern Campaign Medal with 2 battle stars, Bronze Star Medal, Good Conduct Medal, Victory Medal

AINSLIE, JOSE J.

Tec5, U.S. Army

Honors: Asiatic-Pacific Campaign Medal, Victory Medal, Army of Occupation Medal (Philippines)

ALDAPE, FELIPE M.

ALDRIDGE, EDWIN E.

Colonel, U.S. Army, 57th Infantry (Filipino Scouts)

Battles: Philippines-Bataan

The Eagle Pass News Guide on January 21, 1943, Colonel Aldridge was cited as a hero in the historic defense of the Bataan Peninsula. The Eagle Pass News Guide stated "Col Aldridge was last heard from on March 1, 1942. He was among the group of officers who performed the feat of bringing 20,000 Filipino troops from southern Luzon province, where the Japanese intended to trap them, all the way to Bataan Province, where the men became hardened brave fighters." Col Aldridge was taken as a POW of the Japanese Government in Taiwan.

Colonel Aldridge's sons, Captain Edwin Aldridge Jr. and 1LT Herbert Aldridge also served in the military.

ALDRIDGE Jr., EDWIN E.

Colonel, U.S. Army; military personnel officer

Son of Edwin E. Aldridge. Excerpt from The Eagle Pass News Guide, November 26, 1942, he served as assistant personnel officer at Ellington Field until July 1942 when he was transferred to Blackland Army Flying School as head of the personnel section.

ALDRIDGE, FRANCIS G.
Private First Class, U.S. Army
After the war, PFC Aldridge became mayor of Eagle Pass

ALDRIDGE, HERBERT JAMES
Lieutenant, Squadron E
Duty Station: Keesler Field, Louisiana

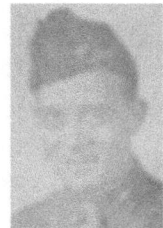

ALVARADO, ALVARO L.
Private First Class, U.S. Army, 2nd Infantry Division, Co. L, 168th Infantry Regiment
Honors: Purple Heart Medal, Combat Infantry Badge
Killed in action in Italy on April 18, 1945. First buried at U.S. Military Cemetery near Mt. Benji, Pietramala, Italy, reburied at his final resting place at Ft. Sam Houston in San Antonio, TX on January 24, 1949. PFC Alvarado was originally from Piedras Negras, Coahuila Mexico.

ALVARADO, BLAS

ALVARADO, EDUARDO C.
Private, U.S. Army; military police
Honors: Army Occupation Medal, Victory Medal; 1 Overseas Service Bar

ALVARADO, JULIO C.
Private, U.S. Army, 106th Infantry Division (one of the last divisions formed in WW II), Anti-tank Company, 422nd Infantry; portable power generator operator
Qualifications: Sharpshooter
Battles: Sicily, Naples-Foggia, Rome-Arno, Northern France, Rhineland
Honors: European-African-Middle Eastern Campaign Medal with 5 battle stars, Good Conduct Medal

ALVARADO, RITO C.
Private First Class, U.S. Army, 41st Infantry Division, Company B, 162nd Regiment; rifleman
Qualifications: Marksman
Battles: Southern Philippines, Philippine Islands
Honors: Purple Heart Medal, Good Conduct Medal, Asiatic-Pacific Campaign Medal, Philippine Liberation Medal, Combat Infantry Badge
PFC Alvarado was wounded on March 20, 1945 at the Asiatic-Pacific Campaign.

ARRELLANO, CRUZ R.
Sergeant, U.S. Army, 506th Anti-aircraft Artillery Battalion attached to USMC 5th Amphibious Corps
Qualifications: Marksman
Battle: Iwo Jima, Western Pacific
Honors: Asiatic-Pacific Campaign Medal, Victory Medal, Good Conduct Medal

ARRELLANO HEREDIA, CLAUDIO
Private First Class, U.S. Marine Corps
Qualifications: Sharpshooter
PFC Arrellano was born in Sabinas, Coahuila, Mexico and was stationed in the Pacific.

ARIZPE, EDUARDO
Corporal, U.S. Army, Guard Squadron

ARMENDAREZ, REYNALDO R.

ARQUETTE, LEROY ARTHUR
First Lieutenant, U.S. Army Air Forces, 8th Army Air Force; bombardier

1 Lt Arquette flew the B-17 Flying Fortress in 25 missions over Europe. "The sky was so full of Flying Fortresses that day as Lt Arquette would put it, "they needed a few traffic cops up there." "Formations were jockeying with each other for positions over the various targets. As one put it, "it was like a scavenger hunt with everyone trying to get the biggest prize." (San Antonio Express Newspaper 1944)

1 Lt Arquette found himself in many tight spots as stated in The Eagle Pass News Guide, dated March 23, 1944. "Last September, for instance, "Old Battle Axe," engaged in the running fight over enemy territory (Germany). Badly crippled, with two engines shot out, the tail assembly torn up, and the waist riddled with shells, the Old Battle Axe fell out of formation. Her guns were still going, however, and they accounted for at least four German fighters- later officially confirmed and credited by intelligence. The pilot dived the heavy bomber 10,000 feet to shake off the fighters, then he Old Battle Axe skirted the Brest Peninsula all alone. Going over German Held Island at 700 feet the crew strafed the gun emplacements and threw their empty guns out. By that time, one of the engines caught fire. It was wind milling so badly that the whole airplane shook. Just after, we crossed the friendly coast (England) another engine went out-the-third- so we went back out to sea and ditched. No one was injured. It wasn't long before some fishermen came along and picked up the crew.

By mid-1944, the unit had a total strength of more than 200,000 people, and it could send more than 2,000 four-engine bombers and 1,000 fighters on a single mission against enemy targets in Europe. For this reason, 8th Air Force is commonly known as the "Mighty Eighth." From May 1942 to July 1945, the 8th planned and precisely executed America's daylight strategic bombing campaign against Nazi-occupied Europe. The 8th suffered about half of the U.S. Army Air Force's casualties (47,483 out of 115,332), including more than 26,000 dead."

AUSTIN, ODIE R.
Tec5, U.S. Army, Company A, 2nd Combat Engineer Battalion

Tec5 Austin died of non-battle wounds. His unit came ashore on D-Day on June 6, 1944 at H-hour to blow obstacles in the path of assault boats and landing craft carrying the infantry. On June 16, 1944, the battalion was committed as Infantry in support of the 38th Infantry on Hill 192, St. Lo, France. On July 4, 1944, the Engineers reverted to engineer work, but many times were called upon to fight with the infantry troops. The 2nd Engineer Battalion saw action at the seaport of Brest, France and was pitted against the German 2nd Engineer Battalion. Tec5 Austin died in the vicinity of Brest, France. According to the individual deceased personnel file of the Department of the Army, Tec5 Odie Austin was "killed by an accidental discharge of a German pistol which one of the men of Company "A" of this organization was examining on August 24, 1944.

AVERY Jr., ALBERT J.
Lieutenant Colonel, U.S. Army Air Forces, 2514 Army Air Force Base Unit; training officer

Duty Station: Randolph Field, San Antonio, Texas

AVILA, ANTHONY R.
Sergeant, U.S. Army, 43rd Infantry Division, 271st Field Artillery Battalion; clerk typist

Qualifications: Marksman

Battles: Bismarck Archipelago, New Guinea, Luzon, Southern Philippines

Honors: Asiatic-Pacific Campaign Medal with 4 battle stars and 1 bronze arrowhead, Philippine Liberation Medal with 2 battle stars, Good Conduct Medal.

The 271st Field Artillery Battalion used the 105mm Howitzer. The Battalion was attached to the 1st Calvary Division which landed in the Philippines on October 20, 1944.

AVILES, MOISES
Private, U.S. Army

BACKUS, ARTHUR
Sergeant, U.S. Army, 2nd Infantry Division, K Company, 9th Regiment; rifleman

Medals: Bronze Star Medal, Purple Heart Medal, European-African-Middle Eastern Campaign Medal with 2 battle stars, Good Conduct Medal, American Defense Medal, Combat Infantry Badge

Sergeant Backus participated in the liberation of France and landed on Omaha Beach on D-Day + 1. He was wounded at St. Lo on July 28, 1944 and returned to England to recuperate before returning to duty.

BACKUS, CHARLES
U.S. Navy, aircraft Mechanic

BACKUS, EDWARD
Tec5, U.S. Army, Company B, 99th Signal Battalion; teletype operator

Battles: Bismarck Archipelago, New Guinea, Southern Philippines Liberation

Honors: Philippine Liberation Medal with 1 battle star, Good Conduct Medal, Victory Medal, 1 Service Stripe, 5 Overseas Service Bars

BACKUS, JOSEPH WILLIAM
Tec5, U.S. Army, Troop B, Engineer Squadron; Jackhammer Operator (1941); cook (1942)

Having enlisted in the Army on September 19, 1940 at Ft. McIntosh, Texas, Tec5 Joseph Backus was discharged from active duty on October 1943, Ft. Bliss, El Paso, Texas' William Beaumont General Hospital for disabilities obtained after being severely burned in an explosion while on duty.

BACKUS, OSCAR V.
Private First Class, U.S. Army, Cannon Company, 9th Infantry Regiment, 2nd Infantry Division

Honors: Combat Infantry Badge, Purple Heart Medal

Killed in action in Les Bruyeres, France on July 3, 1944 by gunshot wound to the head, PFC Oscar Backus was buried on July 4, 1944 at St. Laurent Sur Mer #1, U.S. Armed Forces Cemetery (20 miles northeast of St. Lo, France). Oscar was Arthur Backus younger brother.

BALBOA, APOLONIO S.
Private, U.S. Army, Service Battery, 721st Field Artillery Battalion; barber

Battles: Rhineland

Honors: American Campaign Medal, European-African-Middle Eastern Campaign Medal, Good Conduct Medal, Victory Medal

BALBOA, ARTURO S.
Private First Class, U.S. Army, 85th Infantry; medical aidman

Qualifications: Medical Badge

Battles: North Apennines, PO Valley

Honors: European-African-Middle Eastern Campaign Medal, Victory Medal, American Campaign Medal, Bronze Star Medal, Purple Heart Medal

PFC Balboa was wounded at February 20, 1945 in the European Theater.

BARBA, ROGELIO
Private First Class, U.S. Army, Company B, 49th Engineer Combat Battalion; rifleman

Qualifications: Marksman

Battles: Normandy, Northern France; Ardennes, Rhineland, Central Europe

Honors: European-African-Middle Eastern Campaign Medal with 5 battle stars and 1 bronze arrowhead, Asiatic-Pacific Campaign Medal, Good Conduct Medal, Victory Medal

BARBOSA, EDWARDO

BARNHEART, ORVILLE HERMAN
Fireman First Class, U.S. Navy
Served on USS Granville

BARNHART, JOHN EDWARD

BARKSDALE, JOE FRANK
2nd Lieutenant, U.S. Marine Corps
Qualifications: Marksman, Bayonet Expert, Spanish Interpreter

BARKSDALE, WANDA M.
U.S. Navy Reserve

BARON, MAURICE W.
Private First Class, U.S. Army Air Forces, 1177th Military Police Company; military police
Battles: Normandy, Northern France, Rhineland, Central Europe
Honors: American Campaign Medal, European-African-Middle Eastern Campaign Medal with 4 battle stars, Good Conduct Medal, Meritorious Unit Award, 1 Service Stripe, Victory Medal
PFC Baron was a sophomore student at The University of Texas, but the excitement of ongoing war was too much for him to focus on his studies. He enlisted in the Army Air Forces on January 8th and headed to bombardier training.

BARRERA, ENRIQUE

BARRERA, RAUL
Barrera served in India during WWII.

BARRIENTOS, AUGUSTO L.
Private First Class, U.S. Army Air Forces, 9th Air Force Service Command; truck driver
Battles: Rhineland, Ardennes
Honors: European-African-Middle Eastern Campaign Medal with 2 battle stars, Good Conduct Medal, Purple Heart Medal, Combat Infantry Badge
PFC Barrientos earned a Purple Heart medal after being wounded in the Battle of the Bulge, January 1945 in Belgium. He was subsequently discharged from O'Reilly General Hospital, Springfield, Mo, July 17, 1946.

BARRIENTOS, FRANK A.
Sergeant, U.S. Army Air Forces, First Air Intransit Depot Squadron, Field Lightning Office; clerk

Battles: Normandy, Northern France, Rhineland

Honors: American Defense Service Medal, American Campaign Medal, Good Conduct Medal, European-African-Middle Eastern Campaign Medal with 3 battle stars, Victory Medal.

In a letter, Sgt Barrientos stated:

It is 6:30pm and TSgt Albert McKay, department head of Field Lightning, is received last minute instructions over the phone . . . They knew that they (Brooks Field Airdrome Illumination Personnel) must get the right information in order to lay out the runway on the right direction and on the number of degrees specified. They are now checking their equipment for they know that the lives of the pilots depend upon them. All the lights are on; the airplanes are coming in to land. All the crews are on the alert, waiting to change the runways on a minute's notices. The department is composed of experience men and they are doing an excellent work in KEEPING THEM FLYING AT NIGHT. They are working as a unit, for they know that only by team work they are able to keep all the fields lighted and in tip-top condition.

BARRIENTOS, JUAN
Private First Class, U.S. Army

Honors: Combat Infantry Badge

BARRIENTOS, MARIO M.
Tec4, U.S. Army, Army Service Field Training Center Signal Corps; high voltage lineman

Battles: Ardennes, Rhineland, Central Europe

Honors: American Campaign Medal, European-African-Middle Eastern Campaign Medal, Victory Medal, Good Conduct Medal

BARRIENTOS, PEDRO
Private, U.S. Army, Company K, 322 Infantry

BARRIENTOS, ROMUALDO
Tec4, U.S. Army, Company D, 32nd Medical Battalion; cook

Honors: American Campaign Medal, Victory Medal

BARRY Jr., ARTHUR
Private First Class, U.S. Army

BARRY, DWIGHT W.
First Lieutenant, U.S. Army Air Forces; B-24 pilot

The Eagle Pass News Guide on February 24, 1944 stated that 1Lt Barry received preliminary flight training at Bonham Field, Greenville, Texas and Frederick, Oklahoma. The rigorous B-24 piloting school specialized in four-engine aircraft, which included many hours of ground training, a brisk athletic program, and long cross-country navigation flights under simulated battle conditions. Most of the B-24 pilots will either become flight instructors, assisting in the training of other bomber pilots, or be sent to tactical schools for the final phases of pre-combat flight training.

BASS, JACOBO M.
Private First Class, U.S. Army Air Forces, 3505th Army Air Force Unit; duty soldier

BASS, JOSEPH A.
Sergeant, U.S. Army, HQ Company, 2nd Signal Training Battalion; supply clerk
Qualifications: Marksman

Battles: Asiatic-Pacific Campaign

Honors: American Defense Service Medal, American Campaign Medal, Asiatic- Pacific Campaign Medal, Good Conduct Medal, Victory Medal, 1 Service Stripe

BEARD, CHESTER F.

BEARD, LELAND
Beard was killed in action in Okinawa, 1945.

BEARD Jr., RALPH E.
Colonel, U.S. Army Air Forces; engineering officer

Duty Station: Eagle Pass Army Air Force Base

Beard, a sub-depot engineering officer at Eagle Pass Army Air Force Base, investigated and inspected a plane that crashed 5 miles into Mexico. Air Cadet Murray flew a proposed cross- country flight from Eagle Pass to Hondo to Cotulla and back to Eagle Pass. After taking off from Eagle Pass Air Force Base, Cadet Murray apparently went the wrong way and went to Uvalde, presuming it to be Hondo. Believing that his radio was possibly mal-functioning, he took up the supposedly correct heading to Cotulla, however this carried him to the American Mexican Border. There were no towns or lights or other objects on the ground with the exception of the Rio Grande River to identify his location. Upon radio contact with Lt. Richard Taylor, since Murray did not know where he was and he only had 20-30 gallons of fuel left, Lt. Richard Taylor told him if he did not find any check points to know where he was, or did not find a field to gain plenty of altitude, he should jump out instead of trying to land the plane in unknown territory when he runs out of fuel.

Col. Beard met his wife, Elby Leighton while stationed in Eagle Pass and lived most of his adult life in Eagle Pass.

BEATTIE, ADALBERTO
Sergeant, U.S. Army, Troop E, 7th Cavalry; clerk typist

Battles: Luzon, Southern Philippines, Bismarck Archipelago, New Guinea

Honors: Good Conduct Medal, Purple Heart Medal, Philippine Liberation Medal, American Defense Service Medal, Asiatic-Pacific Campaign Medal, Combat Infantry Badge

BEATTIE, ANDRES W.
Private First Class, U.S. Army, Company B, 505th Military Police Battalion

Battles: Ardennes, Rhineland, Central Europe

Honors: European-African-Middle Eastern Campaign Medal with 3 battle stars, Victory Medal, Good Conduct Medal

BECKER, GERALD D.
Master Sergeant, U.S. Army Air Forces, 2518th Army Air Forces; synthetic trainer operator instructor

Honors: American Defense Medal, American Campaign Medal, Victory Medal, Good Conduct Medal

BELL Jr., WILLIAM

BENAVIDES, CM

BENAVIDES, RAUL "El Comandante"
Corporal, U.S. Army Air Force, 528th Bombardment Squadron; cook

Battles: Bismarck Archipelago, New Guinea, Luzon, Southern Philippines, Northern Solomon

Honors: Asiatic-Pacific Campaign Medal with 5 battle stars, Philippine Liberation Medal with bronze star, Good Conduct Medal

CPL Benavides registered for the draft in Montana when he was working in the fields during harvest season.

While he was in Montana he met another soldier from Eagle Pass, Jose Garza. They became instant friends and stuck together like glue until one night they were called out to leave and board a train with their duffle bags. He never saw his friend again. It was not until years later that he learned that his friend had lived in Uvalde, Texas; but unfortunately, by that time he had already passed away.

While in the Army Air Force he took care of the "big guns" as he put it, and he served in New Guinea, Okinawa, the Philippines, and the Northern Solomon. He rode in B-24 bombers as they moved back and forth from island to island. He also remembered spending time in Australia where soldiers found themselves eating small kangaroos. Benavides left the Army Air Force in 1945. He came back to live in Eagle Pass where he trained as a mechanic. He ended up working for one of the town's auto dealerships for more than 30 years.

BENAVIDEZ, FORTUNATO J.
Private First Class, U.S. Army, 1804th Detachment Service Command Unit, Prisoner of War Camp; range section operator

Qualifications: Marksman

Battles: Bismarck Archipelago, New Guinea, Southern Philippines

Honors: American Campaign Medal, Asiatic-Pacific Campaign Medal, Philippine Liberation Medal, Victory Medal, Good Conduct Medal, Purple Heart Medal

BERNAL, LOUIS

BERRELEZ, JUAN H.

BERRELEZ, TORIBIO

Corporal, U.S. Army Air Forces, 364th Air Service Group, 612th Air Engineer Squadron; airplane armorer

Battles: Western Pacific-Ryukyus

Honors: American Campaign Medal, Asiatic-Pacific Campaign Medal with 2 battle stars, Good Conduct Medal, Victory Medal, Meritorious Unit Award, 3 Overseas Service Bars.

BARRY, HAYES D.

BERTEAU Jr., SAMUEL LEE

Private First Class, U.S. Army, Battery C, 226th Field Artillery Battalion; field lineman

Qualifications: Sharpshooter

Battles: Southern Philippines, Ryukyus

Honors: American Defense Service Medal, Asiatic-Pacific Campaign Medal, Philippine Liberation Medal, Good Conduct Medal

PFC Berteau Jr. entered service on October 18, 1941. He served in the Battle of Breakneck Ridge on November 6, 1944 in Leyte, Philippine Island with the purpose of securing the mountain passes that led to the Leyte Valley.

BIBB, ALVARO

Tec5, U.S. Army, Administrative Clerical School; instructor

Honors: Victory Medal, 1 Overseas Service Bar, Good Conduct Medal, Asiatic- Pacific Campaign Medal

BIBB, WILLIAM H. "La Rana"

Tec3, U.S. Army, 20th Station Hospital; surgical technician

Honors: American Campaign Medal, Asiatic-Pacific Campaign Medal, Good Conduct Medal, Victory Medal

BINGHAM, EDMOND D.

Private First Class, U.S. Army

Qualifications: Machine Gunner

Battle: South Pacific

Honors: Purple Heart Medal

PFC Bingham was wounded twice in the Papuan Campaign in the Southwest Pacific.

BINGHAM, PERCY

Second Lieutenant, U.S. Army Air Forces, 83rd Fighter Squadron; P-47 Thunderbolt pilot

2Lt Bingham was killed in a tragic airplane accident at the Eagle Pass Army Air Force Base (EPAAF) only 4 miles from his home. After many combat missions overseas, 22 year old 2Lt Bingham was killed on April 15, 1945 while flying a Bell P-63A fighter

at an airshow celebrating the final graduation class of Eagle Pass Army Air Field and a memorial ceremony for President Franklin D. Roosevelt. Among the spectators were his two brothers, Benson and Edmond Bingham and his parents.

Percy Bingham was an outstanding young man. During his short life, he accomplished and excelled at so much more than most people his own age. He was a popular student and football star at Eagle Pass High who was regarded as an "all around good fellow" to his schoolmates. He graduated in 1942 and like most 1942 graduates, he was affected by the events at Pearl Harbor in 1941. He was eager to serve his country and attend the prestigious United States Military Academy in West Point. He had the support of his friends and recommendations from highly influential people to get him an appointment to West Point or Annapolis. Before he was accepted, he enrolled in Southwestern University at Georgetown, Texas and was also a star football player and a member of the Phi Delta Theta fraternity.

Percy could not wait any longer to serve his country which led him to enlist in the Army (Air Corps). Lt. Bingham graduated from the advanced single engine pilot school, receiving his wings at Eagle Pass Army Air Force Base on October 2, 1944. Under Lt. Abe Houston, his high school football coach, the physical training director at EPAAF, Percy won the physical fitness trophy for the National Physical Fitness Championship in the Army.

Lt. Bingham started his combat career as a fighter pilot in the European Theater of Operations where he joined the P-47 thunderbolt fighter group. In one of the raids with the 9th Air Force, Bingham was shot down over occupied Belgium. With the help of the French Marquis (the French Underground), he worked his way back to the Allied territory. His friends had dressed him in women's clothes and hid him during the day. As they got closer to the Allied lines, they gave him men's clothing and a gun. Armed with only a Belgium rifle given to him by the Marquis, Lt. Bingham bluffed 15 Nazis into surrendering and his Marquis friends helped him escort the Nazis to the American lines. During his short career as a fighter pilot based in England, he was credited for shooting down at least one Nazi plane and for shooting 3 enemy locomotives.

While Percy was still missing, his parents learned in a roundabout way that he was "alive and well. Lt. Robert Nance, serving with the bombardment squadron based in England was considered missing in action following a mission over Germany. After Lt. Nance reappeared, he sent a cable to his mother, living in Eagle Pass at the time, saying that he was well and alive in England. He mentioned in the letter that he had spent a couple of days with Lt. Percy Bingham and that "Bingham, is in wonderful health and he is plenty rugged." A later communication for the War Department sent to Percy's parents confirmed that he was safe.

After the war ended and after Bingham was killed in the tragic plane accident in Eagle Pass, 2 of his Belgium friends (brothers) from the French Marquis who helped him escape wrote Lt. Bingham a letter. They were eager to hear how their "American friend" was doing. Percy's mother wrote them back to thank them. The Eagle Pass News Guided stated that she said "If it hadn't been for them, I don't believe we'd have Percy as long as we did."

In 1959, 14 years after Lt. Bingham's tragic death, it was decided that a 3,400 foot runway would be constructed east of Eagle Pass. There was a strong push by the Jay Cees (JC) to name the newly paved airstrip after Percy Bingham. Most of the JC's had known Percy and agreed that he was "one of the finest gentlemen you'll ever meet." In June 1959, there was a unanimous approval by the Maverick County residents (which is a rare occurrence) to dedicate the new municipal airport to Lt. Percy Bingham. A granite marker was placed at the airport in his honor.

When the Eagle Pass Airport was moved to their present location at the prior Eagle Pass Army Air Force Base, 12 miles south of Eagle Pass, the County Commissioner decided to continue to honor Lt. Bingham. However the name of the airport was changed to Maverick County Memorial International Airport and the granite marker was not moved. Alvin E. Stock Contractors from Eagle Pass rescued the granite marker and as of April 2015, the marker was placed at the base of the Flag Pole at Ft. Duncan museum.

BLACK JR., THOMAS EDWARD

Captain, U.S. Army, 103rd Infantry Division; company commander

Battles: France, Germany

Honors: American Defense Medal, European-African-Middle Eastern Campaign Medal with 2 battle stars, Purple Heart Medal, Bronze Star

Captain Black lost the use of his arm on February 2, 1945 in the European Theater.

BLAIR, ROLAND

Corporal, U.S. Marines, 4th Marine Division; marksman

Battles: Roi-Namur, Saipan, Iwo Jima

Honor: Good Conduct Medal

Corporal Blair' nickname was "Pop" because he was the oldest soldier at 30 years old in his squad. In the battle of Iwo Jima, he was the only survivor from his squad. His daughter, Sammy Blair Smallwood said he always told her that he survived the battle because he came home for her. He always carried his bible, lighter, pocket knife and wallet wherever he went. Other artifacts that he came home with was a Japanese doll and gold teeth.

BLANCO, LUIS

BOLDING, LEROY L.

BONNET JR., ELLIS ANDREW

Missing in Action in Germany on November 27,1944

BOWLES, FRANK O.

Tec5, U.S. Army, 105th Infantry Regiment, 27th Infantry Division; surgical technician

Battles: Eastern Mandates-Marshall Islands, Ryukyus

Tec5 Bowles was inducted on December 11, 1941, just four days after Pearl Harbor. He was stationed in Hawaii over two years and three months. Tec5 Bowles was a first-aid man with the detachment of the Medical Corps. He was in the Makin Island where the Carlson Raiders performed their daring feats. In a letter to his Mom, Tec5 Bowles stated, "Well, mom, I never thought that I would make it. I think I am very lucky. I was in one of the bloodiest battles in history. Lot of my buddies got killed. I have seen lots of action. I also have killed seven Japs. I didn't want to kill anybody, but it was the Japs or me. I'll tell more about our last battle in my next letter or maybe you don't want to hear from me after what I have done. I am writing this letter in a fox hole. I am on the Island of Saipan."

BOWLES, HAROLD
Corporal, U.S. Army Air Forces, 421st Tech School Squadron; mechanic

Cpl Bowels volunteered for the Air Corps in August, 1941. He attended technical training at Sheppard Field, Wichita Falls, Texas. He was stationed in Corsica after being in Rome, Italy on D-Day.

Frank and Harold Bowels are brothers.

BOWEN, LEWIS L.
Captain, U.S. Army Air Forces; pilot

Honors: Distinguished Flying Cross, Air Medal

Capt. Bowen was a P-40 Warhawk pilot who flew 76 combat missions over Egypt, Libya, Tunisia, Sicily, Italy, and England. He was shot down twice in the course of five days. According to The Eagle Pass News Guide, October 28, 1943, "P-40 outfit commanded by Col Arthur G. Salisbury "known as the American Desert Rats," this group has fought the German Air Force from Egypt to Central Italy and on October 20, 1943 carried the air war into Yugoslav territory in support of patriot forces. US Fighter bombers, for the first time in history attacked enemy shipping in the "island passage" between two German strongholds along the Dalmatian Coast. Swooping down the machine gun fire, the raiders wrecked one enemy power boat and damaged five others. Last Palm Sunday they destroyed 74 German JU52 transports and escort fighters in a sizzling ambush off Cam Bon, Tunisia. In addition, the Salisbury Squadron did the following: exploded an ammunition train near Anaconda on the Italian Coast destroying approximately 50 railroad cars, received three Distinguished Flying Crosses in a personal presentation by Maj General James H. Doolittle and celebrated the safe return of their squadron member, Lt Bowen.

Lt Bowen was the husband of Jan Mathis Bowen of Eagle Pass.

BRAITHWAITH, JR., RAYMOND

BRIGHTWELL, JOHN
Lieutenant, U.S. Army Air Forces

BROCKMAN, DAVID PAUL
Seaman First Class, U.S. Navy

Seaman Brockman served 14 months of sea duty on the U.S.S. Facility and U.S.S. Samaritan.

BROOKE, RICHARD C.
First Lieutenant, Army Air Force, 1154th Navigation Training Squadron, combat navigator

BROOKS, TROY SYRIL
Ship fitter Third Class, U.S. Navy

BUCKLEY, EDWARD A.
First Lieutenant, U.S. Army Air Forces

Assigned to administrative duties, 1Lt Buckley, who volunteered as an officer candidate, attended basic training at Keesler Field on September 5, 1942. He served as a drill instructor, platoon leader and flight leader.

BUCKLEY, RAYNAR

BUFORD, ROBERT H.
Technical Sergeant, U.S. Army Air Forces, 342nd Bomb Squadron, 97th Bombardment Group; radio operator/gunner

TSgt Buford's plane, a B-17F, exploded following a mid-air collision after returning from a bombing mission to Piraeus, Greece on January 11, 1944. All crew members were killed.

BURKHARDT, FEDERICO
Private First Class, U.S. Army, 108th QM Bakery Company; baker

Qualifications: Marksman

Honors: Victory Medal

BURNETT, PRICE GEORGE

BUTLER, CLIFTON
Master Sergeant, U.S. Army Air Forces, 1504th Army Air Force Base Unit Fairfield, California; administrative specialist

Qualifications: Marksman

Honors: American Defense Medal, American Campaign Medal, Victory Medal, 1 Service Stripe, Good Conduct Medal

BYNUM, ACE T.
Tec4, U.S. Army, Battery C, 67th Anti-aircraft Gun Battalion; truck driver

Qualifications: Marksman

Battles: Normandy, Northern France, Ardennes, Rhineland, Central Europe

Honors: European-African-Middle Eastern Campaign Medal with 5 battle stars, Good Conduct Medal, Victory Medal, 1 Service Stripe, 4 Overseas Service Bars

CABALLERO, FRANCISCO
Sergeant, U.S. Army, 531st Bombardment Squad, 380th Bombardment Group H Sergeant Caballero died in a plane crash in Darwin Area, Northern Territory, of Australia on January 17, 1945.

CABRERA, ANDRES

CADDEL, HOMER HENRY

CADENA, JESUS LUIS
Private

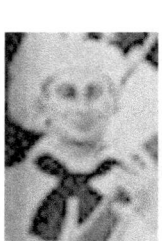

CAMPA, RALPH
Seaman First Class, U.S. Navy

Seaman First Class Campa was killed in action when aboard the U.S.S. Arizona as it was attacked by the Japanese during the attack on Pearl Harbor, Hawaii. The U.S.S. Arizona was bombed and torpedoed and within the first five minutes after the attack began, the fate of the Arizona was sealed. A bomb which was dropped into the Arizona's stack exploded in the boilers and set off the vast amount of powder stored decks cracked upon as fire and debris shot skyward and the Arizona rapidly settled in the water. Fires immediately enveloped the forward part of the ship and a futile attempt was made to put out the fire. The U.S.S. Arizona could not be saved. His remains are interred, along with his shipmates, on the wreckage of the U.S.S. Arizona in the bottom of the harbor. The mother of Seaman Campa moved to San Diego, California (Independence Hill) shortly after he was killed. His name on the U.S.S. monument at Pearl Harbor, Hawaii erroneously listed him as from California instead of Texas.

The Veterans of Foreign Wars Post (VFW) in Eagle Pass was officially named in his honor, Campa VFW.

CAMPOS, ANDREW
Sergeant, U.S. Marine Corps, supply clerk

Qualifications: Marksman, Sharpshooter Battles: Samoa, Maji, Guadalcanal, Guam

Honors: Honorable Service Lapel Button

A graduate of Eagle Pass High School class of 1941, Sgt Campos enlisted in the U.S. Marine Corps on December 8, 1941. Sgt Campos participated in Foreign Service from July 19, 1942 to December 10, 1944. He saw combat action against the Japanese in Guam and also participated in battles in Samoa, Maji, and Guadalcanal.

CAMPOS, JOSE B. "LA MONJA"
Sergeant, U.S. Army, Company I, 350th Infantry Regiment, 88th Infantry Division; rifle NCO

Battles: Rome-Arno, North Apennines, PO Valley

Honors: American Campaign Medal, European-African-Middle Eastern Campaign Medal, Purple Heart Medal with Oak Leaf Cluster, Good Conduct Medal, Victory Medal, Combat Infantryman Badge

Sgt Campos was discharged at Fort Sam Houston due to a serious leg wound. According to his daughter, Margot Ricks, "Dad loved to dance and due his sheer determination to dance again, he danced again."

CANO, EDULIO OYERVIDE
Private First Class, U.S. Marine Corps Reserves
Qualifications: Sharpshooter

CANO, PABLO
Corporal, U.S. Army, Corporal Battery B, 276th Coast Artillery Battalion; heavy machine gunner

Qualifications: Marksman

Battles: Northern Solomons

Honors: Asiatic-Pacific Campaign Medal with 1 battle star, Philippine Liberation Medal, Good Conduct Medal, Victory Medal, 1 Service Stripe, 5 Overseas Service Bars

CARBAJAL, MARGARITO
U.S. Army, 105TH Infantry Regiment, 27th Infantry Division, Company B

Battles: Makin Island. Saipan/Tinian

Honors: Purple Heart Medal

Carbajal enlisted in the Army at Ft. Bliss, Texas on October 17, 1941. He was assigned to the 27th Infantry Division to the Hawaiian Islands in February of 1942. Their mission was to guard against further Japanese attack following the bombing of Pearl Harbor. The 27th Infantry Division was the first division to leave the continental United States after Pearl Harbor.

During the invasion of Saipan, Carbajal was wounded on June 23, 1944 and he received the Purple Heart Medal. After Saipan, his division was assigned to clear the beaches and to fight any snipers in Tinian. Because of the loud noises from the artillery during the war, Carbajal lost part of his hearing.

After the war, he became a sheep herder in Wyoming, Montana, and Idaho.

CARDENAS, ALBERT R.
U.S. Navy

Born in Eagle Pass, but raised in San Antonio, Cardenas enlisted in the Navy in October 1942. He attended aircraft school and was assigned to Duncan Field, San Antonio, Texas, where he served for a year. According to the Texas State Historical Association, Duncan Field was used as an aircraft-repair depot and became part of the Kelly Army Air Field in 1942. He was later appointed Recruiting Chief Petty Officer and was stationed in San Diego, California.

CARDENAS, ARTURO V.
Private First Class, U.S. Army, Company G, 34th Infantry Regiment; scout

Battles: Luzon, New Guinea, Southern Philippines

Honors: Asiatic-Pacific Campaign Medal, Philippines Liberation Medal, Purple Heart Medal, Combat Infantryman Badge

PFC Cardenas was assigned to the Philippines in January, 1945 and was wounded there on May 31, 1945. Cardenas was from Allende, Coahuila, Mexico.

CARDENAS, GILBERTO J.
Seaman Second Class, U.S. Navy
Seaman Cardenas enlisted in the Navy on October 2, 1943.

CARDENAS, MARGARITO J.
Sergeant, U.S. Army Air Forces, 580 Air Material Squadron, 73rd Air Service Group; supply clerk
Qualifications: Marksman
Honors: American Campaign Medal, Asiatic-Pacific Campaign Medal, Victory Medal, Good Conduct Medal

CARDENAS, MICHAEL ANGELO
Sonarman Third Class, U.S. Navy

CARDWELL JR., CLARENCE MADISON
Corporal, U.S. Marine Corps; anti-tank gun crewman
Qualifications: Sharpshooter
Battles: Okinawa, Ryukyu Island
Decorations: Good Conduct Medal, Occupation of Japan

CARPENTER, RICHARD

CARRANZA, RAMIRO R.
Private, U.S. Army Air Forces, 576th Signal Aircraft Warning Battalion; base maintenance
Battles: New Guinea; Luzon, Philippines
Honors: American Campaign Medal, Asiatic-Pacific Campaign Medal, Philippine Liberation Medal, Victory Medal, Good Conduct Medal

CARRASCO, GILBERT
Private, Company B, 330th Infantry Regiment, 83rd Infantry Division
PFC Carrasco was reported as "missing in action" on December 25, 1944 and reclassified to "Killed In Action" on January 25, 1945 in Hurtgen, Germany, located 10 miles west of Aachen. He was buried in a U.S. Military Cemetery in Margraten, Holland. His family requested his remains be returned to Eagle Pass as his final resting place.

CARRASCO, FRUCTUOSO TALAMANTES
U.S. Coast Guard
On January 27, 1944, Fructuoso Carrasco was sworn in at Ft. Worth Coast Guard Aviation Station. He was on CG cutter Norma II, CG Aviation. He was shot down over Greenland and was treated at Chelsea Naval Hospital near Boston where he met his wife.

CARROL, ANTONIO P. "Tony"

Sergeant, U.S. Army, 435th Field Artillery Battalion

Qualifications: Sharpshooter

Honors: American Campaign Medal, American Defense Service Medal, Asiatic- Pacific Campaign Medal with 1 battle star, Good Conduct Medal

CARROLL, JOHN P.

Private First Class, U.S. Army Air Forces, 15th Replacement Squadron, 15th Air Depot Group; airplane/engine mechanic

Qualifications: Army Air Force Technical Badge

Battles: New Guinea, Southern Philippines (Liberation)

Honors: American Campaign Medal, Asiatic-Pacific Campaign Medal with 2 battle stars, Philippine Liberation Medal with 1 battle star, Good Conduct Medal, Victory Medal, 1 Service Stripe, 2 Overseas Service Bars

CARROLL, ROY PINA

Sergeant, U.S. Army, Company A, 201st Quartermaster Battalion; quartermaster supply technician

Qualifications: Sharpshooter

Battles: D-day-Plus 2, Normandy, Northern France, Ardennes, Rhineland, Central Europe

Honors: European-African Middle Eastern Company Medal with 5 battle stars

Sgt Carroll served overseas from November 24, 1943 to November 1, 1945. After the war, Sgt Carroll owned the Ford dealership in Eagle Pass and his daughter Minerva stated that he had an uncanny ability to remember the location and prices of parts in the service department. As quartermaster in the army he had to keep track of parts for all the jeeps, tanks, and trucks to keep the various vehicles running. He had excellent training for his auto dealership.

CARPENTER, GILBERT IRA

CARTER, GEORGE M.

Tec4, U.S. Army, 498th Replacement Company; cook

Qualifications: Marksman

Battles: Ardennes, Rhineland

Honors: American Campaign Medal, European-African Middle Eastern Campaign Medal with 2 battle stars, Asiatic-Pacific Campaign Medal, Philippine Liberation Medal, Good Conduct Medal, Victory Medal, Lapel Button Issued, 3 Overseas Service Bars

CARTER, RODOLFO "PAPO"

CARVAJAL, MANUEL E.

Private First Class, U.S. Army, 704th Engineers Petroleum Distributing Company
Battles: Rome-Arno

Honors: Victory Medal, American Campaign Medal, European-African Middle Eastern

Medal, Good Conduct Medal

PFC Carvajal departed for Europe on August 21, 1943 and returned to the USA on August 31, 1945.

CARVER, JAMES W. "SCOOTIE"

First Lieutenant, U.S. Army Air Forces, 30th Bombardment Squadron, 19th Bombardment Group; pilot/navigator

Honors: Purple Heart Medal, Air Medal

1Lt Carver turned 22 years old just a few weeks before his plane disappeared while in route to Port Moresby, Papua New Guinea, after a night bombing raid on Rabaul, a key base for the Japanese on New Britain Island. 1Lt Carver was a navigator, but substituted as the co-pilot, when the pilot fell sick, on what turned out to be his last flight. His plane was reported "missing in action" in the southwestern Pacific on November 1, 1942 near Faisi Island, Solomon Islands. Five years later, all eight were given up for dead and presumed drowned in the Pacific. Until 1Lt Carver's parents, Winnie and Ike Carver died, they believed that one day "Scottie," their only son, would return home. Ike Carver died in 1953 and Winnie died in 1979.

In 1998, a villager living in a remote area of Papua, New Guinea (P.N.G) found the wreckage of a World War II aircraft beneath canopy of trees in a remote area in New Guinea rain forest while searching for betel nuts. The villager found the dog tags from Carver and presented it to a United States excavating team investigating a crash site on another part of the island. Soon thereafter, the Central Identification Laboratory, Hawaii, was notified. 1Lt Carver's navigation kit and lighter with his initials were also recovered.

In May 2001, Kay Cunningham, Scottie's niece received a call from the Army's genealogy research division asking her to donate some DNA. His remains were identified through the use of mitochondrial DNA taken from his niece of Quemado, Texas. Kay was a baby, less than 3 months old, when her uncle was shot down. Seven other men, among them, another Texan, were on board the plane. Of those, the remains of only six were identified by JPAC's (Joint POW/MIA Accounting Command) Central Identification Laboratory. More than 60 years after he disappeared, "Scootie" Carver came home. He was buried at the foot of his mother's grave in the family plot of the City Cemetery in Eagle Pass with full military honors, including a flyover by jets from Laughlin AFB in Del Rio, Texas. Other pieces of bone were not large enough to identify and were buried at Arlington National Cemetery. A single headstone bear the names of the crew members.

In a letter sent to his father on October 27, 1942, four days before he was reported missing in action (MIA) "Dearest Daddy:

I am writing you this letter 'cause I know it will go through uncensored. The squadron I am in is going home (all except) the new boys like myself-we are being transferred. All the others were in Java and the Philippines so they really deserve to be going home, believe me.

I am sending this letter by my first pilot-I have flown 19 combat missions with him over Rabaul and the Solomon Islands and we have sunk two enemy battleships and cruisers since we have been together. I just want you to know. I am doing my part in this damned war and that I am safe and O.K. So don't worry about me. We are stationed at Mereeba (North Australia) and operate from an advanced base in Port Moresby. I have seen everything this war has to offer and am confident we can lick the hell out of the Japs if we just had a pursuit ship to match their "Zero" fighter and some pilots as good as those yellow b_____. But we will manage.

I haven't been in real danger but once since I have been here and that was when a formation of 6 (B17's-American planes) of us were attacked by 30 zero's (Japanese planes) over Rabaul- they got one B-17 and we got ten zero's. My plane only got 2 holes in it but the rest were all shot to hell. I think we are all going to be decorated for gallantry in action-probably the "silver star" but don't say a word about it to anyone cause I will get court martialed if it is know that I told I was in a combat area. And especially don't breathe a word of this to mama- cause it will make her worry.

Dad, write to me and let me know if you get this o.k. – without it being opened. Remember, I love you all more than anything and I'll be back to prove it. I have taken two complete physicals and am o.k. beyond any doubt so – don't worry about that fighter. The Solomon situation is pee-poor we get hell bombed out of us over there but it's also vice versa. Write me and tell me all the cold dope.

Love, Your son. Scootie

CASTANEDA, ANTONIO DE LEON

Sergeant, U.S. Army Air Forces, 37th Bomb Squadron; flight maintenance gunner

Qualifications: Army Air Force Air Crew Member Badge

Battles: Northern France, Ardennes, Rhineland, Central Europe

Honors: Distinguished Unit Badge, European-African-Middle Eastern Campaign Medal with 4 battle stars, Air Medal with 3 Oak Leaf Clusters, American Campaign Medal, Victory Medal

CASTANEDA, FELIPE DE LEON

Private First Class, U.S. Army Air Forces

CASTANEDA, OSCAR

Seaman First Class, U.S. Navy

Seaman Castaneda served 17 months of sea duty aboard the U.S.S. Kenton out of San Diego, California.

CASTANUELA, RAMON

Technical Sergeant, U.S. Army, 141st Regiment (The Alamo Regiment), 36th Infantry Division; platoon sergeant

Battles: Rhineland, Naples-Foggia, Rome-Arno, Southern France

Honors: American Defense Service Medal, European-African-Middle Eastern Campaign Medal with 4 battle stars, Good Conduct Medal, Combat Infantryman Badge

Sergeant Castanuela was drafted on February 25, 1941. He departed in support of the European- African-Middle Eastern campaign on April 2, 1943 and returned to the U.S. on May 6, 1945.

CASTILLO, CRESPIN

CASTILLO, GUILLERMO

Private First Class, U.S. Army, 507th Engineer Company; outboard motor operator

Qualifications: Marksman

Battles: Normandy, Northern France, Ardennes, Rhineland, Central Europe

Honors: American Campaign Medal, European-African-Middle Eastern Campaign Medal with 5 battle stars, Good Conduct Medal, Bronze Star Medal, Victory Medal, 3 Overseas Service Bars

CASTRO, ENRIQUE LEONEL
Private, U.S. Army, HQ 466th Parachute Field Artillery Battalion, 101 Airborne Division (Screaming Eagles); gunner/cannoneer

Battles: Rome-Arno, Southern France, Ardennes, Rhineland, Central Europe

Honors: European-African-Middle Eastern Campaign Medal with 5 battle stars and 1 bronze arrowhead, Distinguished Unit Badge, Bronze Star Medal with 1 Oak Leaf Cluster, American Defense Medal, Good Conduct Medal, Croix De Guerre (a French honor), Meritorious Award Citation

In August 1944, Private Castro was awarded a Bronze Star Medal for heroic achievement in action against the enemy near St. Tropez, France. He was awarded another Bronze Star for his actions in Bastogne, Belgium (Battle of the Bulge) on December 25, 1944 while under heavy enemy small arms and machine gun fire. Private Castro assisted in the destruction of two enemy tanks and forced a third crew to surrender their tank intact. He also served in Italy and North Africa.

CASTRO, RAUL RODRIGUES
Staff Sergeant, U.S. Army Air Forces, 1562nd Army Air Forces Base Unit; airplane and engine mechanic

Battles: New Guinea

Honors: American Defense Medal, American Campaign Medal, Asiatic-Pacific Campaign Medal, Good Conduct Medal, Victory Medal

CAUGHMAN, D. ARTHUR

CAUGHMAN, ROBERT EMANUEL
Staff Sergeant, U.S. Army Air Forces, 2132 Army Air Force Base Unit; supply clerk

Honors: American Defense Medal, American Campaign Medal, Good Conduct Medal, Victory Medal

CAULEY, IRVIN

CERNA, DAVID
Corporal, U.S. Army, 702nd Military Police Battalion; military police

Honors: Asiatic-Pacific Campaign Medal, American Defense Medal

Before his enlistment in the Army, Corporal Cerna could be found daily behind the counter of Cerna Money Exchange on Commercial Street in Eagle Pass. He, along with his brother Felix, were in the money exchange business.

CERVANTES, MONICO A.
Tec4, U.S. Army, 142nd Armored Signal Company; radio operator

Qualifications: Sharpshooter

Battles: Central Europe

Honors: American Campaign Medal with 1 battle star, Good Conduct Medal, Victory Medal, 1 Service Stripe, 2 Overseas Service Bars

CERVANTEZ, ADOLFO
Private First Class, U.S. Army, Battery D, 211th Anti-Aircraft Artillery Automatic Weapons Battalion; truck driver
Honors: American Campaign Medal, Asiatic-Pacific Campaign Medal, Good Conduct Medal, Victory Medal

CHAPA, JOSE

CHAPA, JULIAN
Corporal, U.S. Army Air Forces, 82nd Air Engineer Squadron, 6th Air Service Group; heavy equipment operator
Honors: Asiatic-Pacific Campaign Medal, Philippine Liberation Medal, Good Conduct Medal, Victory Medal, 2 Overseas Service Bars

CHARRO, FRANCISCO

CHAVARRIA, FRANCISCO M.
Tec5, U.S. Army, Headquarters 204th Medical Detachment; cook
Honors: Good Conduct Medal, Asiatic-Pacific Campaign Medal, American Defense Medal

CHAVEZ, IGNACIO B.
Private First Class, U.S. Army, 439th Anti-Aircraft Artillery Battalion; bugler
Battles: Naples-Foggia, Rhineland, Central Europe, Rome-Arno, Southern France
Honors: European-African-Middle Eastern Campaign Medal, Good Conduct Medal

CHAVEZ, JESUS S.
Private, U.S. Army, 19th Ordnance Medium Maintenance Company
Honors: American Campaign Medal, European-African-Middle Eastern Campaign Medal, Good Conduct Medal, Victory Medal

CHISUM, LOUIS
Corporal, U.S. Army, 1392nd Engineer Forestry Company; meat cutter
Battles: Normandy, Northern France, Ardennes, Rhineland, Offensive Europe
Honors: European-African-Middle Eastern Campaign Medal with 5 battle stars, Good Conduct Medal, Victory Medal

CHISUM, RICHARD

CHITTIM, JACK
U.S. Navy

CLARKE, J.C.

CLAY, ROBERT R.
Third Officer, Merchant Marines

The Eagle Pass News Guide, dated September 3, 1942: "Officer Clay was on a 75,000 barrel tanker which was shelled, torpedoed and sunk off the Cuban coast on August 22. Eleven crew members are still missing. The survivors floated for 8 hours in a lifeboat and finally were picked up by a fishing vessel. Officer Clay said that the German U-Boat followed the tanker for an hour firing shells at it and trying to catch it broadside for a torpedo shot. Finally, crippled by the shells, the tanker was hit by two torpedoes. As the men tried to get away in the lifeboat, they were machine gunned and a number of them were wounded and killed."

COOPER, JOHN FOWLEY

CONNALLY, WILLIS

CONTRERAS, RAFAEL SOTO
Seaman First Class, U.S. Navy

CORONADO, ANTONIO NEIRA

CORTEZ, PEDRO
Private, 548th Medical Motor Ambulance Company

Battles: Normandy, Northern France, Rhineland, Central Europe

Honors: European-African-Middle Eastern Campaign Medal with 4 battle stars, Victory Medal, 3 Overseas Service Bars

CORTEZ, ROMAN S.
Tec5, Battery C, 166th Anti-Aircraft Artillery Gun Battalion; heavy machine gunner
Qualifications: Marksman

Battles: New Guinea, Southern Philippines

Honors: Asiatic-Pacific Campaign Medal with 2 battle stars, 1 Bronze Arrowhead, Philippine Liberation Medal with 1 battle star, Good Conduct Medal, Victory Medal

CORTINAS, JUAN
Private, U.S. Army, Medical Detachment, 1811th Service Command Unit; hospital orderly

Honors: Victory Medal

CORTINAS, LUIS
Private First Class, U.S. Army, 433rd Signal Construction Battalion; telephone/telegraph lineman

Qualifications: Marksman

Battles: Normandy, Northern France, Ardennes, Rhineland, Central Europe

Honors: European-African-Middle Eastern Campaign Medal with 5 battle stars, Good Conduct Medal

CORTINAS, MARTIN

Private First Class, U.S. Army, Medical Detachment, 161 Infantry, litter-bearer
Qualifications: Medical Badge

Battles: Northern Solomon, Guadalcanal, Luzon

Honors: Asiatic-Pacific Campaign Medal, Philippine Liberation Medal, Good Conduct Medal

COVARRUBIAS, JUAN

Corporal, U.S. Army Air Forces

Corporal Covarrubias died during a nighttime, cross-country navigation flight on April 7, 1944, near Tonopah Nevada Army Air Field. His airplane, a B-24 Liberator, crashed into a mountain side. All crew members were killed. As a member of the Army Air Forces Training Command, Corporal Covarrubias was qualified as a combat bomber crew member. He had recently graduated from Flexible Gunnery School in Laredo, Texas, where he earned a pair of Aerial Gunner's Silver Wings.

COVARRUBIAS, LUCAS A.

Sergeant, U.S. Army, 164th Infantry Regiment; heavy motor crewman

Battles: Guadalcanal, Northern Solomon, Southern Philippines

Honors: Asiatic-Pacific Campaign Medal with 3 battle stars, Philippine Liberation Medal with 1 battle star, Good Conduct Medal, 1 Service Stripe, 5 Overseas Service Bars, Combat Infantry Badge

COX, CARLOS CLAUDE

CROWDER, SIMON J.

CRUZ, ELIAS

CRUZ, PEDRO

Private First Class, U.S. Army, Company B, 194th Glider Infantry Regiment; rifleman

Battles: Central Europe

Honors: American Campaign Medal, European-African-Middle Eastern Campaign Medal with 1 battle star, Good Conduct Medal, Victory Medal, 1 Service Stripe, 1 Overseas Service Bar, Combat Infantry Badge

CUNNINGHAM, EMIL Y.

Tec5, U.S. Army, 116th Infantry Regiment, 29th Division, Army Quartermaster Corps; light truck driver

Honors: Good Conduct Medal, American Defense Service Medal, European African Middle Eastern Campaign Medal

Tec5 Cunningham enlisted in the Quartermasters Corps at Fort Clark in 1940 at the age of 15. He was stationed in England. When released from active duty in 1945, he was a 5 year veteran at the age of 20.

CUNNINGHAM, MARY JANE

Cunningham was a member of Women Accepted for Volunteer Emergency Service (WAVES).

CUNNINGHAM, RAYMOND

Corporal, U.S. Army, 31st Infantry Division, Machine Gun Company

Corporal Cunningham, brother of Tec5 Emil Cunningham, enlisted in December of 1939. He served in the 5th Calvary at Ft. Clark with General Jonathan Wainwright. Raymond's Cavalry unit rode horses and mules from Ft. Clark near Brackettville to El Paso and then was sent to the Philippines under General Douglas McArthur in the 31st Infantry Division.

In a letter to his parents, date December 27, 1940 from Estado Mayor in Manila on the Philippine Islands.

"I expect it (the war) for sure next year. It worries me so much, I can't sleep at night. We're making plenty of preparations here in case the Japs attack us. We all know here that we're doomed in case of war with Japan. P.I. is only 600 miles from China, 1,000 miles from Japan and 7,000 from the USA. They could wipe us off the map before aid could reach us. But let us all hope for the best. All these miseries and tragedies that the war is suffering convinces me that there must be a Christianity and a supreme being and that the end of time is not too far away, because all of this is predicted in the bible. I am through with the Army if I ever get back, and everything else that refers to war. But naturally if our Country is threatened we must fight for all we have, because it is about the last country in the world where there is any freedom,...I'm saving my money, so I can buy me a farm when I get back to Quemado. I mean I'm going to appreciate the U.S. when I get back after seeing how these people live. We have the best Country and government in the world. I think only most of us don't appreciate it. Well, I guess that's enough politics. I hope you all had a good Christmas."

After Japan bombed Pearl Harbor on December 7, 1941, they went on to attack the Philippine Islands where he was stationed. For four months they fought the Japanese, but at the end they were no match for them. The U.S., having lost most of its ships during the bombing of Pearl Harbor, had no way of getting them food supplies and ammunition. So on April 9, General Wainwright surrendered to the Japanese, rather than see his men starve and die of malaria and dysentery. This became the largest surrender in U.S. military history. The Eagle Pass News Guide stated "In November 1941, he (Raymond Cunningham) was listed in the War Department record as one of the heroes of Bataan. The famous 31st Infantry of which he as a member fought for months against overwhelming odds, manning machine guns form fox-holes, fighting the Japs in fierce hand to hand encounters in the dense jungle and finally blasted from above all sides, fired their last ammunition and surrendered on Corregidor."

This marked the beginning of the Bataan Death March. Both Americans and Philippines were marched in groups of 100 to Camp O'Donnell, which was 65 miles away. This became one of the worst atrocities in modern wartime history. As the emaciated men were marched like cattle in the blistering heat, they were shot and bayoneted if they fell, attempted to escape, or stopped to quench their thirst. Some men were tied to trees or fences, and shot to death to serve as examples to the others. The Japanese killed between 7,000 and 10,000 men. CPL Cunningham managed to survive the ordeal.

At Camp O'Donnell, the men were nearly starved with very little food, and hardly any water. They had received no medical attention and had to use trenches for sanitation purposes. Flies flew out of the trenches and latrines and covered the soldier's food and their bodies. Malaria, dysentery and beriberi ran rampant among the soldiers. Men began to die at the rate of 400 per day. In July of 1942, the Japanese then decided to move the men to Camp Cabanatuan, a prisoner of war camp. Here some of the men managed to receive some medical attention.

As described by John Allen McCarty, one of the very few that survived the Cabanatuan prison camp, the men who had managed to crawl to Cabanatuan from Camp O'Donnell were now nothing but skin and bones. The hospital at Cabanatuan was crowded with men with malaria, beri beri, and other diseases. Dysentery was also a major problem. Men suffering from this were placed in what was called the "Zero Ward" because there was no hope of them walking out of there alive. The patients there were naked, lying on the floor usually on their own vomitus and dysentery stool. Flies crawled all over them. Many were unconscious, their hair and beards tangled and soiled with feces. Flies were in their eyes and mouth. Dead men were carried out each day and were placed in common graves.

It was there in Cabanatuan that CPL Cunningham died of dysentery on November 14, 1942 at the age of 25 according to the records. He was buried in the Cabanatuan Prisoner of War Camp Cemetery in the Philippines in a mass grave with 13 other solders. His remains were later recovered by an American Graves Registration Unit and moved to the United States Armed Forces Cemetery, Manila # 2, Luzon, a more suitable location where consistent care could be given to the grave. But it would not be until August 14, 1949 when his remains would be shipped to his father, Roy Cunningham, in Quemado, Texas where he would be finally laid to rest for the very last time.

CURI, TOMAS

DALLAS, FREDERICK W.

Captain, U.S. Army Air Forces

Captain Dallas was the commander of six different Flying Fortress aircrafts. As a small boy, he lived in Eagle Pass with his parents. According to The Eagle Pass News Guide, "Failing to make the necessary high average for a Presidential appointment to West Point, Dallas enrolled at Kelly Field and subsequently won his wings, although at graduation he was still too young to be commissioned as an officer. However, he became an instructor there until his 21rst birthday when he was commissioned, and went into active service." According to The Eagle Pass News Guide, on October 3, 1942, "the Fortress' activities were part of a continuing air offensive over England and France. The flying men told how a formation of six Boeing Flying Fortresses fought off 35 crack German fighter planes over France yesterday (October 7, 1942), destroying a record-breaking total of 13-and possibly 12 more- in a 10-minute duel at 25,000 feet. The Flying Fortresses fired all of their guns simultaneously to break up the German attack without the aid of fighter plane."

DANIEL, ARMANDO

Private First Class, U.S. Army, Nigata Military Government Team; rifleman

Battles: Luzon

Honors: Asiatic-Pacific Campaign Medal with 1 battle star, Philippine Liberation Medal with 1 battle star, Good Conduct Medal, Victory Medal, 2 Overseas Service Bars, Army of Occupation Medal (Japan), Meritorious Unit Award

DANIEL, HOMERO

Tec4, U.S. Army, Medical Detachment, 100th Infantry Division; surgical technician
Battles: Northern France

Honors: American Campaign Medal, European-African-Middle Eastern Campaign Medal with 1 battle star, Good Conduct Medal, Victory Medal

DANIEL, REINALDO

Seaman First Class, U.S. Navy

Seaman Daniel served on both the U.S.S. Heritage and U.S.S. LST 476th with 3 months of overseas duty.

DANIEL, RICARDO

Private First Class, U.S. Army, 363rd Infantry Division, Company F; machine gunner

Battles: Rome-Arno, Northern Apennines, PO Valley

Honors: European-African-Middle Eastern Campaign Medal with 3 battle stars, Good Conduct Medal, Victory Medal

DANIEL, ROBERT A.

DAVIES, DAVID OWEN

Staff Sergeant, U.S. Army Air Forces, 15th Air Depot Group, Repair Squadron; administrative clerk

Battles: Southern Philippines, Philippines Liberation

Honors: Asiatic-Pacific Campaign Medal, Victory Medal, Good Conduct Medal, American Defense Service Medal, Philippine Liberation Medal

As reported in The Eagle Pass News Guide: "He was sent after 1 month of basic training to Lincoln Aeronautical Institute at Lincoln, Nebraska where he took airplanes to pieces and learned what made them tick." Afterwards, SSGT Davies became an aeronautical technician to "Keep em flying" with special instructions on assembly lines in Detroit, Michigan."

DAVIS, FRANCISO G.
Private First Class, U.S. Army, 305th Infantry Division, rifleman

Battles: Ryukyus, Southern Philippines (Liberations)

Honors: Philippines Liberation Medal, Asiatic-Pacific Campaign Medal with 2 battle stars and 1 bronze arrowhead, 3 Overseas Service Bars, Combat Infantryman Badge

DAVIS, VANN B.
Captain, U.S. Army Calvary Replacement Training Center, Ft. Riley Kansas, horse cavalry unit commander

Battles: New Guinea, Admiralty Islands

Honors: American Defense Service Medal, Asiatic-Pacific Campaign Medal with 2 battle stars, Combat Unit Badge, Combat Infantryman Badge

On March 21, 1944, a Jap submarine shelled the Admiralty Islands. Shortly after dark Captain Van Davis dug in on the south shore of the island, two miles from the airfield and heard a sound of a vessel off shore. He called the squadron command, asking if any of our crafts were patrolling there. The command said none was reported, but if any craft were there it is either ours or a Jap barge. The sound came closer. Then about 200 yards of shore, the men could make not one ship but two. One was a Jap barge and one was a submarine. The Yanks fired and the Japs responded. A PT boat came to aid. (The Eagle Pass News Guide)

DA BONA, HAROLD ROCCO
Second Lieutenant, U.S. Army, Cavalry Ft. Riley, Kansas; mechanized cavalry unit commander

Honors: American Campaign Medal, Victory Medal

DE HOYOS, RAUL
Private, U.S. Army Air Forces, 104th Army Air Force Base Unit

Honors: Victory Medal

DE LA CRUZ, JULIO F.
Private First Class, U.S. Army, Company C, 379th Infantry Division; machine gunner
Battles: Northern France, Rhineland, Central Europe

Honors: European-African-Middle Eastern Campaign Medal, Good Conduct Medal, Purple Heart Medal

Julio was wounded on November 14, 1944 in the European Theater.

DE LA GARZA, JESUS "Chuy"
Private First Class, U.S. Army, 152nd Quartermaster Laundry Detachment; record clerk
Qualifications: Marksman

Battles: Northern France, Ardennes, Rhineland

Honors: American Campaign Medal, European-African-Middle Eastern Campaign Medal, Good Conduct Medal, Victory Medal

DE LA GARZA, OSCAR
Tec5, U.S. Army, Battery B 453rd Coast Artillery Battalion Anti-Aircraft; duty soldier
Qualifications: Marksman
Battles: Normandy, Northern France, Ardennes, Rhineland, Central Europe
Honors: American Campaign Medal, European-African-Middle Eastern Campaign Medal with 5 battle stars, Good Conduct Medal

DE LA GARZA, PRAXEDIS
Private, U.S. Army, Company I, 39th Infantry Division; light machine gunner
Qualifications: Marksman
Battles: Germany
Honors: European-African-Middle Eastern Campaign Medal, Good Conduct Medal, Combat Infantry Badge

DE LA ROSA, JOSEPH L.
Private; truck driver
Honors: Victory Medal

DE LEON, JESUS R. "El Ladrillo"
Private First Class, U.S. Army Air Forces, 1504th Army Air Force; duty soldier
Honors: Asiatic- Pacific Campaign Medal

DE LEON, MIGUEL M.
Tec5, U.S. Army, 966th Ordnance Depot Company; clerk typist
Qualifications: Marksman
Honors: Army of Occupation Medal, Victory Medal

DE LEON Jr., PATRICIO
Private First Class, U.S. Army, 134th Infantry Regiment, 35th Infantry Division; machine gunner
Battles: Northern France
Honors: American Theater Service Medal, European-African-Middle Eastern Campaign Medal, Good Conduct Medal, Victory Medal, Purple Heart Medal,
PFC De Leon was wounded on September 10, 1944 in the European Theater.

DE LA PAZ, TRINIDAD
Seaman First Class, U.S. Navy

DEL RIO, JOHN M.
Private First Class, U.S. Army, 1962nd Ordnance Depot Company
Battles: Rhineland
Honors: European-African-Middle Eastern Campaign Medal with 1 battle star, Good Conduct Medal, Victory Medal, 1 Overseas Service Bar, Combat Infantryman Badge

DEL TORO, GABRIEL

DEL TORO, JAVIER

DENIKE, JERRY M.
Master Sergeant, U.S. Army, 31st Tank Battalion, administrative NCO

Qualifications: Carbine

Battles: Northern France, Ardennes, Rhineland, Central Europe

Honors: European-African-Middle Eastern Campaign Medal with 4 battle stars, Good Conduct Medal, Purple Heart Medal, Bronze Star Medal

M/Sgt Denike was wounded in Deurne, Holland on October 19, 1944.

DE WALD, IMMANUEL
Seaman, U.S. Navy, 76th Naval Construction Battalion, Seabees

Seaman De Wald was discharged after he received a badly broken leg while sliding into a base while playing baseball in Hawaii. He used his GI bill to go to school and for many years worked as a Border Patrol officer.

Upon retirement from the Border Patrol, Seaman De Wald became a Municipal Judge in Eagle Pass. He died in January 1982 and was buried in the Masonic Cemetery in Del Rio, Texas.

DIAZ, ADOLFO CASARES
Private First Class, U.S. Army, 243rd Quartermaster Depot Company; water supply filter operator

Battles: Mandated Islands (Mariana Island, Carolinas & Marshall Islands)

Honors: Asiatic-Pacific Campaign Medal with 1 battle star

DIAZ, PORFIRIO
Sergeant

Sgt Diaz was stationed in Australia.

DIAZ, TOMAS C.
Private, U.S. Army, Battery D, 554th Anti-Aircraft Artillery Battalion; truck driver

Qualifications: Marksman

Battles: Normandy, Northern France, Ardennes, Rhineland, Central Europe

Honors: European-African-Middle Eastern Campaign Medal with 5 battle stars, American Campaign Medal, 3 Overseas Service Bars

DICKERSON, C.W.
Lieutenant, U.S. Army Air Forces, 505th Bomb Group; left gunner B-29

The unit served primarily in the Pacific Ocean Theater of World War II as part of 20th Air Force. The 505th Bomb Group's aircraft engaged in B-29 Super fortress bombardment operations against Japan. Its aircraft were identified by a "K" (January to March 1945) or "W" (April to September 1945) inside of a circle painted on the tail.

After World War II, Dickerson attended University of Texas at Austin to become a teacher. Afterwards, he volunteered back into the U.S. army and served in the Korean War in Germany. When he was discharged from the Army, he became a teacher and later a principal with the Eagle Pass Independent School District.

DICKEY, ISAAC V.
Sergeant, 1643rd Ordnance Company; welder

Battles: Algeria-French, Moroccan, Tunisia, Rome-Arno

Honors: European-African-Middle Eastern Campaign Medal with 3 battle stars and 1 bronze arrowhead, Good Conduct Medal

DICKSON Jr., RAY E.
Captain, U.S. Army

Before the War, Capt Dickson came to Eagle Pass in 1940 to assist in planning and organizing the fair. Ultimately, Capt Dickson was killed in action in France.

DODGE, HAROLD R.
Technical Sergeant, U.S. Army Air Forces, 558th Bombardment Squadron; airplane maintenance

Qualifications: Army Air Force Technician Badge

Battles: Normandy, Northern France, Ardennes, Rhineland, Central Europe, Air Offensive Europe

Honors: American Campaign Medal, European-African-Middle Eastern Campaign Medal, Good Conduct Medal, Victory Medal, Distinguished Unit Badge, Bronze Star Medal

DOLAN, BUZZ
U.S. Army

Dolan helped negotiate the German surrender in Italy.

DOLCH, ALLAN B.
Sergeant, U.S. Army Air Forces, 9th Air Force, 9th Troop Carrier Command; expert mechanic

Battles: Sicilian Campaign

Honors: American Defense Service Medal, European-African-Middle Eastern Campaign Medal with 1 battle star, Good Conduct Medal

After his enlistment on December 4, 1940, Sergeant Dolch was one of the first seven soldiers assigned to the newly activated troop carrier squadron.

DOLCH, ELMER H.
Sergeant

DOMINGUEZ, ARTURO L
Private First Class, U.S. Army; medical aidman
Honors: Victory Medal

DOOLEY, KENNETH L.

DOVALINA, HECTOR F.
Private First Class, U.S. Army, HQ 3rd Squadron, 124th Calvary, truck driver
Battles: Central Burma, India Burma
Honors: American Campaign Medal, Asiatic-Pacific Campaign Medal with 2 battle stars, Good Conduct Medal, Victory Medal

DOWNING, CHARLES G. "CHARLIE"
Captain, U.S. Army Air Forces, Headquarters Squadron 5th Air Force; adjutant
Battles: Luzon, Bismarck, Archipelago, New Guinea, Southern Philippines Liberation
Honors: Philippine Liberation Medal with 1 service star, Asiatic- Pacific Campaign Medal with 4 battle stars, American Campaign Medal, Victory Medal, Army of Occupation Medal (Japan)

DRAKE, ROYCE A.
Lieutenant Colonel, U.S. Army, 5th Calvary Regiment; commanding officer

Lt Col Drake was killed in action during the retaking of Leyte in the Philippine Islands on October 21, 1944. After the surrender of Japan, one of the twenty military installations around Tokyo area in Japan was named Camp Drake in his honor. Camp Drake was active until the 1970s where it contained a hospital, handling troops from Vietnam.

DUEY, NEWELL H.
First Lieutenant, U.S. Army Air Forces

DURAN, JUAN S.
Technical Sergeant, U.S. Army Air Forces, 339th Fighter Squadron; airplane maintenance technician
Battles: Bismarck Archipelago, China, Guadalcanal, New Guinea, Northern Solomon, Southern Philippines (Liberation), Western Pacifica Anti-Submarine
Honors: American Defense Medal, Philippine Liberation Medal, Asiatic-Pacific Campaign Medal, Good Conduct Medal

SSgt Duran was a crew chief with the famed "Sun Setter" squadron of the 13th Fighter Command in the South Pacific. According to The Eagle Pass News Guide, "The "Sun Setters" have blasted 1656 Japanese planes from the South Pacific skies...have proved themselves to be one of the top squadrons in the Army Air Force." SSgt Duran, brothers, Corporal Marcelino S. Duran and Private Marcos Duran, were also in the armed forces.

DURAN, LUIS SALINAS
Electricians Mate Third Class, U.S. Navy

DURAN, MARCELINO S.
Corporal, U.S. Army Air Forces, 462nd Army Air Force; radio repairman
Qualifications: Marksman Carbine
Honors: American Campaign Medal, Good Conduct Medal, Victory Medal

DURAN, MARCOS S.
Private, U.S. Army, Signal Corps
Private Duran is the brother of Marcelino and Juan Duran.

EBENSTEIN, WILLIAM E.
Private, U.S. Army Air Forces, 834th Air Engineer Squadron; cook
Honors: European-African-Middle Eastern Campaign Medal, American Defense Service Medal

ELGUEZABAL, ARTURO
Private First Class, U.S. Army, Battery A, 459th Coast Artillery Battalion; cannoneer
Qualifications: Marksman
Battles: Normandy, Northern France, Ardennes, Central Europe
Honors: European-African-Middle Eastern Campaign Medal with 5 battle stars, Good Conduct Medal

EIGUEZABAL, JOSE
Private First Class, Company F, 276th Combat Infantry Division
Qualifications: Marksman
Battles: Rome-Arno
Honors: European-African-Middle Eastern Campaign Medal with 1 battle star, Combat Infantryman Badge

ENRIQUEZ, EDUARDO P.
Corporal, U.S. Army Air Forces, 321st Bomb Group; cook
Battles: Bismarck, Archipelago, New Guinea, Northern Solomon, Southern Philippines (Liberation), Luzon, Western Pacific
Honors: Asiatic Pacific Theater, Philippine (Liberation), Good conduct

ESCONTRIAS, GERARDO
Sergeant, U.S. Army, Company B, 259th Infantry Division; rifleman
Battles: Rhineland, Central Europe
Honors: African-Middle Eastern Campaign Medal with 2 battle stars, Good Conduct Medal, Purple Heart Medal, Bronze Star Medal, Victory Medal, 2 Overseas Service Bars, Combat Infantryman Badge
Sgt Escontrias was wounded April 22, 1945 in the European Theater.

ESPARZA, FRANCISCO LUIS
Cpl Esparza volunteered to serve in WWII in 1944, in exchange he was given U.S. citizenship. He was stationed at Charleston Army Air Field and was responsible for the cargo shipments that came on the Liberty Ships.

ESPARZA, JUAN Z.
Private First Class, U.S. Army, HQ Company, 148th Infantry Regiment; rifleman

Battles: New Georgia Campaign, Bougainville, Luzon

Honors: Asiatic-Pacific Campaign Medal, American Defense Service Medal, Purple Heart Medal, 6 Overseas Service Bars, Good Conduct Medal, Philippine Liberation Medal, Combat Infantryman Badge

PFC Esparza started his tour of overseas service on May 26, 1942. He was stationed on Fiji Islands, Guadalcanal, Russell Islands and a veteran of the New Georgia Campaign.

ESPARZA, LOUIS
Private, U.S. Army

Private Esparza was a former salesman of the J.C. Penny Co. According to The Eagle Pass News Guide- "Since the 1st of July 1943, all J.C. Penny stores had been conducting an intensive drive aimed a selling $10,000,000 worth of War Bonds and Stamps during the month. Pictures of service men, including the picture of Private Esparaza, were on display at J.C. Penny stores. These pictures had been borrowed for the occasion from local people—relatives and friends".

ESPARZA, PAULO Z.
Tec5, U.S. Army, 142nd General Hospital; medical technician

Honors: American Campaign Medal, Asiatic-Pacific Campaign Medal, Good Conduct Medal, Victory Medal, 1 Service Stripe, 2 Overseas Service Bars

Esparza entered active duty service on January 19, 1943 and attended Army service training at Camp Barkley, Texas.

ESPINOSA, JESUS M.
Tec5, U.S. Army, 145th Engineer Battalion

Qualifications: Sharpshooter

Battles: Northern France, Europe, Rhineland, Ardennes, Normandy

Honors: European-African-Middle Eastern Campaign Medal with 5 battle stars, American Defense Service Medal, Good Conduct Medal

ESQUIVEL JR. , PILAR
Private First Class, U.S. Army, Battery C, 867th Field Artillery Battalion; gun crewman

Qualifications: Sharpshooter

Battles: Rhineland, Central Europe

Honors: American Campaign Medal, European-African-Middle Eastern Campaign Medal with 2 battle stars, Good Conduct Medal, Victory Medal

ESQUIVEL, RAUL

ESTRADA JR., AUGUSTIN
Tec4, U.S. Army, 758th Engineer Parts Supply Company; clerk typist
Battles: Southern Philippines
Honors: Victory Medal, Good Conduct Medal, American Campaign Medal, Asiatic-Pacific Campaign Medal with one battle star, Philippine Liberation Medal

ESTRADA, FRANCISCO L
Private, U.S. Army, 345th Military Police Escort Guard Company; military policeman
Honors: Asiatic-Pacific Campaign Medal, Victory Medal

ETHERIDGE, H.C.
H.C. Etheridge was killed in action.

ETTER, HENRY W.
Corporal, U.S. Army Air Forces, 3rd Emergency Rescue Squadron; airplane and engine mechanic
Battles: Air Offensive Japan, Southern Philippine (Liberation), Luzon, Western Pacific, Ryukyus
Honors: American Campaign Medal, Asiatic-Pacific Campaign Medal with 5 battle stars, Philippine Liberation Medal with 2 battle stars, Victory Medal, 1 Service Stripe, 1 Overseas Service Bar

ETTER, ROY JAMES
Sergeant, U.S. Army Air Forces, 462nd Army Air Force Base Unit; radio mechanic
Qualifications: Army Air Force Technician Badge, Marksman
Honors: American Campaign Medal, Victory Medal, Good Conduct Medal

EVISTON, FRED

FALCON, ADOLFO H.
Tec5, U.S. Army, Medical Detachment, 359th Infantry Division; surgical technician
Qualifications: Medical Badge
Battles: Normandy
Honors: American Campaign Medal, European-African-Middle Eastern Campaign Medal with 1 battle star and 1 bronze arrowhead, Good Conduct Medal, Victory Medal

FALCON, FRANCISCO H.
Private First Class, U.S. Army, Company A, 2nd Engineer Combat Battalion; cook
Qualifications: Sharpshooter
Battles: Normandy, Northern France
Honors: American Defense Service Medal, American Campaign Medal, European-African-Middle Eastern Campaign Medal with 2 battle stars, Victory Medal

FALCON, MIGUEL H.
Private, U.S. Army

FARHAT, GEORGE
British 8th Army

Battles: North Africa, Greece, 4-year prisoner of war

George Farhat was a long term resident of Eagle Pass. Around 1960 George Farhat opened a very successful Western wear Store in downtown Eagle Pass. The following story was told by George Farhat's brother, Fred Farhat.

"George was born in California. When he was a teenager, he decided to work for his uncle who was a building contractor in Palestine. He was getting tired of working with his uncle when World War II started in 1939. George decided to enlist in the British Army in 1940 when he was 17 or 18. He served until 1945, when he returned to Palestine for a short time prior to returning to the United States in 1946.

George's first military assignment in the British Army was in Saudi Arabia. Next, he served with the British 8th Army under General Montgomery, fighting in Egypt, Libya and Tobruk. About everyone had left Tobruk, except for the Italians. They said that everything was nice and quiet, so we (the British Army) will give you a 30-day furlough to go to Egypt. Instead of his boat going to Egypt, his unit ended in Athens Greece. Because of an unsuccessful Italian invasion on October 28, 1940 in Greece, Winston Churchill sent troops including George's unit to reinforce Greece in anticipation of a German attack. Germany attacked Greece and George's unit fought the German Troops in this area for about six months. The Greek army with the British, Australian and New Zealand troops were outnumbered and could not defend itself against both the Italian and German troops. The British troops were to be evacuated. However, before a ship came to pick up George and the rest of his unit, the German soldiers surrounded the British troops and the British army officers ordered their troops (7,000 soldiers) to lay down their weapons and surrender to the German Army. One month later, Crete and Greece was captured by Germany.

After surrendering, he and the other soldiers became interned in the prisoner of war camp at Serrai, Greece. While there, the soldiers all became very badly infested by lice. They had very little to eat and if it had not been for the Red Cross gift packages that they received while there, more of them would have died of starvation. These packages included about 50 cigarettes, a can of condensed milk mixed with chocolate syrup (Carnation Brand) or plain condensed milk, chocolate, sometimes coffee, dried tea, canned ham or bully beef, canned sardines, and crackers. The cigarettes, coffee and chocolate were the most prized by their German guards and they could trade these to the Germans for a loaf of bread or other needed items.

Their usual breakfast while in this camp was hot tea made of Eucalyptus tree leaves, which no one would have drunk except that it was hot and it warmed their stomachs. For lunch they were supposed to get a bowl of soup with vegetables. However, the soup usually never had any vegetables and was mostly only hot water. For supper they had a slice of bread, a slice of baloney or ham, a spoon of butter, a spoon of sugar and a bowl of soup. The soup was usually made by boiling horse bones in hot water. George said that he thought they would never leave this camp alive. They were always cold, especially their fingers, hands and toes and sickness of many different kinds was a frequent event while they were there. They were required to work out of doors without gloves or overshoes and many did not have warm coats. The German Soldiers kept telling them that they were going to capture and imprison the world. They were the superior race and if you did not do as they said, they would kill you and so-on. George firmly believes that in effect the United States of America saved the World by furnishing arms and supplies to England, Russia and the other Allies. George said that while in the POW camp, the commanding German officer was controlling the Black Market in the area, including the Red Cross packages. Apparently his superior officers found out about it and came to investigate him. However, the commanding officer shot himself rather than face his superiors. After that, they did receive more of their Red Cross packages.

The British prisoners were in this camp for about 4 months. They were then sent to Germany. There they had all their hair shaved off, their clothes taken from them and deloused, much to their relief and the comfort of everyone. Their primary work for about a year was shoveling sand into open-topped railroad cars with scoop shovels day after day. This sand was used to build more railroad tracks. Each morning they would walk from the prisoner of war camp without warm clothes or gloves, work all day and then walk back to camp again that evening.

Next, they were transferred to a camp near the center of Berlin to work in a factory named Solex. The prisoners did a variety of work but George's group would blow a mixture of aluminum and other metals into a machine that molded the metal into machine parts. Someone said the part that they were making was carburetors for tanks. They would then remove the parts from the machines when they had cooled and place them into barrels to be taken to another part of the factory. They had work shifts both at night and during the day. They were here for about a year.

Then they were moved to Italy where they would go up into the mountains to plant trees. It was a crazy place to be and there was much confusion, like the day when all the Italian guards just threw their arms down and left the camp. The prisoners were without any guards and in effect they were free. However, there was really no place for them to go and no place to get food from. Some of the guys went down into the town just to look around, where some German soldiers on motorcycles saw them. The soldiers knew that they were Prisoners of War because all of them had large red circles painted on their trousers. The Germans told these prisoners to return to camp and that they would pick them up from there. The prisoners returned to camp and told the others at camp what had happened. There was considerable confusion, with men running every which way and no one really knowing what to do. Some prisoners decided to stay on at Camp, others went back into town and still others went into the nearby mountains. George and a couple of other guys that he knew very well decided to walk up to the top of the mountain and try to escape that way.

They could not go all of the way up the mountain the first day and had to spend the night on the side of the mountain. The next morning when they looked back toward the Camp, the German Soldiers were in the process of surrounding it. They fired a number of rounds of shells over the Camp and when no firing was returned, they took the Camp over. The prisoners that remained at Camp were taken back to Germany. The Germans made no effort to locate any of those who had escaped. There were about 200 who had fled into the mountains. George and two others ended up in a small village with just a few houses adjacent to small villages nearby. The townspeople felt sorry for them and fed them regular meals daily. When the Germans heard of this, they surrounded the village, captured the prisoners and returned them to Germany.

They were then taken to Austria for about 6 months. They were taken into the mountains daily to a rock quarry. Here they made small rocks out of large rocks with sledge-hammers. Then the group was transferred to France to repair bomb damaged airfields, roads, railroads and other such places. They did this until 1944 when the War was going against the Germans. They started leaving to return to Germany. The prisoners were all loaded into crowded train boxcars. While still in France, many of the prisoners were able to carve and break holes in the doors of the boxcars so they were able to reach outside of the doors and unlock them. This enabled them to jump off of the slow moving trains and escape into the surrounding countryside. Many of them just jumped off the train and hide in the brush adjacent to the train tracks until the train had passed them by so that the guards riding on top of the train would not shoot them.

George and two other guys ended up in a small village with just a few houses adjacent to small farms. After hiding in the nearby brush for 2 or 3 days, they ran out of water. George said that they had seen a young girl working nearby shoveling hay off a wagon. The next time that they saw her working, George said that he approached her and, in French, he asked her for some water. She pointed to a large concrete water tank with a faucet sticking out from its side. George said that he took a big drink, filled their water bottles, thanked the girl and returned to their hiding place. In a short while, three Frenchmen with rifles came to where the girl had seen them go into hiding. George and the other two men told them that they were Englishmen that had escaped the "Prisoner of War" train that was returning them back to Germany. The Frenchmen told them that they were welcome and that they were glad to see them. They were fed and cared for by the French and eleven days later the Americans showed up. George told the Americans that they wanted to be returned to England.

The Americans put them on a troop carrying trucks and transported them to a camp on the coast of France where other British Soldiers were waiting to be taken to England. From there they were sent on the two hour boat trip across the English Channel back to England. They mostly just laid around and did very little work for the first two months that they were there. They were however, questioned daily about what they had seen in Europe, the German troop movements, the number and kind of German troops, the amount and type of equipment, the amount and type of damage to airports, bridges, railroads and all other types of damage, etc. Almost the same questions were asked over and over again each day. They were also given complete medical examinations and treatment, rest and care to return them back to good health. They stayed in England for six months before being returned to Palestine.

Once back in Palestine, they were told that they had a choice of either staying in the British Army or being discharged from the Army. George told them that he would prefer to get out.

The war was still not over but it did end in about a month. He found out later that the British really did not want them to stay in the Army because the war was nearly over and by letting these soldiers choose to get out, the British Government did not have to pay them the discharge pay that was promised to soldiers still serving at end of the War. This would have amounted to about 500 pounds to each soldier. George said that he did not mind too much as what he really wanted was to get out of the Army."

After the war, Sandra Farhat, daughter of George Farhat said that George would donate $1,000 a year to the Red Cross because he felt that the Red Cross helped saved his life.

FERNANDEZ, SANTOS

Private, U.S. Army, Company A, 550th Infantry Airborne Battalion

Battles: Rome-Arno, Southern France, Germany

Honors: Purple Heart Medal, European-African-Middle Eastern Campaign Medal

Pvt Fernandez was wounded on October 18, 1944 in the European Theater.

Santos Fernandez volunteered along with many other young Mexican immigrants for military service once the U.S. declared war on Japan and entered war in Europe. Even though some were not yet American citizens, he used to say, "We HAD to go do our part too!" Santos was naturalized as an American citizen in Algeria (not Nigeria), North Africa on his way to France by way of Italy. He would talk about his experience as "rough". Marching in the bitter cold was really harsh he'd say. He and others found ways to keep their feet from frost bite by using old letters to insulate their boots. He suffered with foot issues the rest of his life from having to keep going with wet socks in their boots for miles and miles. He'd say there was no getting around it . . . "we had to keep moving or become a target". He learned to speak a little French and Italian by conversing with the locals as they entered and secured towns and villages. He was injured on the French side of the Alps, having marched over from Italy. I'm not sure where but he remembers the French Alps as his last stand. He had just minutes before replaced a buddy on guard duty when a shell hit the area he was guarding. He remembers a lieutenant, name unknown, being his savior as he recalls going in and out of consciousness as the lieutenant went up the hill to where he was and dragged and carried him (Santos) over his shoulder down to safety and medic and again going up to and back down with at least one other. My dad would often say his regret was not knowing who that lieutenant was that saved his life. He remembers his body on fire and telling the lieutenant to just leave him there and he remembers the lieutenant saying "hang in there, I got you." His next memory is that of being told by a field medical team that he was going to lose his right arm and left leg. He remembered telling them in no uncertain terms that if was going to die, he was going to go whole, in one piece. He was patched up best as possible and sent home on a medical ship. He says that trip was almost as bad as the injuries themselves. Everyone suffered from sea sickness as they must have traveled through very rough seas. He says all the guys injured and laying in those bunks were miserable the entire trip. His injuries consisted of missing 3 ribs and a lung and his body littered with shrapnel. He endured many, many surgeries at the VA hospital in El Paso, Texas where he stayed for an extended period of time first in a full body cast and then slowly enduring many months of physical rehabilitation. Shrapnel fragments continued to move around in his body and some literally to the surface of his skin, where Drs. at the Long Beach, CA VA Hospital would occasionally extract these jagged edged metal fragments and stitch him up. This continued up to his early 80's. He passed away March 7, 2012 at home in Whittier, CA, one month short of his 92 birthday. (written by Estelle Lester, daughter)

FISHER, BYRON G.
Major, U.S. Army

FITCH, LENOX ALEXANDER
Seaman First Class, U.S. Navy

Honors: Victory Medal

Seaman First Class Fitch entered service September 8, 1944 and served at the Naval Training Center in San Diego, California.

FLETCHER, Sr., DOUGLAS
Airman 2nd Class, U.S. Navy, Utility Squadron Seven, Utility Squadron Fourteen, Utility Squadron One

Airman 2nd Class Fletcher entered service on April 2, 1944 and served at the Naval.

FLORES, ANTONIO JACOB

FLORES, BELISARIO J.
Major General, U.S. Army, Headquarters, 38th Field Artillery Battalion, 2nd Infantry Division.

Honors: Victory Medal

After WWII, Major Gen Flores attended St. Mary's University in San Antonio, Texas and served in the Army ROTC and gained an officer's commission in 1950. He also served in the Korean War and joined the Texas Air National Guard in 1954 where he was only one of three Hispanic officers. During the Korean War he earned a Bronze Star as an Artillery Forward Observer. Major General Flores held the position of Assistant Adjutant General for Air for the state of Texas from September 1971 until he retired in July 1986. He was the first Hispanic to hold the position of Assistant Adjutant general. He was also the first Hispanic to hold the rank of general in the Texas Air National Guard.

FLORES, CARLOS GARZA

FLORES, ENRIQUE
Seaman 1st Class, U.S. Navy, Company 33 A-7

Seaman 1st Class Flores served on the tank landing ship U.S.S. LST 30

FLORES, GILBERT D.
Staff Sergeant, U.S. Army, Company A, 931st Signal Battalion; mess sergeant

Battles: China, Central Burma, India Burma

Honors: American Campaign Medal, Asiatic- Pacific Campaign Medal, Good Conduct Medal, Victory Medal, Meritorious Unit Award

FLORES, GUADALUPE S.
Private First Class, U.S. Army, Company G, 101st Infantry; demolition specialist

Qualifications: Sharpshooter

Battles: Ardennes, Rhineland, Central Europe

Honors: American Campaign Medal, European-African-Middle Eastern Service Medal with 3 battle stars, Good Conduct Medal, Victory Medal

FLORES, GUILLERMO
US Navy

FLORES, JUAN C "EL PURRAQUE"
Tec5, U.S. Army, Company G, 1915th, Engineers Aviation Battalion; electrician

Battles: Ryukyus

Honors: American Campaign Medal, Asiatic-Pacific Campaign Medal, Good Conduct Medal, Victory Medal

The Army of the U.S. described Tec5 Flores' position as maintaining electricity generator field, connecting wiring to light up landing fields at night, repairing wiring when needed, minor repairs of generator motors, and operating and maintaining refrigerators and generators.

FLORES, LOUIS CASARES
Tec5, U.S. Army, Troop A, 8th Engineers; truck driver
Qualifications: Marksman
Battles: New Guinea, Bismarck Archipelago, Southern Philippines, Luzon
Honors: Asiatic-Pacific Campaign Medal with 4 battle stars, Philippine Liberation Medal with 2 battle stars, Good Conduct Medal, American Defense Service Medal

FLORES, MIGUEL
Private First Class, U.S. Army Air Forces, 807th Army Air Force; duty soldier
Honors: American Theater, Victory Medal, Good Conduct Medal

FLORES, REFUGIO H.
Private First Class, U.S. Army, 32nd Infantry Division (Red Arrow Division), Company E, 127th Infantry Regiment; combat infantryman

The men of the 32nd wore the Red Arrow patch signifying that their division had pierced every line it had encountered. The 32nd logged a total of 654 days of combat during WWII, more than any other US Army division. The division was among the first to enter the war and were still engaging Japanese soldiers after the official Japanese surrender. PFC Flores' division was engaged in jungle combat for months in New Guinea and the Battle of Leyte Campaigns. They only had only three weeks rest after the Battle of Leyte before they invaded Luzon, Philippines on January 30, 1945. PFC Flores was killed in action by a shell fragment to the chest and head on April 28, 1945 on the Villa Verde Trail near Santa Maria, Luzon, Philippines.

FOSTER, COZEL
U.S. Marine Corps, 3d Division

In 1945, Corp. Foster sailed from Pearl Harbor to San Diego on the U.S.S. Texas, the only battleship to serve in both WWI and WWII.

After WWII, in 1955 until he retired in 1993, Foster joined the faculty of Eagle Pass High School, where he led the football team to a district championship. He was inducted into the Texas High School Coach Hall of Fame in 1996.

FRANCE, ARTHUR T.

FRICK, HENRY WILLIAM
Private, U.S. Army, Southern Personnel Reassignment Center; ammunition carrier
Battles: North Africa and Sicily
Honor: European-African-Middle Eastern Campaign Medal with 2 battle stars, Good Conduct Medal

FRICK, JULIUS
Private First Class, U.S. Army, Medical Detachment Department, 1977th Service Command Unit; field lineman
Qualifications: Marksman Honors: Good Conduct Medal

FUENTES, CELESTINO

FUENTES, EDUARDO
Tec4, U.S. Army, HQ Company, 4th Infantry Division; cook
Qualifications: Sharpshooter
Honors: American Campaign Medal, Good Conduct Medal, Victory Medal

FUENTES, RAFAEL
Private, U.S. Army, 1st Service Squadron, 3rd Service Group; automotive equipment operator
Battles: Algeria, France, Morocco, Naples-Foggia, Rome-Arno, Tunisia
Honors: European-African-Middle Eastern Campaign Medal, Good Conduct Medal

FUENTES, SAM

GAINE, ENRIQUE

GALAN, JESUS GARCIA
Seaman Interior Communication Electricians(S/IC), U.S. Navy
Seaman Galan was appointed squad leader on August 1, 1944, assigned to the U.S.S. Gosper. He served 13 months of sea duty.

GALAN, ROBERTO
Private First Class, U.S. Army, 820th Military Police Company; military policeman
Qualifications: Driver and Mechanic Badge
Honors: 1 Service Stripe, Army of Occupation Medal (Germany), Victory Medal, 3 Overseas Service Bars, American Campaign Medal, European-African-Middle Eastern Medal, Good Conduct Medal

GALINDO, O.G.

GAMERO, RAMON P.
Private, U.S. Army, 815th Quartermaster Gas Supply Company; truck driver
Qualifications: Sharpshooter
Battles: Normandy, Northern France, Ardennes, Rhineland, Central Europe
Honors: 3 Overseas Service Bars, European-African-Middle Eastern Campaign Medal with 5 battle stars

GAMEZ, FRANK FLORES
Carpenter's Mate Second Class, U.S. Navy

GARCIA, ALCALA

GARCIA, ARMANDO S.
Private First Class, U.S. Army, 11th Infantry Company D, Medical Detachment; ammunition handler

Battles: Central Europe, Rhineland

Honors: American Defense Service Medal, European-African-Middle Eastern Campaign Medal with 2 battle stars, Good Conduct Medal, Combat Infantry Badge

GARCIA, ANTONIO

Private, U.S. Army, 4473rd Quartermaster Truck Company; truck driver

Qualifications: Driver and Mechanic Badge

Battles: Normandy, Ardennes, Rhineland, Central Europe

Honors: American Campaign Medal, European-African-Middle Eastern Campaign Medal with 4 battle stars, Victory Medal

GARCIA, ARNOLDO ORTIZ

GARCIA, ARNULFO S.

Sergeant, U.S. Army, 442nd Anti-aircraft Artillery Battalion

Qualifications: Sharpshooter

Battles: European-African-Middle Eastern Campaign Medal

GARCIA, ARTURO

Radioman First Class, U.S. Navy

Honors: European-African-Middle Eastern Campaign Medal with 2 battle stars, Victory Medal, Good Conduct Medal

Radioman First Class Garcia served aboard the CVE-25 escort carrier, U.S.S. Croatan. From October 17-December 29, 1943, the Croatan made two voyages to Casablanca, Morocco, ferrying aircraft and airplane crewmen in support of the North African operations. U.S.S. Croatan made a most successful patrol from March 24- May 11, 1944. On April 7, 1944, her airplanes spotted and identified U-856 enemy submarine, which was sunk by her escorts, Champlin and Huse. On April 25-16, 1944, her four escorts joined in sinking U-488. Seaman Garcia recalls when a torpedo was fired at his carrier, the captain took evasive action and everything not bolted down was moving. Following the war, Seaman Garcia became a biology teacher at Eagle Pass High School. Years later, Arturo Garcia became the Mayor of Eagle Pass.

GARCIA, ESTEBAN

Private, U.S. Army

Private Garcia was inducted into the Army on June 1, 1943, Grand Island

GARCIA, JACOBO L.

Private First Class, U.S. Army, 815th Quartermaster Sterilization Company; truck driver

Qualifications: Marksman

Battles: Normandy, Northern France, Ardennes, Rhineland, Central Europe

Honors: European-African-Middle Eastern Campaign Medal with 5 battle stars, 3 Overseas Service Bars

GARCIA, RAMON DE LOS SANTOS
U.S. Army, Battery B, 442nd Anti-aircraft Artillery Battalion; truck driver

Battles: Northern Apennines, PO Valley

Honors: European-African-Middle Eastern Campaign Medal with 2 battle stars, Good Conduct Medal, Victory Medal, 1 service stripe, 5 Overseas Service Bars, Combat Infantry Badge

GARCIA, JESUS CELESTINO
Ship Serviceman Third Class, U.S. Navy

GARCIA, JOSE S.
Private First Class, U.S. Army, Anti-Tank Company, 387th Infantry Regiment; Anti-Tank Gun Crew

Battles: South Philippines (Liberation), Luzon

Honors: Asiatic-Pacific Campaign Medal with 2 battle stars, Philippine Liberation Medal with 1 battle star, Good Conduct Medal, Army Occupation Medal (Japan), Victory Medal, 2 overseas Service Bars, Combat Infantryman Badge

GARCIA, RAMON D.
U.S. Army, Battery B, 442nd Anti-aircraft Artillery Battalion; truck driver

Battles: Northern Apennines, PO Valley

Honors: European-African-Middle Eastern Campaign Medal with 2 battle stars, Good Conduct Medal, Victory Medal, 1 Service Stripe, 5 Overseas Service Bars, Combat Infantry Badge

GARCIA, RAUL SANTOS
Private First Class, U.S. Army, Battery B, 130th FA Battalion; cannoneer

Qualifications: Expert Gunner

Honors: Good Conduct Medal

GARCIA, RAUL T.
Private First Class, U.S. Army, Company B, 806th Replacement Battalion

Qualifications: Sharpshooter

Honors: American Campaign Medal, European-African-Middle Eastern Campaign Medal, Good Conduct Medal, Victory Medal

GARCIA, RODRIGO
Private First Class, U.S. Army, 27th General Hospital; hospital orderly

Qualifications: Marksman

Battles: Philippines (Liberation)

Honors: American Campaign Medal, Meritorious Unit Award, Victory Medal, Good Conduct Medal

GARCIA, VIRGIL V.

GARDNER Jr., ROBERT JAMES
Ensign, U.S. Navy

Ensign Gardner was stationed in Alaska in 1942. In 1943, he graduated from the Naval Reserve Officers Indoctrination School in Tucson, Arizona with the 13th Battalion, completing 60 days of training in navigation ordinance, and communications. Ensign Gardner was a former football coach at Eagle Pass High School.

GARZA, ALBERT K.
Qualifications: Marksman

Honors: American Campaign Medal, Asiatic-Pacific Campaign Medal with 1 battle star, Good Conduct Medal, Victory Medal with 2 Overseas Service Bars

Tec5 Garza met Mary Orta in 1942 at Kelly AFB, San Antonio, Texas. Mary worked in the fabric department making ailerons for airplanes, including trainers and B-29's. Albert and Mary were married after the war on November 21, 1948.

GARZA, ALBERTO M.
Staff Sergeant, U.S. Army, Exchange Section; clerk

Honors: American Campaign Medal, Asiatic-Pacific Campaign Medal, Good Conduct Medal, Victory Medal

GARZA, ALFREDO MARSHALL
Lieutenant, U.S. Army Air Forces; Assistant Engineering Officer and Air Contract Liason Officer at the 36th Street Army Base in Miami, Florida

Before entering the Army, Lt Garza worked at Pan American Airways and Braniff Airways as a maintenance and aircraft engineer.

GARZA, BRISIDO

GARZA, DANIEL

GARZA, ENCARNACION G.
Private First Class, U.S. Army Air Forces, 1288th Engineer Battalion

Qualifications: Marksman

GARZA, FRANCISCO M.
Private, U.S. Army, Company D 508th Parachute Infantry; paratrooper, automatic rifleman

Battles: Rome-Arno, Southern France; Ardennes, Rhineland, Central Europe

Honors: European-African-Middle Eastern Campaign Medal with 5 battle stars, Good Conduct Medal, Distinguished Unit Badge, Victory Medal, 3 Overseas Service Bars, Combat Infantry Badge

GARZA, GUADALUPE I.

Corporal, U.S. Army, Battery B, 58th Field Artillery; gun crewman

Qualifications: Marksman

Battles: Tunisia; Sicily; Normandy, Northern France; Ardennes, Rhineland

Honors: American Campaign Medal, European-African-Middle Eastern Campaign Medal with 6 battle stars and 1 bronze arrowhead, Distinguished Unit Badge, Good Conduct Medal, Victory Medal, 4 Overseas Service Bars, 1 Service Stripe, Purple Heart Medal

Letter (The Eagle Pass News Guide June 24, 1943 Vol 1, 7033)

"I left New York November 2 landed in Casa Blanca in French Morocco on November 18th. The Vichy French put up a three day fight but it did not amount to much. From Casa Blanca we moved into Rabat. It was a smaller town than Casa Blanca. Casa Blanca is one of the largest towns in North Africa. We stayed in Rabat approximately three weeks when we got the train and went to Tebessa a town in Southern Tunisia. Tebessa was occupied by the Germans about three days before we got there. From Tebessa we convoyed into a position between some mountains. We moved at night almost every time. First day we captured twenty Italian prisoners. From this place we moved into the famous town of Maknossy a place I won't forget the rest of my life. At this certain place we had our main battle. We stayed 21 days under enemy bombing and artillery shelling continuously every day. After three weeks the Jerries, which are the Germans evacuated the place and we took the town. It was considered as the "Battle of El Guetar." It was here where the British Eighth Army joined the Americans on the right and the French on the left side of the Bizerte. We took Matuer after a week's battling. Yanks went through Matuer on May 8th and on Mother's Day we were fifteen miles from Bizerte when the Germans surrendered. From May 9th we just waited with our guns pointed at the Germans in case they would try to fight again. On May 12th we moved back for a rest. Next day I went on a tour into Tunisia. All the people were glad to see us. We all had a swell time. I met a couple of French girls and with my amateur French I started to talk to them and I was lucky they could understand me fairly well."

Cpl Garza was wounded on September 5, 1944 in the European Theater.

GARZA, JESUS R.

Private First Class, U.S. Army, 709th Tank Battalion; medium tank crewman

Qualifications: Marksman

Battles: Rhineland, Central Europe

Honors: European-African-Middle Eastern Campaign Medal with 2 battle stars, Good Conduct Medal, Victory Medal, 2 Overseas Service Bars

GARZA, JOSE "EL APARATO"

Staff Sergeant, U.S. Army, 6th Engine Overhaul Squadron; cook

Qualifications: Marksman

Battles: New Guinea

Honors: Overseas Service Bar, American Campaign Medal, Asiatic-Pacific Campaign Medal with 1 battle star, Good Conduct Medal, Victory Medal, 1 Service Stripe

GARZA, LUIS B.
Private First Class, U.S. Army, 317th Infantry Regiment; rifleman
Battles: Rhineland; New Guinea
Honors: European-African-Middle Eastern Campaign Medal with 1 battle star, Asiatic-Pacific Campaign Medal with 1 battle star, Good Conduct Medal, Purple Heart Medal
PFC Garza was wounded in France on November 14, 1944.

GARZA, MANUEL B.

GARZA, MANUEL M
Sergeant, U.S. Army, Company A, 117th Infantry Regiment; machine gunner
Qualifications: Marksman
Battles: Northern France, Europe, Rhineland, Ardennes
Honors: Distinguished Unit Badge, European-African-Middle Eastern Campaign Medal, Good Conduct Medal, Combat Infantry Badge

GARZA, MELECIO M.
Sergeant, U.S. Army Air Force, 370th Bombardment Squadron; baker
Qualifications: Marksman
Battles: Bismarck, Archipelago; Eastern Mandates, New Guinea, Northern Solomon, Luzon, Southern Philippines (Liberation), Western Pacific, Air Offensive Borneo
Honors: Distinguished Unit Badge, Asiatic-Pacific Campaign Medal with 8 battle stars, Good Conduct Medal, Victory Medal, 3 Overseas Service Bars

GARZA, OSCAR T.
Private First Class, U.S. Army, 142nd Infantry; truck driver

GATES, MACARIO "EL TORO"
Private First Class, U.S. Army, 62nd Bombardment Squadron; duty soldier
Qualifications: Sharpshooter
Battles: Western Pacific, Air Offensive Japan
Honors: American Campaign Medal, Asiatic-Pacific Campaign Medal with 2 battle stars, Good Conduct Medal, 1 Overseas Service Bar, Victory Medal

GIL, ALBERTO
Tec5, U.S. Army, 56th Medical Detachment; medic
Battles: European Theater of Operations
Honors: Purple Heart Medal, Bronze Star Medal, Silver Star Medal

Tec5 Gil sent many letters via V-mail from England, France and Germany to his family before he was tragically killed. The letters are very sentimental in that he said that he

missed them and that he never forgets them for one moment. He also asked his family to fatten up a "cabrito" (kid goat) and that he misses his mom's stuff chicken at Christmas time. His mom kept all his letters in a box which was handed down to his younger sister, Petra Gil.

Gil was killed in action on April 5, 1945 in Bohl, Germany. The war ended May 8, 1945.

GIL, CARLOS
Tec5, U.S. Army, HQ and Service Company 50th Engineer Battalion; water supply filter operator

Qualifications: Marksman

Battles: Aleutian Islands, Eastern Mandates, Southern Philippines, Ryukyus

Honors: Asiatic-Pacific Campaign Medal with 4 battle stars and 1 bronze arrowhead, Philippine Liberation Medal with 2 battle stars, Good Conduct Medal, Victory Medal, 4 Overseas Service Bars

GIL, ELISEO
Private First Class, U.S. Army, 4278th Quartermaster Depot Company; supply clerk
Battles: Aleutian Islands

Honors: American Campaign Medal, Asiatic-Pacific Campaign Medal, Good Conduct Medal, Victory Medal

GILLILAND, OSCAR C.
Private First Class, U.S. Army; ammunition bearer

Honors: European-African-Middle Eastern Campaign Medal, 1 Overseas Service Bar

GOODSON, WILLIAM A.
U.S. Army Air Forces; airplane maintenance

Goodson completed his aviation mechanic training, while learning military drills, tactics and defense, in the Army Air Forces Technical Training School at Amarillo

GONZALES, ARMANDO T.
Private First Class, U.S. Army, Company I, 19th Infantry; rifleman

Battles: New Guinea; Southern Philippines, Luzon

Honors: Asiatic-Pacific Campaign Medal with 3 battle stars, Philippine Liberation Medal with 2 battle stars, Victory Medal, 2 Overseas Service Bars, Combat Infantryman Badge

GONZALES, JOSE M.
Private First Class, U.S Army, Battery D, 459th Anti-Aircraft Artillery Battalion; cannon operator

Qualifications: Marksman

Battles: Normandy (Northern France), Rhineland, Central Europe

Honors: European-African-Middle Eastern Campaign Medal with 4 battle stars, Good Conduct Medal

GONZALES, JOSE R.
Tec5, U.S. Army, 598th Signal Air Warning; cook

Battles: Tunisian, Naples-Foggia, Rome-Arno, Northern Apennines, PO Valley, Southern France

Honors: American Defense Medal, European-African-Middle Eastern Campaign Medal with 1 battle star and 1 silver star, Good Conduct Medal, Victory Medal

GONZALEZ, ALFREDO D.
Corporal, U.S. Army, Battery C, 559th Anti-Aircraft Artillery Battalion; truck driver

Qualifications: Marksman

Battles: Central Europe

Honors: European-African-Middle Eastern Campaign Medal with 1 battle star, American Campaign Medal, Good Conduct Medal, Victory Medal, 1 Service Stripe, 1 Overseas Service Bar

GONZALEZ, ANTONIO R.
Private First Class, U.S. Army, 529th Engineer Light Pontoon Company; baker

Qualifications: Marksman

Battles: Normandy, Northern France, Ardennes, Rhineland, Central Europe

Honors: American Campaign Medal, European-African-Middle Eastern Campaign Medal with 5 battle stars, Good Conduct Medal, Victory Medal, 3 Overseas Service Bars

GONZALEZ, EUGENIO E. "Green Eyes"
Staff Sergeant, U.S. Army, Company M, 382nd Infantry; squad leader

Battles: Southern Philippines (Liberation): Ryukyus

Honors: American Theater, Asiatic-Pacific Campaign Medal, Philippines Liberation Medal with 1 bronze arrowhead, Victory Medal, Combat Infantryman Badge

GONZALEZ, FRANCISCO G.

GONZALEZ, GILBERT G.

GONZALEZ Jr., JESUS R.
Private First Class, U.S. Army, Company A, 4th Signal Battalion; telephone/telegraph lineman

Qualifications: Marksman

Battles: Northern France; Rhineland, Central Europe

Honors: European-African-Middle Eastern Campaign Medal with 3 battle stars, Good Conduct Medal, Victory Medal, 3 Overseas Service Bars

GONZALEZ, JOE M.
Corporal, U.S. Army Air Forces, 18th Air Service Squadron; mechanic

Qualifications: Marksman

Battles: American Theater

Honors: American Campaign Medal, Good Conduct Medal

GONZALEZ, LEOPOLDO V.
Private, U.S. Army, Company A, 177th Battalion, Infantry Replacement Training Center
Qualifications: Marksman
Honors: Victory Medal

GONZALEZ, PORFIRIO
Private First Class, U.S. Army, 377th Station Hospital; military police
Battles: Pacific
Honors: American Campaign Medal, Asiatic-Pacific Campaign Medal, Good Conduct Medal, Victory Medal

GONZALEZ, RAUL
Private First Class, U.S. Army, Company A, 382nd; rifleman
Battles: Southern Philippines
Honors: Purple Heart Medal, Asiatic-Pacific Campaign Medal, Philippines Liberation Medal, Combat Infantryman Badge
PVC Gonzalez was wounded in action on November 4, 1944 in Leyte, Philippines

GONZALES, RICARDO
Sergeant

GOODMAN, CARL
Corporal

GOODSON, ELMER
U.S. Army, 71st Infantry Brigade

GOODSON, HENRY C.
Tec5, U.S. Army, 1847th Service Unit; military policeman
Qualifications: Marksman
Battles: Rome-Arno, Naples-Foggia: Southern France, Rhineland
Honors: European-African-Middle Eastern Campaign Medal with 4 battle stars, Purple Heart Medal, Distinguished Unit Badge, Bronze Star Medal, Good Conduct Medal, American Defense Service Medal.

An excerpt from The Eagle Pass News Guide, issued June 1, 1944, recalling an incident involving Tec5 Henry Goodson: "Four soldiers went to the rescue of the comrades after the half-track in which they have been riding received a direct hit by an enemy artillery shell, setting the vehicle on fire. One of the men was thrown under the burning truck and the other two were trapped inside. They successfully removed the victims and carried them to a nearby stations." Tec5 Goodson was wounded in Italy on August 17, 1944. He also served as General Patton's driver.

GOODSON, OSCAR
U.S. Army, 71st Infantry Brigade
All three Goodson brothers, Elmer, Henry, and Oscar, began active duty service on November 25, 1940, as members of the Texas National Guard.

GRAVES, ROBERT VICTOR

GREENBERG, THEODORE
Pharmacist Mate Third Class, U.S. Navy

GREER, HAROLD QUENTIN

GROSSENBACHER, CURTIS J.
2nd Lieutenant, U.S. Army Air Forces; administrative clerk; cannoneer

GUAJARDO, ARTURO R.
Sergeant, U.S. Army Air Forces, 236th Army Air Force Base Unit; electrician
Qualifications: Marksman
Honors: Good Conduct Medal

GUEDEA, ARTURO CASTRO
Private First Class, U.S. Army, 5th Tank Battalion; gun crewman
Qualifications: Marksman
Battles: Normandy, Northern France, Ardennes, Rhineland, Central Europe
Honors: European-African-Middle Eastern Campaign Medal with 5 battle stars, Good Conduct Medal, 1 Service Stripe, 4 Overseas Service Bars

GUERRA, PEDRO
Tec4, U.S. Army, HQ Detachment, 4th Tank Destroyer; cook
Battles: Asiatic-Pacific Campaign
Honors: Asiatic-Pacific Campaign Medal, Good Conduct Medal, 2 Overseas Service Bars
After being inducted in to the army on July 4, 1942, Tec4 Guerra spent 19 months in Alaska and the Aleutian area.

GUERRERO, AMBROSIO CASTILLO

GUERRERO, CARLOS
Sergeant, U.S. Army, Company B, 327th Glider Infantry; rifleman
Battles: Ardennes, Rhineland, Central Europe
Honors: European-African-Middle Eastern Campaign Medal with 3 battle stars, Good Conduct Medal, Distinguished Unit Badge, Victory Medal, 2 Overseas Service Bars
Sgt Guerrero attended parachutist school.

GUERRERO, JESUS
Motor Machinist Mate 2nd Class, U.S. Navy
Battles: Asiatic-Pacific Campaign
Honors: Asiatic-Pacific Campaign Medal, Victory Medal

GUNNARSON, MARY JANE
Ensign, U.S. Navy (WAVES "Women Accepted for Volunteer Emergency Service")

Ensign Gunnarson, the first "WAVES" from Eagle Pass, was assigned to the U.S. Naval Training School to study communications in October 19, 1943 in South Hadley, Massachusetts. A graduate of the University of Texas, she was a teacher in the Eagle Pass public school system. Ensign Gunnarson was also a member of the Motor Corps and the American Association of University Women.

GUILLOT, E.V.
Petty Officer, U.S. Navy, Signal Corps

Battles: European Theater

Petty Officer Guillot served on the destroyer U.S.S. Gheradi which was a convoy escort destroyer stationed offshore of Normandy Beach (Utah) in France at the kick-off of "D-Day," June 6, 1944.

GUTIERREZ, ROBERT F.
Private First Class, U.S. Army Air Forces, 468th Air Service Squadron; truck driver

Battles: Rhineland

Honors: Victory Medal, Good Conduct Medal, European-African-Middle Eastern Campaign Medal and 1 bronze service star

HANDLEY, DAVID W.
Sergeant, U.S. Army-Air Forces, 13th Bombardment Squadron; airplane crew chief

Qualifications: Sharpshooter

Battles: New Guinea, Southern Philippines, Luzon, Western Pacific

Honors: American Campaign Medal, Asiatic-Pacific Campaign Medal with 4 battle stars, Philippine Liberation Medal, Good Conduct Medal, Victory Medal, 1 Service Stripe, 3 Overseas Service Bars

David William Handley, born 09-05-1921 in Eagle Pass Texas, entered the service on May 27, 1942 in San Antonio, Texas. He received his basic training in Gainesville, Florida under General Patton and General Patch in the 930th Signal Battalion Company C. He repaired and maintained military telephone and telegraph wire systems, erecting poles, strung and spliced wires as a Lineman.

Leaving Florida they rode a train for 7 days and nights through Canada down to Redland, California and ending in Bend, Oregon doing maneuvers for several months before going to Desert Center, California.

His company was shipped out for New Guinea. He worked on the switchboard at Headquarters for several months when the company broke up. He always wanted to work on airplanes and was transferred to the 5th Air Force 3rd Bomb Group. As an Airplane and Engine Mechanic, he made inspections, repair and did general maintenance work on aircrafts. He removed and replaced airplane engines and faulty mechanical equipment. There he worked on Col Dick Ellis's plane. Col Dick Ellis was an Austrian-born British intelligence officer, who is alleged to have also been a double agent for Nazi Germany and the Soviet Union. Sgt. Handley worked on his plane as a Crew Chief supervisor with the 3rd Bomb Group in the Philippines and Okinawa until the end of the war.

On September 2, 1945, Sgt Handley witnessed the plane with the Japanese representatives landing in Japan for the surrender ceremony with General Douglas MacArthur, who accepted the surrender on behalf of the Allied Powers.

They were shipped back to the states to Seattle before going to Ft Sam Houston Texas and honorably discharged on November 26, 1945.

After returning to Eagle Pass Texas he went to work for Shell Oil Company in March 1946 for 39 years, 9 1/2 months when he retired in 1985. He made his home in San Antonio Texas. He's 94, still driving and mowing his yard and walking his dog. (Written by Sgt Handley's daughter, Mary Kay Pfullman)

HARDT, JOHN HARRY
Seaman First Class, U.S. Navy
S1/C Hardt served 27 months of sea duty on the U.S.S. San Diego.

HARPER, RICHMOND C.
Second Lieutenant, U.S. Army Air Forces; pilot, single-engine
Trained at the Eagle Pass Army Air Force Field, 2LT Harper received his pilot's wings on May 23 1944 as a member of class 44E. He was later stationed at Perin Air Field, Denison, Texas.

HARPER, WILLIAM J.
Corporal, Detachment Medical Department Brooks General Ft. Sam Houston, TX; athletic instructor
Battles: New Guinea
Honors: American Defense Medal, Victory Medal, Good Conduct Medal

HARVEY, ERNEST LEE
Staff Sergeant, U.S. Army, Medical Detachment, 1811th Service Command Unit; duty NCO
Honors: Good Conduct Medal

HAUSMAN, ARTHUR J.
Sergeant, U.S. Marine Corps, Aviation Ordinance Service, marksman
Sgt Hausman served his tour of duty in the Solomon Islands.

HAUSMAN, HAROLD LAWERENCE
Major, U.S. Army, Headquarters 81st Battalion; chemical warfare unit commander
Battles: Normandy, Rhineland, Northern France, Ardennes, Central Europe
Honors: American Campaign Medal, European-African-Middle Eastern Campaign Medal with 5 battle stars and 1 bronze arrowhead, Purple Heart Medal, Bronze Star Medal with 1 Oak Leaf Cluster, Presidential Unit Citation, Victory Medal

Major Hausman was wounded on November 1944 in France.
He graduated Texas A&M University with a degree in chemical engineering.

HAYES, JAMES VIRGIL

Tec4, U.S. Army, Medical Detachment, 180th General Hospital; x-ray technician
Battles: Central Europe
Honors: Victory Medal, American Campaign Medal, European-African-Middle Eastern Campaign Medal with 1 battle star, Good Conduct Medal, Meritorious Unit Award
Tec4 Hayes was a school teacher in Eagle Pass before and after the war.

HAYNES, THOMAS A.
Staff Sergeant, U.S. Army Air Forces, 58th Fighter Squadron; quartermaster supply technician
Qualifications: Marksman
Battles: Central Burma Theater, India-Burma
Honors: American Defense Service Medal, American Campaign Medal, Asiatic-Pacific Campaign Medal with 2 battle stars, Good Conduct Medal, Victory Medal, 1 Service Stripe, 2 Overseas Service Bars

HEDDELSTON, ROBERT

HEDGE, WILE BERNARD
Lieutenant, U.S. Navy Reserve

HELMS, CHARLES

Corporal, U.S. Marine Corps, HQ Battalion, 5th Marine Division; military police, truck driver
Battles: Iwo Jima, Okinawa,
Honors: Victory Medal

Cpl Helms participated in the battle at Iwo Jima. Hunkered down in a fox hole for many days with a direct view of Mount Suribachi, he was hurt while unloading ammunition. While in the hospital, he crafted two bracelets with a drawing of Mount Suribachi. The bracelets were given to his wife and to his little sister.

In a letter from Cpl Helms's little sister, Lola J. DeWald - "One time I remember well, it was about 1955 and Charles came to our house at the Hydro Electric Plant. He was so shook up, he was hysterical and for the first few minutes we could not even understand him. Daddy finally got him to calm down enough that Charles told us this story. During the war I cannot remember where his lieutenant was shot so badly that he was left for dead but Charles would not leave his body. Charles carried the body for a long way until they came across some medics. He had to leave the body there so Charles could continue to fight. The day he came to our house, he had met the Lieutenant in Eagle Pass. He had thought for about 10 years that his lieutenant was dead. I have never seen a man cry like Charles cried that day and it was the only time I ever saw Charles shed even one tear". Before WWII began, Charles moved to Maverick County around 1936 and lived there, except for the years he was in the armed forces, until he retired from the Maverick County District Irrigation Canal in the early 1980s. He then ran the Rancho Rio Grande Ranch between Del Rio and Quemado until he died in December 16, 1990.

HENSON, RAYMOND

HENSON, THURMAN LEE

HERNANDEZ, ANTONIO

HERNANDEZ, COSME
Tec5, U.S. Army, 1707th Ordnance Company; automobile mechanic
Qualifications: Marksman
Honors: American Campaign Medal, European-African-Middle Eastern Campaign Medal, Good Conduct Medal, Victory Medal, 1 Service Stripe, 3 Overseas Service Bar

HERNANDEZ, DOMINGO
Private First Class, U.S. Army, 117 Station Hospital; duty soldier
Honors: Victory Medal

HERNANDEZ, GUILLERMO
Corporal, U.S. Army Air Forces, 462nd Army Air Force; duty soldier
Battles: Aleutians Island
Honors: Asiatic-Pacific Campaign Medal with 1 battle star, Good Conduct Medal

HERNANDEZ, HOMERO
Private

HERNANDEZ, JESUS

HERNANDEZ, JORGE F.
Private First Class, U.S. Army, Battery C, 755th Field Artillery Battalion, 101st Airborne Division "Screaming Eagles"

On December 26, 1944, as a member of the 101st Airborne Division "Screaming Eagles," commanded by General Maxwell D. Taylor, PFC Hernandez was killed in action by multiple gunshot wounds to the arms and legs at the Battle of Bastogne (Battle of the Bulge). His unit received the Presidential Unit Citation. He was originally buried at the Grand Failly France Cemetery, but was later moved to his final resting place in Luxembourg's Hamm US Military Cemetery.

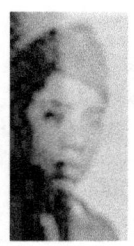

HERNANDEZ JR., JOSE R.
Private First Class, U.S. Army 2910th Engineer Reproduction Detachment, carpenter
Honors: Victory Medal, Army of Occupation Medal

HERNANDEZ JR., JOSE
Private, U.S. Army, Company A, Reception Center

HERNANDEZ, JUAN ALVAREZ
Seaman First Class, U.S. Navy, PSC Camp
S1/C Hernandez served 18 months of sea duty aboard the U.S.S. Serene.

HERNANDEZ, NASARIO
Private First Class, U.S. Army, Company G, 119th Infantry Regiment; messenger
Battles: Normandy, Northern France: Rhineland, Central Europe; Ardennes
Honors: Purple Heart Medal, European-African-Middle Eastern Campaign Medal, Good Conduct Medal, Bronze Star Medal, Combat Infantryman Badge
PFC was wounded on October 16, 1944 in Germany.

HERNANDEZ, NICANOR C.

HERNANDEZ, OCTAVIANO
Sergeant, U.S. Army Air Forces, Detachment Medical Department; medical technician
Battles: India, Burma
Honors: American Defense Service Medal, Asiatic-Pacific Campaign Medal, Good Conduct Medal
Born in Piedras Negras, Coahuila, Mexico, Sgt Hernandez graduated from Eagle Pass High School and completed one year at The University of Texas before entering the service.

HERNANDEZ, OSCAR T.
Captain, U.S. Army Air Forces, 74th Army Air Force Base Unit; weather forecaster
Honors: American Campaign Medal, Victory Medal

HERNANDEZ, SOSTENES A.
Private First Class, U.S. Army Air Forces, HQ 39th Division, Company A, 145th Infantry; automatic rifleman

Battles: Northern Solomon, Luzon

Honors: Asiatic-Pacific Campaign Medal with 2 battle stars, Philippine Liberation Medal with 1 battle star, Good Conduct Medal, Victory Medal, Purple Heart Medal, Combat Infantryman Badge

HERNANDEZ, THOMAS

Staff Sergeant, U.S. Army Air Forces, 2539th Army Air Force; airplane armorer, gunner

Qualifications: Aircrew Member Badge (wings)

Battles: Rome-Arno, Northern Apennines, Southern France, Rhineland

Honors: American Campaign Medal, European-African-Middle Eastern Campaign Medal with 4 battle stars, Victory Medal, Good Conduct Medal, Air Medal with 2 bronze clusters

HERNANDEZ, TOMAS R.

Tec4, U.S. Army, Company F, 409th Infantry; radio operator

Qualifications: Radio Operator

Battles: Naples-Foggia, Rome-Arno, Southern France, Rhineland, Central Europe

Honors: American Defense Service Medal, European-African-Middle Eastern Campaign Medal with 5 battle stars, Good Conduct Medal, 1 Service Stripe, 4 Overseas Service Bars

HERRERA, ALEJANDRO

Private First Class, U.S. Army Air Forces, HQ Company 876th Aviation Engineer Battalion; duty soldier

Battles: Normandy, Northern France; Rhineland, Central Europe

Honors: Good Conduct Medal, 6 Overseas Bars, 1 Service Stripe, European-African-Middle Eastern Campaign Medal with 4 battle stars, Distinguished Unit Badge

PFC Herrera was a liberator of one of the camps of the Holocaust. His Story is included in the Holocaust section of this book.

HERRERA, ENRIQUE

TEC 5, U.S. Army, Company I, 309th Infantry; truck driver

Qualifications: Marksman

Battles: Germany, Ardennes

Honors: European-African-Middle Eastern Campaign Medal, American Defense Service Medal, Combat Infantryman Badge

HERRERA, NACASIO B.

HERRERA, RICARDO

Private First Class, U.S. Army, 116 Station Hospital; dining room orderly

Honors: Asiatic- Pacific Campaign Medal, Victory Medal

HERRERA, RODOLFO "RUDY" LOZANO

Master Sergeant, U.S. Army Air Force, 1st Army Airways Communication System Wing; radio operator mechanic.

Battles: India, Burma, Central Burma

Honors: Asiatic-Pacific Campaign Medal with 2 battle stars, American Defense Service Medal, Victory Medal, Good Conduct Medal,

M/Sgt Herrera furnished all types of radio and navigational aids to aircrafts in flight- follows a plan from time of take off until it safely lands at its destination. They also furnish weather reports to the aircrafts. According to The Eagle Pass News Guide "Rudy saved a stricken plane in India. He was in the radio control tower of an AAF field engaged in the responsible work of keeping radio check on the various flights in and out of his field. Suddenly the pilot of a cargo ship radioed that it was lost. Immediately, Herrera went into action, giving the pilot a radio bearing and getting him back on beamon- course to the field."

HERRERA, VALERIANO O.

Staff Sergeant, U.S. Army, 16th Combat Cargo Squadron, 4th Combat Cargo Group; aerial engineer

Qualifications: AAF Air Crew Member Badge

Battles: China Offensive, Central Burma

Honors: American Campaign Medal, Asiatic-Pacific Campaign Medal with 2 battle stars, Good Conduct Medal, Victory Medal, 1 Service Stripe, 1 Overseas Service Bar

HERRING, CAROL EUGENE

U.S. Navy

HERRING, EDGAR

U.S. Navy

HERRING, FERDINAND RALPH

Corporal, U.S. Army, Repair Squadron, 20th Air Depot Group; engineer mechanic

Qualifications: Army Air Force Technology Badge

Battles: Rome-Arno

Honors: European-African-Middle Eastern Campaign Medal with 1 battle star, Good Conduct Medal

HERRING, HERBERT J.

Sergeant, Army Air Force, 301st Bomb Group, 419 Squadron, 15th Air Force

Sgt Herring was killed in action July 26, 1944 near Ratten, Austria. He was on a mission to bomb Wiener Neudorf aircraft facility in Austria. The following are statements by the other airman from his group:

"We were about five minutes from our target when we were attacked from the rear by numerous of German fighter planes. We thought at first it was flack but someone called over the inter-phone that it was Nazi fighter planes.

The Nazi planes made a direct hit on the nose of our B-17 causing the oxygen tanks to explode and killing the navigator and bombardier, instantly. Also starting a tremendous fire in the nose of the ship (plane). When Lilligren (a crewmember) saw the fire, he immediately called for everyone to bail out and the inter-phone went blank and everyone had to act on his own. I hurried to the rear of the plane and as I passed the ball turret to look to me like Brenneman was already dead so I didn't stop. When I got to the Waist of the plane, I could see that Bishop was frozen to his gun. I hit him twice but he just kept staring out the window like he was made out of stone. That is the last thing I remembered until I hit the ground and was captured by the Land Watchmen." This is part of a letter from Mr. and Mrs. Charles J. Allison (Radio Operator) on June 18, 1947 to Mrs. Thompson (widow of co-pilot):

"I bailed out, Allison and Lewis bailed out. Lilligren set the automatic stabilizer and he bailed out. All others apparently were killed and went down with the ship. There is some question about Lt Thompson. The four of us were rounded up and sent to Frankfort. Bishop, Brennan, Herring, Stever, and Tracer were in the aircraft when it struck the ground."

Statement from Richard August Longo, S Sgt, AC to the War Department

HERRING, LEWIS HOMER
Fireman First Class, U. S Navy

Fireman 1/C Herring served 10 months on sea duty aboard the U.S.S. Dade and U.S.S. Cassipeia

HESLES, ALFREDO
Private, Headquarter (HQ) Company Tank Destroyer Replacement Training Center; anti-tank gun crewman

Honors: Victory Medal

HESS, BRIJIDO URESTE
Tec5, U.S. Army, Company C, 2d Engineers Battalion; carpenter

Qualifications: Sharpshooter

Battles: Normandy, Northern France, Rhineland

Honors: European African Middle East Campaign Medal with 3 battle stars, Purple Heart Medal, Distinguished Unit Badge, American Defense Service Medal, Good Conduct Medal.

Tec5 Hess was wounded on August 25, 1944.

HEYES, JOHN D.
Corporal, 1046th Basic Flying Training Squadron

HILL, HARVEY H.
Captain, U.S. Army, POW Camp at 19047 SCU Ft. Lewis.LA; prison officer

Honors: American Campaign Medal, Victory Medal

HOBBS, LAWRENCE "LORENZO"
Private, U.S. Army Air Force, 462nd Army Air Force
Battles: Aleutians Island
Honors: American Theater Medal, Asiatic-Pacific Campaign Medal with 1 battle star, Good Conduct Medal, Victory Medal

HOGAN, WILLIAM M.
Tec5, U.S. Army, 815 Quartermaster Sterilization Company; squad leader
Qualifications: Marksman
Battles: Normandy, Northern France, Ardennes, Rhineland, Central Europe
Honors: European-African-Middle Eastern Campaign Medal with 5 battle stars, Good Conduct Medal, 3 Overseas Service Bars.

HOUSTON, JOHN ALBERT "Abe"
Lieutenant, U.S. Army

Originally from Carrizo Springs, Lt Houston moved to Eagle Pass in 1940 and was the football and basketball coach at Eagle Pass High School for two years before the war. Coach Houston was quoted as saying, "I don't guarantee to make winners out of any of you, but I will make good players." Under his training, the Eagles football team grew into a powerhouse. Although they were one of the lightest teams in the district, they won second place in the zone, both seasons. In basketball, they won many tournaments and in the 1942 season, won the district championship. The International News Guide, August 20, 1942 said, "Lucky will be the men who received training under Abe Houston in the Air Corps. They will have courage, endurance, and a fighting heart, and they will win, because Abe will impress them with his oft-repeated motto: "A strong offense is the best defense. It's the fellow who is standing still who gets hurt in a collision." Abe Houston resigned from Eagle Pass High School on July 31, 1942 to become Lt Houston, a physical training instructor for the Air Corps. Upon arrival to his post at Eagle Pass Army Air Field, he came face to face with one of his football players, Cadet Bingham Percy. They found themselves back together as coach and student.

HOWARD, EDWIN ERNEST
Qualifications: Marksman
Honors: European-African-Middle Eastern Campaign Medal, Good Conduct Medal, 1 Service Stripe, 4 Overseas Service Bars

HOWARD, MARELLOUS JONES
Lieutenant Colonel, U.S. Marine Corps

HOYOS, CONCEPCION C.
Tec5, U.S. Army, Company B, 543rd Engineer Boat and Shore Regiment; diesel engineman
Battles: New Guinea, Luzon

Honors: American Campaign Medal, Asiatic-Pacific Campaign Medal with 2 battle stars and 1 bronze arrowhead, Philippine Liberation Medal with 2 battle stars, Good Conduct Medal, Victory Medal, 1 Service Stripe, 3 Overseas Service Bars

HUDDLESTON Jr., ROBERT EMMETT

HUERTA, ENRIQUE

Private First Class, U.S. Army, Company F, 10th Infantry; scout

Battles: Northern France, Rhineland

Honors: European-African-Middle Eastern Campaign Medal with 2 battle stars, Good Conduct Medall

HUFFMAN, EDWARD C.

Staff Sergeant, U.S. Army Air Forces, 1020th Army Air Force Base Unit; armorer

Qualifications: Air Crew Badge

Battles: Northern France, Rhineland, Ardennes

Honors: European-African-Middle Eastern Campaign Medal with 3 battle stars, Good Conduct Medal, Air Medal with 6 Oak Leaf Clusters

SSgt Huffman graduated from Eagle Pass High School in 1941. He served as a turret gunner aboard a B-17 Fortress and as an assistant radio operator for his crew. (The Eagle Pass News Guide)

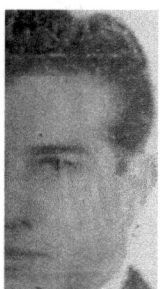

HUFFMAN, LEON C.

U.S. Army Air Forces; pilot

Brother of SSgt Edward C. Huffman

HUNTER, TOMAS RAY

Corporal, U.S. Army, Quartermaster Corps

Before his enlistment into the Army on February 23, 1942, Cpl Hunter was the manager of S.H. Kress & Co. for 2 1/2 years.

HUNTSMAN, EMETT B.

Sergeant, U.S. Army, Quartermaster Detachment Center

Sgt Huntsman was stationed at Camp Swift, Texas.

HUME, DAVID
Lieutenant, U.S. Navy

Lt Hume was the captain of a gunnery crew on a destroyer. He wrote in a letter, "his ship has just arrived in New York after a thrilling round-the-world jaunt, in which they were on convoy duty in the Mediterranean and through the Suez Canal took part in the successful attack on the island of Martinique, and in general gave their guns a good workout on the enemy."

HUME, EVAN B.
Major, U.S. Army, Army Medical Corps

HUTCHENS, BRUCE MARION
Private, U.S. Army, 1984th Quartermaster Truck Company; auto equipment operator

Qualifications: Marksman

Battles: Bismarck Archipelago, New Guinea, Northern Solomon, Southern Philippines, Luzon

Honors: American Campaign Medal, Asiatic-Pacific Campaign Medal with 5 battle stars, Philippine Liberation Medal with 1 battle star, Good Conduct Medal

HUTCHENS, Jr., JOHN B.
Staff Sergeant, U.S. Army Air Forces, 9th Fighter Squadron, 49th Fighter Group; sheet metal worker

Qualifications: Army Air Force Technician Badge

Battles: New Guinea, Northern Solomon, Southern Philippines, Luzon, Western Pacific

Honors: Asiatic-Pacific Campaign Medal with 5 battle stars, Philippine Liberation Medal with 1 battle star, Good Conduct Medal, 4 Overseas Service Bars, Victory Medal

IBARRA, ADRIAN V.
Sergeant

IRELAND, HARRY B.
Captain, U.S. Army, Coast Artillery Corps

Honors: American Campaign Medal, European-African-Middle Eastern Campaign Medal, American Defense Service Medal, Victory Medal

IZQUIERDO, RAMON
Private, U.S. Army

JACKSON, O.N. "Tip"
U.S. Navy; medic

"Tip" Jackson enlisted in the US Navy from 1943-1946. He was attached to the Marine Corps and was stationed at Nanumea Atoll in an underground hospital. Nanumea is part of the Polynesian nation of Tuvalu, a group of nine islands and atolls (series of islands sitting on a coral reef surrounding a lagoon). The Nanumea Atoll lies near the Gilbert Islands. In 1943, the women of the Atoll were moved across the lagoon to Lakena Island as Navy Seabees began constructing an airfield and hospital on Nanumea. As many as 2,300 servicemen were stationed there at the time of the Invasion of Tarawa. "Tip" was also a boxer in the Navy with 50 fights under his belt, only 5 losses, all by decision. He sparred with a future welterweight champion, Dr. Bobby Venter.

After the war, Jackson played football at Southern Methodist University in Dallas, Texas.

JEFFERS, BILLY LLOYD
Yeoman Second Class, U.S. Navy, 52nd Naval Construction Battalion, "Seabees"

The Sea-Bees transformed barren isles into well-equipped military bases. Yeoman 2/C Jeffers quoted, "Weather is the greatest enemy there, making it difficult to build the various installations. Fog, rain, sleet, snow and of course the ever present Williawaw (sudden blast of wind) were as common as sunshine around here and the sun, when and if it shown, was one of the rare luxuries that just didn't seem to show up on the scene at any time. He served 18 months of sea duty in the Aleutian Isles. (The Eagle Pass News Guide May 25, 1942)

JIMENEZ, CARMEN M.
Private, U.S. Army, 402nd Company, 18th Replacement Battalion

Originally from Guerrero, Coahuila, Mexico, Pvt Jimenez died of tuberculosis on February 14, 1945 at the 17th General Hospital in Naples, Italy while on tour. He was originally buried at Naples Allied Cemetery then reinterred in his final resting place at Ft. Sam Houston Cemetery in San Antonio, Texas.

JIMENEZ, ENRIQUE A
Private First Class, U.S. Army, 561st Motor Ambulance Battalion; crewman

Qualifications: Sharpshooter

Battles: Normandy, Northern France, Ardennes, Rhineland, Central Europe

Honors: American Campaign Medal, European-African-Middle Eastern Campaign Medal with 5 battle stars, Good Conduct Medal, Victory Medal, 2 Overseas Service Bars

JIMENEZ, JESUS P.
Corporal, U.S. Army Air Forces, 1466th Army Air Force Base Unit; cook
Qualifications: Marksman
Honors: Good Conduct Medal, Victory Medal, American Campaign Medal, Asiatic-Pacific Campaign Medal

JIMENEZ, JUAN
Private First Class, U.S. Army, HQ Company Base K; supply clerk
Qualifications: Marksman
Battles: New Guinea, South Philippines
Honors: 6 Overseas Service Bars, Asiatic-Pacific Campaign Medal with 2 battle stars, Philippine Liberation Medal with 1 battle star, Good Conduct Medal, Victory Medal, 1 Service Stripe

JIMENEZ, MARGARITO
Private, U.S. Army, Service Battery, 155th F, A Battalion; ammunition server
Honors: American Defense Service Medal, European-African-Middle Eastern Campaign Medal

JIMENEZ, SALVADOR A.
Staff Sergeant, U.S. Army, Company M, 23rd Infantry; machine gunner
Battles: Normandy
Honors: Bronze Star Medal, Purple Heart Medal, European-African-Middle Eastern Campaign Medal, American Defense Service Medal, Combat Infantryman Badge
S/Sgt Jimenez was wounded on August 1, 1944 in the European Theater.

JOBES, H.B.
Battles: China, Burma, India
After WWII, Jobes became Deputy Sheriff in Maverick County.

JOHNSON, CHARLES E.
Private, U.S. Army, 8th Service Detachment, and Medical Department; x-ray technician
Honors: Good Conduct Medal

JOHNSON Jr., HORACE H.
Staff Sergeant, U.S. Army Air Forces, 2532nd Army Air Force Base Unit; airplane, engine mechanic
Qualifications: Army and Air Force Member Badge (wings) Gunner
Battles: China, Central Burma, India, Luzon, Western Pacific
Honors: Distinguished Flying Cross, 2 Overseas Service Bars, Asiatic-Pacific Campaign Medal with 1 silver battle star, Good Conduct Medal

JOHNSON, JOHNNY ZALETA
Private, U.S. Army, Coast Artillery

JOHNSON, JUAN Z
Private First Class, U.S. Army, 1550th Service Command Unit Prisoner of War Camp; heavy machine gunner

Qualifications: Sharpshooter

Honors: Good Conduct Medal, Victory Medal, American Defense Medal, American Campaign Medal, European-African-Middle Eastern Campaign Medal

JOHNSTON, Jr., CHARLIE
Private First Class, U.S. Army, Company B, 748th Tank Battalion; truck driver

Battles Naples-Foggia, Rome-Arno, Southern France, Rhineland, Central Europe

Honors: European-African-Middle Eastern Campaign Medal with 5 battle stars, Good Conduct Medal

JOHNSTON, RAMON MENCHACA
Private First Class, U.S. Army, Company H, 165th Infantry; ammunition bearer

Battles: Central Pacific, Eastern Mandates

Honors: Asiatic-Pacific Campaign Medal with 2 battle stars, Good Conduct Medal, Victory Medal, 1 Service Stripe, 6 Overseas Service Bars, Combat Infantryman Badge

JONES, Jr., EMMETT C.
Corporal, U.S. Army Air Forces, Accessories Section, Air Service Command Depot, England

"Cpl Jones is one of the highly trained technicians whose job of overhauling and rebuilding all aircraft instruments and to make sure they are in perfect working order. Daily precision bombing requires delicate instruments, carefully adjusted to get our planes to their pin-point targets." (The Eagle Pass News Guide)

JONES, GEORGE HENRY
Fireman First Class, U.S. Navy

George Jones served 15 months sea duty.

JONES, JACK C.
Private First Class, U.S. Army, Company C, 270th Engineer Battalion; demolition specialist

Qualifications: Marksman

Battles: Rhineland, Central Europe

Honors: American Campaign Medal, European-African-Middle Eastern Campaign Medal with 2 battle stars, Good Conduct Medal, Victory Medal, 1 Overseas Service Bar, Army of Occupation Germany

JONES, WILFORD HORACE

JUAREZ, PEDRO D.
Private First Class, U.S. Army, 1385th Engineers; automatic rifleman

Battles: Central Europe, Rhineland

Honors: European-African-Middle Eastern Campaign Medal with 2 battle stars, 1 Overseas Service Bar, Purple Heart Medal

PFC Juarez was wounded in action on February 19, 1945 in the European Theater

JUVE, VALENTIN
Staff Sergeant, U.S. Army Air Forces, 95th Depot Repair Squadron, 63rd Air Depot Group; classification specialist

Qualifications: Sharpshooter

Honors: American Campaign Medal, European-African-Middle Eastern Campaign Medal, Good Conduct Medal, Victory Medal, 1 Service Stripe, 1 Overseas Service Bar

KELLEY, GEORGE

KELSO, MARTIN
Tec3, U.S. Army, 810th Signal Service Battalion; radio operator

Battles: Northern France, Ardennes, Rhineland, Central Europe

Honors: European-African-Middle Eastern Campaign Medal, Bronze Star Medal, Good Conduct Medal

KENNEDY, ROBERT
Staff Sergeant, U.S. Army

KESSELMAN, LOUIS

KILE, CHARLES L.
Private, U.S. Army, Unit B, Separation Center #45; clerk typist

Qualifications: Marksman, pistol

Honors: Good Conduct Medal, American Theater Service Medal

KIFURI Jr., EMILIO
Private First Class, U.S. Army, 426th Armored Field Artillery Battalion; military police

KIFURI, VICTOR
Private, U.S. Army Air Forces, 306th Training Group

KOWNSLAR, ROBERT CONRAD
Sergeant, U.S. Army

Sgt Kownslar attended cadet training in St Louis, Missouri. He spent more than 14 months on duty in England.

KNIGHT, PAUL W.
Corporal, U.S. Army, Company B, 807th Tank Destroyer Battalion; half-track driver

Qualifications: Marksman

Battles: Rhineland, Central Europe

Honors: European-African-Middle Eastern Campaign Medal with 2 battle stars, Good Conduct Medal, 1 Overseas Service Bar

KYPUROS Jr., FRANCISCO
Private First Class, U.S. Army, Company C, 85th Mountain Infantry; rifleman

Battles: Northern Apennines, PO Valley

Honors: American Campaign Medal, European-African-Middle Eastern Campaign Medal with 2 battle stars, Good Conduct Medal, Victory Medal, 1 Overseas Service Bar, Combat Infantry Badge

KYPUROS, THEODORE V.
Tec5, U.S. Army, HQ Detachment, 935th Signal Battalion; cook

Battles: Rome-Arno, Northern Apennines, PO Valley, Southern France

Honors: American Campaign Medal, European-African-Middle Eastern Campaign Medal with 4 battle stars, Good Conduct Medal, 1 Service Stripe, 3 Overseas Service Bars, Victory Medal

LAMBETH, BOYD O.
Master Sergeant, U.S. Army Air Forces, 729th Heavy Bombardment Squadron; airplane maintenance technician

Qualifications: Sharpshooter

Battles: Air Offensive Europe, Normandy, Northern France, Ardennes, Rhineland, Central Europe

Honors: European-African-Middle Eastern Campaign Medal, American Defense Service Medal

LAMBETH, DAVID
Private First Class, U.S. Army Air Forces; airplane mechanic

LAMBETH, JERREL
Sergeant, U.S. Army Air Forces; airplane mechanic

Brother of Private Boyd Lambeth

LATRIMORE, GW

Latrimore was a former resident of Quemado who was stationed at the Eagle Pass Army Air Force Base on December 10, 1942.

LEAL, FRANCISCO V.

LANE, LOUIS

Private First Class, U.S. Army, chaplain's assistant at Greenville Base, SC ; musician

An accomplished musician, PFC Lane received his Bachelor of Arts Degree in Music with the highest honors from The University of Texas on May 31, 1943. Upon entering a contest, and winning second place, at the Army post in Greenville, South Carolina, PFC Lane wrote: "I am fighting because I want to be part, however small, of this war, the greatest effort for good ever made by mankind. I hope our winning the war will help free all men from the fear of other men, and to prove that a world in which each individual can have a secure place, be happy, and contribute his part toward the common good is really possible of achievement. Perhaps we can demonstrate to our enemies, and convince ourselves that we can set up a world where equality of opportunity is a reality, and which all men know that governments are to serve and not to be served. If this war does make the realization of these great aims possible, then I am grateful for the privilege of helping achieve them, and am glad to be able to fight in the Army of the United States."

LARA, JOSE

Tec5, U.S. Army, 1876th Engineer Battalion; carpenter, construction

Qualifications: Marksman

Battles: New Guinea, Luzon

Honors: Asiatic-Pacific Campaign Medal with 2 battle stars, Philippine Liberation Medal with 1 battle star, Good Conduct Medal, Victory Medal, 3 Overseas Service Bars

LEDBETTER, ELTON LORD

First Lieutenant, U.S. Army, Photographic Signal Corps

A former photographer for Time and Life Magazines, Lt Ledbetter served as a model for posters and magazine illustrations in New York.

LEDBETTER, GARLAND BRANTLEY

First Lieutenant, U.S. Army Air Forces, 489th Bomb Group (B-24), 499th Bomb Group, 878th Bomb Squadron (B-29);pilot

Lt. Ledbetter graduated from the pilot training at Brooks Field, San Antonio, Texas. Soon after, Lt. Ledbetter was stationed overseas. The records of the Department of the Army, disclosed that Lt Ledbetter, with the rest of his crew, was returning to his home base after a mission over Nagaya, Japan, when his B-29 Bomber crashed in to the sea 1500 ft. off the shore on Magicienne Bay, Saipan in the Northern Marianas Islands. Witnessed by a control tower observer, rescue boats were dispatched immediately to the scene, but no survivors or remains of the crew members were ever recovered. All crew members, including Lt. Ledbetter, perished in the crash.

LEDBETTER, HOBART
U.S. Navy

Hobart Ledbetter attended basic training with the Coast Guard in Miami, Florida. Upon graduation, he was transferred to New Orleans, Louisiana to attend flight training.

Hobart Ledbetter is the brother of Lt Elton Ledbetter and Lt Garland Ledbetter

LEDBETTER, ROBERT
U.S. Coast Guard

LEE Jr., CARROL VOLNEY
Seaman, U.S. Navy

Honors: Purple Heart Medal

The Eagle Pass News Guide stated that, "Seaman Carroll V. Lee, Jr. was stationed aboard the battleship U.S.S. Arizona in Pearl Harbor on the fateful Sunday morning December 7, 1941. Without warning, bombs from scores of Japanese planes raked the harbor with fearful detonations. One of the bombs slanted down the smokestack of the Arizona and exploded in her powder magazine. Even as she settled into the water, her gallant Carrol was among the missing. Seaman Lee is entombed with this shipmates on the U.S.S. Arizona at Pearl Harbor, Hawaii."

LEHMANN, ALFRED ROBERT
Tec5, U.S. Army, Battery D, 865th Anti-craft Artillery, Automatic Weapons Battalion; artillery mechanic

Qualifications: Marksman

Battles: Eastern Mandates

Honors: American Defense Service Medal, Asiatic-Pacific Campaign Medal, Good Conduct Medal

Enlisted on October 13, 1941 at Ft. Bliss, Texas, Pvt Lehmann was station in Oahu, Hawaii in 1942. He is quoted by The Eagle Pass News Guide as saying, "The boys are entertained royally two and three times a week, and go on sightseeing trips occasionally."

LEHMAN, FRANK
Private, U.S. Army Air Forces; military police

Battles: North Africa

LEIJA, GUADALUPE R.
Tec5, U.S. Army, 3622nd Quartermaster Truck Company; heavy automotive equipment operator

Qualifications: Driver and Mechanic Badge

Battles: Normandy, Northern France; Rhineland, Central Europe

Honors: American Campaign Medal, European-African-Middle Eastern Campaign Medal with 4 battle stars, Good Conduct Medal, Victory Medal

LERY, GEORGE

LEURA, JULIO
Private First Class, U.S. Army, 96th Chemical Composite Company; gas mask repairman
Honors: Asiatic-Pacific Campaign Medal, Good Conduct Medal, Victory Medal, 1 Service Stripe, 4 Overseas Service Bars

LEVIN, MARTIN "The Jalapeno"
Lt j.g.; U.S. Navy; coding officer

"During the early years of WWII, college enrollment declined because of the men being drafted or volunteered to serve in the armed forces. One of the requirements to become an officer in the U.S. Navy was to complete 2 ½ years of college. Hoping to help the colleges and have a pool of officers, the Navy in July 1943 started the V-12 program. In the course of the war, the Navy enlisted 120,000 students to 131 colleges throughout the country. In High School Martin took a test and was found eligible for the V-12 program. Since Martin had already taken ½ year of college, he was sent to Harvard University for 19 months. The school day was up to 8 hours a day which included some Navy courses Monday to Friday. Saturday was drill instruction and Parades. V12 students were in uniform and were provided food, housing and paid as an able bodied seaman $21 a month, later changed to $50. Robert Kennedy was at Harvard ½ year behind him.

After completing 2 years of college in 19 months, Martin was sent to Asbury Park, N.J. to Pre-Midshipman school. One night Martin and a friend had guard duty on the beach and decided to practice Morse Code. The signal was picked up by a ship at sea who could not understand what was being said so they notified Washington. In no time, the beach was crowded with police, FBI, firemen FBI, and Shore Patrol. It took quite a while to get them to understand what was happening. After 2 months, his platoon took a train ride to Midshipman School in Chicago.

Midshipmen School was all Navy. We had inspection every morning. School all day. Finally in May of 1945, we graduated as Ensigns in the U.S Navy. He had asked for Destroyers, Attack Transports or PT boats, however the Navy gave Martin Communication School. Back to Harvard again. During this time, the War ended but he was not discharge instead he was sent to Pearl Harbor Naval Bases as a Coding Office and later to Wahiawa Naval Radio Station. After learning all about radios, the Navy sent him to an office with 135 teletype machines. Martin gives much thanks to the Chiefs.

After Separation in San Francisco, he went to Eagle Pass to see his cousin Lloyd Munter and his new bride. Martin Levin became an "honorary" Maverick County citizen the night he went to dinner at the Moderno Night Club in Piedras Negras with his cousins Lloyd and Yolanda Munter. Lloyd told his cousin that the jalapeño was like a Jewish pickle that Martin was accustomed to in Brooklyn, New York. Martin took a big bite and he screamed in agony." (Martin Levin 2/14/16)

LEVINE, BEN
U.S. Navy (Sampson Naval Base, New York)

LEWIS, HOMER I.
Major General, U.S. Army Air Forces, Headquarters 486th Bomb Group (H) Drew Field, Tampa Florida; aerial gunnery instructor
Battles: Central Europe

Honors: Air Medal, European-African-Middle Eastern Campaign Medal with 1 battle star, American Defense Service Medal

In July 1941, he was called to active military duty with the Headquarters Gulf Coast Flying Training Command at Randolph Field. In September 1941, he was assigned to the 81st Material Squadron, 75th Air Base Group, Foster Field, Texas. General Lewis was selected for the glider training program at its inception in June 1942 and was assigned as commandant of students, 23d Army Air Force Glider Training Detachment. He was selected for the college training program in February 1943 and was assigned as commander of 93d Army Air Forces College Training Detachment at Spearfish, S.D. In March 1944, he was transferred to Douglas Army Air Field, as commander of cadets for the twin-engine advanced flying school with both Chinese and Americans officers and cadets. After 3 months as an aerial gunnery instructor at Harlington Army Air Field, in February 1945, he went overseas and joined the 3rd Air Division at Thetford, England and later was assigned to the 486th Bombardment Group. He flew combat missions over Central Europe in B-17 aircraft.

After the war, General Lewis remained in the service. On March 8, 1971, General Lewis was nominated by the president of the United States to serve as chief of Air Force Reserve. His military decorations and awards include the Legion of Merit, Air Medal and the Air Force Outstanding Unit Award Medal. He was promoted to permanent grade of major general effective May 12, 1970. (Web site of the U.S. Air Force)

LEYJA, IGNANCIO R,

Corporal, U.S. Army, Battery A, 313th Field Artillery Battalion; gun crewman

Battles: Northern France, Ardennes, Rhineland, Central Europe

Honors: 3 Overseas Service Bars, Distinguished Unit Badge, Good Conduct Medal, Victory Medal, European-African-Middle Eastern Campaign Medal with 4 battle stars, American Campaign Medal

LEYJA, MARCELINO R.

LEVY, FRED

Corporal, U.S. Army Air Forces, 3705th Army Air Force Base Unit; airplane and engine mechanic

Honors: American Campaign Medal, Good Conduct Medal, Victory Medal

LEVY, GEORGE

LEYVA, MARIA ESTELA

First woman from Eagle Pass to join Women Army Corps (WAC)

LIBSON, NOJEM

Private First Class, U.S. Army, 3137th Signal Motor Messenger Company; message center clerk

Battles: Ardennes, Rhineland, Central Europe

Honors: American Campaign Medal, European-African-Middle Eastern Campaign Medal with 3 battle stars, Good Conduct Medal, Victory Medal, 2 Overseas Service Bars

LINDENBORN, IVY LOUIS
Seaman First Class, U.S. Navy, HQ Troop; radio operator

PFC Lindeborn's unit was attached to an attack transport for 20 months in the South Pacific.

LIRA, MARCELINO M.

LIRA, RAMON
Private, U.S. Army, Armored Tank Company, 363rd Infantry; anti-tank gun crewman

Battles: Rome-Arno, Northern Apennines, PO Valley

Honors: European-African-Middle Eastern Campaign Medal, Good Conduct Medal, Infantry 45th Distinguished Unit Badge, Combat Infantryman Badge

LOCKE, CLARENCE M.
Private First Class, U.S. Army, 185th General Hospital; clerk typist

Honors: European- African-Middle Eastern Campaign

LOFTIN, OSCAR L.
Private First Class, U.S. Army, Company B, 136th Infantry; rifleman

Honors: Asiatic-Pacific Campaign Medal, Good Conduct Medal, Meritorious Unit Award, Army of Occupation (Japan) Medal, 1 Overseas Service Bar, Victory Medal, Combat Infantryman Badge

LOPEZ, ARTURO N.

LOPEZ, BALTAZAR G.
Staff Sergeant, U.S. Army Air Forces, 3018th Army Air Force Base Unit; aerial gunner

Battles: Egypt, Libya, Algeria - French Morocco, Air Combat Balkans, Tunisia, Rome-Arno, Naples-Foggia, Southern France, North Apennines, Air Offensive Europe

Honors: Air Medal with 2 Oak Leaf Clusters, European-African-Middle Eastern Campaign Medal with 9 battle stars, Good Conduct Medal

LOPEZ, DOMINGO F.
Private, U.S. Army, Company B, 1st Battalion, 27th Infantry Regiment; rifleman

Honors: Victory Medal, Army of Occupation (Japan) Medal

LOPEZ Jr., ESTEBAN HERNANDEZ
Private First Class, U.S. Army, Company A, 255th Infantry; rifleman

Battles: Rhineland, Central Europe, Aleutian Islands

Honors: European-African-Middle Eastern Campaign Medal with 2 battle stars, Asiatic-Pacific Campaign Medal with 1 battle star, Combat Infantryman Badge.

LOPEZ, JESUS
Corporal, U.S. Army Air Forces, 49th Supply Squadron, 49th Air Depot Group; supply clerk

Qualifications: Marksman

Honors: American Campaign Medal, Asiatic-Pacific Campaign Medal with 1 battle star, Philippine Liberation Medal, Good Conduct Medal, Victory Medal, 3 Overseas Service Bars

The Eagle Pass News Guide, October 28, 1943, stated, "Jesus Lopez was promoted to corporal at Stinson Field Air Depot Training Station in San Antonio, Texas"

LOPEZ, JOAQUIN
Private First Class, U.S. Army, Company C, 243rd Engineer Battalion; duty soldier

Qualifications: Marksman

Battles: Ardennes, Rhineland, Central Europe

Honors: European-African-Middle Eastern Campaign Medal with 3 battle stars, Good Conduct Medal, Victory Medal, 2 Overseas Service Bars

LOPEZ, JOSE M.
Private, U.S. Army, 1296th Military Police Company Aviation; cook

Qualifications: Marksman, pistol

Battles: Northern France, Rhineland

Honors: European-African-Middle Eastern Campaign Medal, American Campaign Medal, Distinguished Unit Badge, Victory Medal

Pvt Lopez received advanced airplane mechanic training in Sioux Falls, South Dakota

LOPEZ, MARGARITO
Private First Class, U.S. Army, 342nd Infantry, 86th Division; military policeman

Qualifications: Marksman

Honors: American Campaign Medal, European-African-Middle Eastern Campaign Medal with 1 battle star, Asiatic-Pacific Campaign Medal, Good Conduct Medal, Victory Medal, 1 Service Stripe, 1 Overseas Service Bar

LOPEZ, RAUL H.
Corporal, U.S. Army Air force; cook

Battles: Normandy, Northern France, Ardennes, Rhineland, Central Europe, Air Offensive Europe

Honors: European-African-Middle Eastern Campaign Medal, Good Conduct Medal

LOPEZ Sr., REYMUNDO D.
Private First Class, U.S. Army, Company H, 323rd Infantry; heavy mortar crewman

Battles: Southern Philippines, Western Pacific

Honors: American Campaign Medal, Asiatic-Pacific Campaign Medal with 2 battle stars, Philippine Liberation Medal with 1 battle star, Good Conduct Medal, Victory Medal, 1 Service Stripe, 3 Overseas Service Bars, Combat Infantryman Badge

LOPEZ, RUDY
Private, U.S. Army, Infantry Company
Honors: Purple Heart Medal, Combat Infantryman Badge
Pvt Lopez was wounded in action in France.

LOPEZ, SANTIAGO L.
Private, U.S. Army, Company E, 184th Infantry
Battles: Southern Philippines (Liberation)
Honors: 2 Overseas Service Bars, American Campaign Medal, Asiatic-Pacific Campaign Medal with 1 battle star, Philippine Liberation Service Medal with 1 battle star, Victory Medal, Combat Infantryman Badge

LOTHRINGER, LAWRENCE L.
Staff Sergeant, U.S. Army Air Forces, 2532nd Army Air Force Base Unit; auto equipment mechanic
Battles: Asiatic-Pacific, Egypt, Libya
Honors: European-African-Middle Eastern Campaign Medal, Bronze Star, Egypt Liberation Medal, Asiatic-Pacific Campaign Medal

LOUEZ, ESLIO F.

LOUGH, JOHN H. "Pete"
Sergeant, U.S. Army
Honors: Purple Heart Medal, Combat Infantryman Badge
Sergeant Lough was wounded in action in France.

LOZANO Jr., EFRAIN
Mailman Second Class, U.S. Navy
Battles: Asiatic-Pacific
Honors: American Campaign Medal, Victory Medal

LOZANO, GILBERTO M.
Sergeant, U.S. Army Air Forces, Headquarters Air Depot Group; translator
Honors: American Campaign Medal, Good Conduct Medal, Victory Medal, 1 Service Stripe, 3 Overseas Service Bars

LUNA, ALEJANDRO
Private First Class, U.S. Army Air Forces, 62nd Fighter Squadron; carpenter
Honors: European-African-Middle Eastern Campaign Medal

LUNA, GUADALUPE

LYALL, GEORGE A.
Private First Class, U.S. Army, Company B, 643rd Tank Destroyer Battalion; medium tank crewman

Battles: Northern France, Ardennes, Rhineland, Central Europe

Honors: American Campaign Medal, European-African-Middle Eastern Campaign Medal, Victory Medal, Purple Heart Medal

PFC was wounded in Germany on April 17, 1945. After the war, George Lyall published a book named To A Different Drummer. It tells the story about pioneer Texas family from Scotland.

LYNN, ADRIAN L. Sr.,
Private First Class, U.S. Army, 88th Field Hospital

MABE, WILLIAM ROBERT "Bobby"
First Lieutenant, U.S. Army Air Forces, 8th Air Force; B-24 liberator bombardier

Battles: Central Europe, Ploesti, Germany, North Africa

Honors: Air Medal for Meritorious (Award) with Oak Leaf Cluster, Distinguished Unit Medal

Lt Mabe was involved in the 8th Air Force historic "Battle of Ploesti." Ploesti had oil refinery facilities located 30 miles north of Bucharest, Romania. It supplied an estimated 60% of the refined oil necessary to keep the German war machine running. (Eye Witness to History.com) Lt Mabe's unit won the Distinguished Unit Medal from the President and War Department for its role in the battle of Ploesti in August 1943.

According to The Eagle Pass News Guide, Bobby's crew was nicknamed "Hell Cat." The Hell-caters set a bombing record in England by making 4 raids over Europe in 4 days.

Lt. Bobby Mabe spoke on behalf of all the Hell-caters when he said "we is exhausted."

MABE Jr., JAKE MARSHALL
Lieutenant, U.S. Army

According to The Eagle Pass News Guide, June 3, 1943, Lt Mabe Jr. graduated from a course in electrical engineering at Harvard University and ranked in the top 10% of his class. Due to his excellent work and drive, he was selected to take advanced training at the Massachusetts Institute of Technology (MIT).

MACK, FREDDY
TEC 5, U.S. Army, Headquarters Battery 718th Field Artillery Battalion; truck driver

Qualifications: Marksman

Battles: Naples-Foggia, Rome-Arno, Southern France, Rhineland, Central Europe

Honors: European-African-Middle Eastern Campaign Medal with 5 battle stars, Bronze Indian Arrowhead, Good Conduct Medal, American Defense Service Medal

MADDOX, WALTER BENJAMIN
Corporal, U.S. Army Air Forces, 3701st Army Air Force Base Unit; airplane and engine mechanic

Qualifications: Technician's Badge

Battle: Northern Solomon's

Honors: Asiatic-Pacific Campaign Medal with 1 battle star, American Defense Service Medal, Good Conduct Medal

As stated in The Eagle Pass News Guide: "Almost as important as the pilots, are the men at the hangar that keep his plane in the air."

MALDONADO, ALVARO
Private First Class, U.S. Army, Company K, 351st Infantry; duty soldier
Battles: Sicilian Naples-Foggia, Rome-Arno, Northern Apennines, PO Valley
Honors: European-African-Middle Eastern Campaign Medal, Good Conduct Medal, Silver Star Medal, Bronze Arrowhead

MALDONADO, ARMANDO G.
Corporal, U.S. Army, 498 Service Squadron, 44th Service Group; truck driver
Battles: Central Burma, India Burma
Honors; Asiatic-Pacific Campaign Medal, Good Conduct Medal, Victory Medal

MALDONADO, DESIDERIO
Private First Class, U.S. Army, Company B, 555 Engineer Pontoon Battalion; rigger
Qualifications: Marksman
Battles: Normandy, Northern France
Honors: European-African-Middle Eastern Campaign Medal, Good Conduct Medal, Croix de Guerre with Palm battle star

MALDONADO, FEDERICO C.
Private First Class, U.S. Army Air Forces, 1st Army Air Force Base Unit; duty soldier
Honors: American Campaign Medal, Victory Medal, Good Conduct Medal

MALDONADO, FRANCISCO S.
Private First Class, U.S. Army Air Forces, 459th Coast Artillery Battalion
Battles: Normandy, Northern France, Rhineland, Central Europe
Honors: European-African-Middle Eastern Campaign Medal with 4 battle stars, Good Conduct Medal

MALDONADO, EUDELIO G.
Private First Class, U.S. Army, Battery C, 163rd Field Artillery Battalion; crewman
Qualifications: Marksman
Battles: New Guinea, Southern Philippines (Liberation), Luzon
Honors: American Campaign Medal, Victory Medal, Good Conduct Medal, American Defense Service Medal, Asiatic-Pacific Campaign Medal with 3 battle stars and bronze arrowhead, Philippine Liberation Medal, 1 Service Stripe, 3 Overseas Service Bars

MALTOS, VALERIANO F.
Tec5, U.S. Army, 54th General Hospital; medical technician
Battles: New Guinea
Honors: Asiatic-Pacific Campaign Medal, Good Conduct Medal

MANCHA, ALFONSO D.
Private, U.S. Army, Company A, 86th Battalion Infantry Replacement Training Center

MANCHA, JOSE D.
Tec4, U.S. Army, Troop E, 12th Cavalry
Battle: New Guinea, Bismarck-Archipelago, Southern Philippines, Luzon
Honors: European-African-Middle Eastern Campaign Medal with 4 battle stars, Good Conduct Medal, American Defense Service Medal, Philippine Liberation Medal with 2 battle stars

Tec4 Mancha was a member of the 1st Cavalry Division's invasion of Admiralty Islands.

MANCHA, ROBERTO R.
Tec4, U.S. Army, Company C, 863rd Engineer Aviation Battalion; cook
Battles: New Guinea, Southern Philippines, Luzon
Honors: Asiatic-Pacific Campaign Medal with 3 battle stars, Philippine Liberation Medal, Victory Medal, 1 Service Stripe, 5 Overseas Service Bars with 1 battle star

MANCHA, RUBEN
Sergeant, U.S. Army, 860th Engineer Aviation Battalion
Battles: New Guinea

Brother of Tec4 Roberto Mancha and Tec4 Jose Mancha, The Eagle Pass News Guide, August 3, 1944, stated, "CPL Roberto and SGT Ruben were lucky enough to meet somewhere in New Guinea on Christmas Day. While CPL Jose and SGT Ruben missed each other by a matter of hours."

MANCHA, RAUL R.
Private First Class, U.S. Army, Class Troop E, 5th Cavalry
Qualifications: Automatic Rifleman
Battles: New Guinea, Southern Philippines, Luzon
Honors: Purple Heart Medal, American Defense Service Medal, Asiatic Pacific Campaign Medal with 3 battle stars, Philippine Liberation Medal with 2 battle stars, Good Conduct Medal, Distinguished Unit Badge, Combat Infantryman Badge

MARINES, ERASMO

MARINES, FRANCISCO
Private First Class, U.S. Army Air Forces, 3543rd Army Air Force; cooks helper
Qualifications: Marksman Carbine
Honors: Victory Medal

MARINES, HIGINO F.
Tec4, U.S. Army, 133rd Texas Engineer Battalion

Tec4 Higino Marines was killed in action on January 11, 1945, his 20th birthday.

MARINOS, PETER
Lieutenant, U.S. Army Air Forces, 306th Group; pilot

According to The Eagle Pass News Guide, November 18, 1943, Lt Marinos was reported as "missing in action" in Europe. In a letter dated October 27, 1943, he wrote, "...not very long after that I finally got what I longed for so long- raid over enemy territory. I'll probably never forget that first raid. It was to France, the last one Clark Gable went on before he returned to the United States. All the rest I have been on were over Germany except one which was to Poland. I just learned something interesting. Most of the German airmen wear lipstick and rouge and use fingernail polish. That doesn't mean that they are feminine, on the contrary..."

MARTIN, DAVID
U.S. Navy

Battles: South Pacific, Soloman Islands

MARTIN, JOHN ROY
Captain, U.S. Army, Infantry Parachute Unit, 509th Parachute Battalion; unit commander

Battles: Algeria, Morocco, Tunisia, Sicily, Naples-Foggia, Rome-Arno

Honors: Purple Heart Medal, Unit Combat Infantryman Badge

Capt. Martin was wounded in Italy on February 29, 1944.

MARTIN, RICHARD
Private First Class, U.S. Army, 1st Battalion; auto mechanic

MARTINEZ, ANDRES D.
Private First Class, U.S. Army, Company A, 175th Engineer Regiment; artillery gun crewman

Battles: Naples-Foggia, Rome-Arno, Northern Apennines, PO Valley

Honors: European-African-Middle Eastern Campaign Medal with 4 battle stars, Good Conduct Medal, Victory Medal, 4 Overseas Service Bars

MARTINEZ, BLANCO E. L.
Private First Class, U.S. Army, Field Artillery, Demolition Section SCU 1907; cannoneer

Qualifications: Marksman

MARTINEZ, CARLOS S.
Corporal, U.S. Army, Company K, 331st Infantry; combat rifleman

Qualifications: Rifleman

Battles: Normandy, Central Europe

Honors: European-African-Middle Eastern Campaign Medal with 2 battle stars, Victory Medal, Good Conduct Medal, American Campaign Medal, Combat Infantryman Badge

MARTINEZ, DAVID
Private, U.S. Army Air Forces, Battery A, 210th Anti-Aircraft Artillery Automatic Weapons Battalion; heavy machine gunner

Qualifications: Marksman

Battles: New Guinea, Southern Philippines, Luzon

Honors: Asiatic-Pacific Campaign Medal, Good Conduct Medal, Philippine Liberation Medal

MARTINEZ JR., ESPIRIDION "SPEEDY"
Private First Class, U.S. Army, Battery A, 207th Field Artillery Battalion; cannoneer

Battles: Northern France, Germany

Honors: European-African-Middle Eastern Campaign Medal, American Defense Service Medal, Purple Heart Medal, Good Conduct Medal

PFC Martinez was wounded in action in the European Theater on July 13, 1944.

MARTINEZ, FELIX

MARTINEZ, GUILLERMO S.
Private First Class, U.S. Army, Company B, 570th Signal Battalion; guard, patrolman

Qualifications: Marksman

Battles: China

Honors: American Campaign Medal, Asiatic-Pacific Campaign Medal with 1 battle star, Victory Medal, Good Conduct Medal

MARTINEZ, PEDRO R.
Private First Class, U.S. Army

Honors: Purple Heart Medal

PFC Martinez was born in Eagle Pass on May 5, 1921 and lived there until he entered the service on October 30, 1941 as an infantryman. He was killed in action in Leyte, Philippines on October 29, 1944. General Douglas MacArthur wrote a personal letter to Mrs. Maria Martinez expressing his deep sympathy as one of the heroic liberators of the Philippines. He was formerly an employee of the S.M.T. Lines and a softball player for the local N.Y.A. Carpenters.

MARTINEZ, PEDRO ESCOBEDO

Private First Class, U.S. Army, Air Force, 207th Army Air Force Base Unit; munitions worker

Battles: Northern France, Ardennes, Rhineland, Central Europe, Air Offensive Europe

Honors: European-African-Middle Eastern Campaign Medal with 1 battle star and 1 silver battle star, Good Conduct Medal, 3 Overseas Bar

PFC Martinez told his daughter Mary Martinez Trevino that he was in a battle with enemy fire. He and 5 other American soldiers were in a dugout. After it was quiet, PFC Martinez got up and said "Let's go." He looked down and saw that all the other 5 soldiers had been killed.

After WWII, he also entered into the Korean War. He received the Silver Star and Bronze Star for his bravery. (Kewaunee County Star-News, obituary in Wisconsin)

MARTINEZ, REYNALDO G.

Tec5, U.S. Army, 118th General Hospital

Qualifications: Sharpshooter

Battles: New Guinea, Southern Philippines

Honors: Asiatic-Pacific Campaign Medal, Philippine Liberation Medal, Victory Medal, Combat Infantryman Badge

Tec5 Martinez was from Morelos, Coahuila, Mexico.

MARTINEZ, REYNALDO S.

Private First Class, U.S. Army, Company F, 1st Infantry; rifleman

Battles: New Guinea, Luzon

Honors: Philippines Liberation Medal, Good Conduct Medal, Bronze Arrowhead, Victory Medal, American Defense Medal, American Campaign Medal, Asiatic-Pacific Theater Medal, Combat Infantry Badge

MARTINEZ, RODOLFO

Tec5, U.S. Army, 3196th Signal Service Company; telephone/telegraph lineman

Qualifications: Sharpshooter

Honors: Victory Medal, Italy Occupation Medal

MARTINEZ, XAVIER H.

MASTERS, OSCAR E.

Lieutenant, U.S. Army Air Forces, B-24 Liberator Bombers

Lt Masters enrolled in the Army Air Force Training Command technical school with outstanding grades on the Army Mechanical Aptitude Test.

MASTERS, ROBERT

MASTERS, WILLIAM EDWARD

Master Sergeant, U.S. Army Air Forces, 2532rd Army Air Force Base Unit; administration specialist

Honors: American Defense Medal, European-African-Middle Eastern Campaign Medal, Good Conduct Medal, 5 Overseas Bars

MSgt Masters claimed the distinction of being one of the youngest Master Sergeants in England. The Eagle Pass News Guide dated May 25, 1944 stated, "...through his hands comes much administrative material at this bombing repair depot where battered 8th Air Force's bombers are made ready."

MASON, JOHN T.

Private First Class, U.S. Army, 19th Infantry, 24th Division; truck driver

Battles: Luzon, Southern Philippines (Liberation), New Guinea

Honors: Philippine Liberation Medal with 2 Campaign Medals, American Defense Campaign Medal, American Campaign Medal, Victory Medal, Asiatic-Pacific Campaign Medal with 3 battle stars and Bronze Arrowhead, Army of Occupation Medal (Japan), 1 Service Stripe, 4 Overseas Service Bars, Distinguished Unit Badge, Combat Infantryman Badge

MATHIS Jr., HARRY P.

First Lieutenant, U.S. Army Air Forces, 525th Fighter Squadron, 86th Fighter Group; pilot (A-36-dive-bomber)

Battles: Anzio, Cassino, Rome-Arno, Naples-Foggia

Honors: Air Medal with 1 Oak Leaf Cluster, European-African-Middle Eastern Campaign Medal with 2 battle stars, Distinguished Unit Badge

1st Lt Mathis graduated his pilot training at Eagle Pass Army Air Field on July 29, 1943. He flew a total of 57 strafing and dive bombing missions. Quoted from The Eagle Pass News Guide on August 5, 1943, "Aviation Cadet Harry P. Mathis Jr. of Eagle Pass had the Silver Wings of an Army Air Force flying officer pinned on his breast by his mother, Mrs. Harry P. Mathias when Lt. Mathis became the first local boy to finish training at the field. Looking on the ceremony was Col. John H. Bundy, commanding officer, Mrs. L.L. Bowen, sister of Lt. Mathis, John Mathis, younger brother and Harry P. Mathis, father of Lt. Mathis, an employee of the U.S. Engineers at the Eagle Pass Army Air Field. His father was the principal speaker at his graduation ceremonies of this latest class of Aviation Cadet 43-G to finish their advanced flying training at the Eagle Pass Army Air Field. Proceeding graduation ceremonies, during which the cadets received their commissions as officers and orders transferring them to various duties all over the world, the graduating cadets put on a spectacular exhibition of formation flying and attack maneuvers".

MATHIS, ROBERT "Bobby"

General, U.S. Army Air Forces

Upon graduating from Eagle Pass High School in 1944, Gen. Mathis was admitted to the U.S. Military Academy, West Point in New York. He went on to retire as the vice-chief of the U.S. Air Force, the highest ranking officer from Eagle Pass.

MAULE, EDWIN

MAURICIO, FRANCISCO E.
Private, U.S. Army, Troop C, 7th Cavalry

Battles: Australia, New Guinea

Private Mauricio was killed in action during the Admiralty Island Campaign on March 22, 1944 after being wounded by a gun shot on Manus Island. He was identified by a letter from his mother that was found on his body. He was 20 years old.

MAYER, CARL W.
Sergeant, U.S. Army, Military Police Detachment, 2nd Division; military police

Qualifications: Marksman

Honors: Victory Medal, American Defense Service Medal, American Campaign Medal, European- African-Middle Eastern Campaign Medal, Good Conduct Medal, 1 Service Stripe, 4 Overseas Service Bars

MAYER, Jr., CHARLES
Private First Class, U.S. Army, 18th Depot Separation Squadron; carpenter

Battles: Rome-Arno, Tunisia

Honors: European-African-Middle Eastern Campaign Medal, Good Conduct Medal, Victory Medal

MAZUCA, CRUZ S.
Tec5, U.S. Army, 387th Fort Battalion; winch operator

Qualifications: Marksman, Rifle and Bayonet

Battles: New Guinea, Papua, Southern Philippines, Luzon

Honors: Distinguished Unit Badge, Victory Medal, Good Conduct Medal, Asiatic-Pacific Campaign Medal, Philippine Liberation Medal

MCCULLOUGH, TOM

MCBEATH, ANDREW W.
U.S. Marine Corps

MCDAVID, MARVIN
Private First Class, U.S. Army, Company I, 357th Infantry; rifleman

Qualifications: Marksman

Battles: Normandy Campaign

Honors: Good Conduct Medal, Purple Heart Medal, European-African-Middle Eastern Campaign Medal with 1 battle star

PFC McDavid was discharged to McCloskey General Hospital in Temple, Texas due to wounds he sustained during combat on June 12, 1944.

MCDUFF, ALLEN LEE
Seaman Second Class, U.S. Navy

MCDUFF, DANIEL "Dan"
Captain, U.S. Army Air Forces, 12th Bomber Command; pilot (B-17 and B-25)

Capt. McDuff, brother of Seaman Allen McDuff, flew 50 missions over Germany and Europe. He received an Air Medal with 8 oak leaf clusters.

MCKELLER, ALDEN SCOTT

MCLEMORE, THOMAS
Sergeant, U.S. Army Air Forces

MCMILLAN, HENRY TRAVIS
U.S. Marine Corps

Mr. McMillan received a Bronze Star and Silver Star.

MCPHERSON, Jr., WILLIAM
Captain, U.S. Army Air Forces, 95th Bomb Group, 344th Bomb Squadron; B-17 pilot

From The Eagle Pass News Guide dated November 4, 1943, "This outstanding, courageous young Fortress pilot has been decorated with the Distinguished Flying Cross with 2 oak leaf clusters and the Air Medal with 3 clusters. The Distinguished Flying Cross was awarded to him for participating in the long shuttle raid to Regensberg, Germany, thence to North Africa. The 8th Air Force bombing attack on the vital shipping center of Emden in Northern Germany marked the 25th milestone for Capt. McPherson who was recently promoted from 1st Lt. He has flown his Fortress over heavily defended enemy targets on most of the major 8th Bomber Command Operations in which his combat group has participated during the past few months. His ship is named after the detective in the "Lil" Abner comic strip, "Fearless Fosdick IV." Capt. McPherson was captured as a POW on October 14, 1943."

MEDRANO, RAYMUNDO M.
Private First Class, U.S. Army, 148th Infantry Regiment; truck driver

Battles: Luzon, Southern Philippines (Liberation)

Honors: Good Conduct Medal, Victory Medal, American Campaign Medal, Asiatic-Pacific Campaign Medal, Philippine Liberation Medal, Combat Infantry Badge

MENCHACA, ALFREDO R.
Private First Class, U.S. Army, Battery D, 390th Anti-Aircraft Artillery Automatic Weapons Battalion; guard, patrolman

Qualifications: Sharpshooter

Honors: Army of Occupation Medal (Germany), Victory Medal, 1 Overseas Service Bars

MENCHACA, ARMANDO R.

Private First Class, U.S Army Air Forces, 390th Anti-Aircraft Artillery Automatic Weapons Battalion; crewman

Qualifications: Marksman

Honors: Army of Occupation Medal (Germany), Victory Medal, 1 Overseas Service Bars
PFC Alfredo Menchaca and PFC Armando Menchaca are twin brothers.

MENCHACA, JOSE

MENDEZ, JUAN G.

Private First Class, U.S. Army, Company A, 432nd Signal Construction Battalion; telephone/telegraph lineman

Qualifications: Marksman-Carbine

Battles: Central Burma, India Burma

Honors: American Theater, Asiatic-Pacific Campaign Medal, Good Conduct Medal, Victory Medal

MENDEZ, MANUEL

Private First Class, U.S. Army, Company G, 167th Infantry, Fire Direction Center Operations

Battles: Northern Solomon's, South Philippines (Liberation)

Honors: Asiatic-Pacific Campaign Medal, Philippine Liberation, Good Conduct Medal, Victory Medal.

In a letter to Mrs. Jones (published in The Eagle Pass News Guide), Pvt Manuel Mendez wrote:

I was so pleased to receive your letter. I cannot tell you how happy I was to receive an answer from you, because I do not know what words to use. What I am trying to say is, that mail brings a lot of joy to me and to my buddies. Especially to guys like us that are overseas, thousands of miles from the United States.

Well, I know that all of you that are in the United States are doing the best you can. Some are working in defense work and every time they build a new plane or ship, it's a headache to the Axis. Some of you are buying war stamps. Every time that you stick one of those war stamps into a book, you stick the Flag of Freedom a little farther out of reach of Hitler and Tojo.

We who are fighting on foreign soils know why we are fighting this war. We are fighting for the things that made America the greatest place in the world to live in, and that are going to keep America the greatest place in the world to live in. We want to come home to the same America we left behind, where there is freedom and justice and opportunity for all. That's America for us. Keep it that way until we come back.

As you know, this island where I am, is on this side of the equator, I mean south of the equator. The heat here was what got me, but now I am getting used to this climate. Almost always the temperature is well above 100 degrees. The mosquitos are bad around here, we have mosquito nets, but you can hear them buzzing around outside the net all night long.

MENDEZ, OSCAR A.
Private, U.S. Army

Pvt. Mendez, from Piedras Negras, Mexico entered active duty on July 23, 1945, one month before the end of the war.

MENDOZA, JULIO C

Tec5, U.S. Army, 467th Signal Heavy Construction Company Aviation; truck driver

Battle: Luzon, Philippines (Liberations)

Honors: Asiatic-Pacific Campaign Medal with 1 battle star, Good Conduct Medal, Philippine Liberation Medal with 1 battle star, Army of Occupation Medal (Japan), Victory Medal, 2 Overseas Service Bars, Combat Infantryman Badge

MENDOZA, TEODORO "Ted"

Private, U.S. Army

Pvt Mendoza was en route to the Philippines when the Japanese surrendered. His unit received new orders for occupation duty in Korea. Pvt Mendoza remembers in Korea that the Japanese left their barracks so quickly that they forgot to turn off their heaters. Pvt Mendoza could never forget the brutal, cold winters as he told us "muy frio."

MEYER, VAUGHN BENJAMIN
Lieutenant Commander, U.S. Navy

Lt Commander Meyer was a graduate of Cal Tech and was stationed at the Washington Navy Yard. He was part of a team that corrected the guidance systems on defective torpedoes. The torpedoes were misfiring and were not accurate. Lt Meyer's grandson, Casey Lang told us that the Soviet Union wanted to issue him a medal for his work on torpedoes. At the time in 1945, the Soviet Union Embassy did not have any WWII medals to issue but they did have a Czar Medal.

MEZA, PABLO A.
Private First Class, U.S. Army, 1857th Service Command Unit; duty soldier

Battles: New Guinea, Papua

Honors: Asiatic-Pacific Campaign Medal with 2 battle stars, Distinguished Unit Badge

MYERS, JOHN A.
Private First Class, U.S. Army Air Forces, radio operator mechanic

MIKULINSKY, SAM (Sam Michaels)

Seaman Second Class, U.S. Navy, radioman

Seaman Mikulinsky served 12 months of overseas duty aboard the U.S.S. Keosanqua.

Sam Michaels was born in Minsk, Russia in 1924. His family immigrated to Mexico because United States limited the number of immigrants from Russia. His father started a business with two partners, importing radios from the United States to Rosita, Mexico. Because his parents wanted Sam to be educated in the United States they moved to Piedras Negras, Coahuila. They would take him to Eagle Pass every day to school.

When Sam was 14 years old, his family moved to Eagle Pass and went into the cattle and produce business. During high school, Sam played on several sports teams- basketball and football with other future veterans- Richmond Harper, Percy Bingham, David O. Williams, JR Rubio, Nojem Lipson, and Rodolfo Reyes.

On a Sunday drive in December 1941 with his best friend Richmond Harper, the radio announced that Pearl Harbor was bombed. They both did not comprehend the meaning of this event. The next day, the high school had gathered the students in the auditorium and they listened to the radio. President Franklin Delano Roosevelt announced that the United States declared war on the Japanese Empire. Sam and Richmond and all their friends knew that their lives would be changed forever. Upon graduation from High School in May 1942, many of his High School buddies went to college during that summer. However because Sam's family lost money on their onion crop that year, he couldn't afford to go to college. To earn money for college, Sam went to work at Brown & Root Construction Company as a construction worker to build the Eagle Pass Air Force Base. The superintendent, being very impressed with Sam recommended that he should get his civil engineer degree and after he graduates, Brown & Root would hire him. In the fall, Sam went to Texas A&M University to get his civil engineering degree.

After two years as a student at Texas A&M University, Sam enlisted in the Navy. After boot camp, Sam took the Navy radio training program in San Diego, specializing in communications technology. The top two students of the program were selected to advance their training at Texas A&M as a radio technician. Sam ranked as one of the top two in his class and was excited to go back to Texas. However, before the trip to go back to Texas, the Battle of Iwo Jima occurred and many of his colleagues- radiomen were lost. Because of the shortages of radiomen in the Pacific, his unit was quickly shipped overseas.

While on duty in the Pacific, Sam applied and was subsequently accepted to officer's training school. On the same day his transfer papers arrived, he heard that the United States dropped an atomic bomb over Hiroshima. Since Sam figured that the war would be over very soon, he declined officer's training since the Navy requires the officer to serve three additional years.

After the war, Sam graduated at Texas A&M as a civil engineer on the GI Bill. After college, he went to work with some relatives who owned a business that manufactured yarn in New York City. Sam found out he had knack for business and bought and sold several successful businesses in his career. Sam is now retired and lives in Palm Beach, Florida.

MILLER, BENJAMIN

MIRELES, ARMANDO "El Caballo"
Technical Sergeant, U.S. Army
Battles: Italy, France
TSgt Mireles was wounded in action while serving in France. He was captured and was kept as a POW.

MIRELES, GUADALUPE A.
Technical Sergeant, U.S. Army, Company K, 113th Infantry; rifleman
Battles: Naples-Foggia, Rome-Arno, Rhineland, Southern France, Central Europe

Honors: Purple Heart Medal, European-African-Middle Eastern Campaign Medal with silver service star, Good Conduct Medal

TSgt. Was wounded at St. Rafail, France on August 15, 1944.

MIRELES, RAUL S.
Tec4, U.S. Army, Battery A, 764th Field Artillery Battalion; clerk battery

Qualifications: Sharpshooter

Honors: American Campaign Medal, European-African-Middle Eastern Campaign Medal, Good Conduct Medal, Victory Medal

MIRELES Jr., TOMAS
Corporal, U.S. Army, HQ Company Service Command; cannoneer

Honors: Good Conduct Medal, American Theater Service Medal

MONCADA, APOLONIO R.
Private, U.S. Army, HQ 141st Infantry

Qualifications: Sharpshooter

Honors: European-African-Middle Eastern Campaign Medal, Purple Heart Medal

Pvt Moncada was wounded in action on November 27, 1943 near Mont Rotrando, Italy.

MONCADA, JOE R.
Private, U.S. Army, 3372nd Signal Service Battalion; auto equipment operator

Battles: Normandy, Northern France, Southern France, Rhineland, Air Offensive Europe

Honors: European-African-Middle Eastern Campaign Medal with 5 battle stars, 3 Service Bars

MONCADA, RAUL R. "FARRA"
Private First Class, U.S. Army, Troop E, 5th Cavalry; automatic rifleman

Battles: New Guinea, Luzon, Southern Philippines

Honors: Distinguished Unit Badge, Asiatic-Pacific Campaign Medal with 3 battle stars, Good Conduct Medal, American Defense Service Medal, Purple Heart Medal, Philippine Liberation Medal with 2 battle stars, Combat Infantry Badge

MONCADA, RAYMUNDO
Private First Class, U.S. Army, 1857th Service Command; demolition

Battles: Northern France, Central Europe, European-African-Middle Eastern

Honors: American Theater, European African Middle East Campaign Medal, Victory Medal, Good Conduct Medal

PFC Moncada received certification as a radio operator in Washington. According to his

nephew, Jimmy Moncada, PFC Moncada was sent overseas as a tank instructor and had landed on Omaha beach with his tank division for 3 or 4 days.

Before entering the army, Moncada played 2 years with a semi-professional baseball team, the local "Eagles" and played one year professionally with the professional team Rosita Mines and with another professional team at Puebla, Mexico. (The Eagle Pass News Guide)

MONCADA, RODOLFO R.

MONCADA, SANTIAGO
Private First Class, U.S. Army, Military Police Detachment; military police
Qualifications: Marksman rifle
PFC was stationed in New Mexico, guarding prisoners of war from Italy, Germany and Japan. FFC Santiago Moncada and Raymundo Moncada were brothers.

MONTEMAYOR, LUIS
Private First Class, U.S. Army, 45th Signal Company; field lineman
Battles: Naples-Foggia, Rome-Arno, Southern France, Rhineland
Honors: American Defense Service Medal, European-African-Middle Eastern Campaign Medal with 4 battle stars, Good Conduct Medal
As told in The Eagle Pass News Guide, "From Mexico to Texas to California to Florida to Louisiana, Alabama and Georgia, thence to North Carolina. Pvt. Luis Montemayor has seen as much of the U.S. since January 8th of last year as any traveling salesman could on an unlimited expense account. "Life" Magazine carried a half page photo of a famous movie actress singing to the soldiers at camp and who should be right next to her but Pvt. Luis Montemayor, smiling as though he has just adopted her."

MORALES Jr., JOSE MARIA
Seaman Second Class, U.S. Navy

MORAN, FRANCISCO
Private First Class, U.S. Army, Company B, 11th Engineer Combat Battalion; carpenter
Qualifications: Sharpshooter
Battles: Rhineland, Central Europe
Honors: American Defense Service Medal, American Campaign Medal, European African Middle Eastern Campaign Medal with 2 battle stars, Victory Medal

MORIN, JOSE TOVAR

MORIN Jr., RAFAEL

MORENO, ANTONIO R.
Private First Class, U.S. Army, Company I, 9th Infantry; rifleman
Battles: Northern France
Honors: American Campaign Medal, European-African-Middle Eastern Campaign

Medal with 1 battle star, Good Conduct Medal, Purple Heart Medal, 1 Overseas Service Bar, Victory Medal, Combat Infantry Badge

PFC Moreno was wounded at the European Theater on July 31, 1944.

MORENO, CANDELARIO

Private First Class, U.S. Army, HQ Service Company, 926th Engineer Battalion; duty soldier

Qualifications: Marksman

Battle: Normandy, Northern France, Rhineland, Central Europe

Honors: European-African-Middle Eastern Campaign Medal with 4 battle stars, Good Conduct Medal, Victory Medal, 4 Overseas Service Bars

MORENO, EUGENIO

MORENO, JESUS D.

Tec4, Company A, U.S. Army, 144th Infantry; mess sergeant

Qualifications: Sharpshooter

Honors: American Defense Medal, Good Conduct Medal, Combat Infantry Badge

MORENO, JOSE V. "Guero"

Private, U.S. Army, HQ 11th Medical Battalion; litter-bearer

Battles: Italian Campaign

Honors: American Defense Service Medal, Good Conduct Medal, European African Middle Eastern Campaign Medal

As told by his daughter Linda Moreno her father, as a litter bearer carried the wounded soldiers and soldiers who were killed down from the mountains in Italy.

MORENO, JOSE A.

Private, U.S. Army, 7702nd HQ and Service Battalion; cook

Qualifications: Marksman

Battles: Northern France, Rhineland

Honors: Army Occupation Medal, Victory Medal, European-African-Middle Eastern Campaign Medal, Purple Heart Medal

Private Moreno was wounded in action on September 13, 1944 in France. He received a shell fragment wounding his left middle finger.

MORENO, RAMON E.

Private First Class, U.S. Army Air Forces, 245th Army Air Force Base Unit; ammunition handler

Honors: American Campaign Medal, Good Conduct Medal, Victory Medal

MUNTER, LLOYD T.
Private First Class, U.S. Army, mechanic
Honors: Good Conduct Medal, Victory Medal

Originally from Brooklyn, New York, PFC Munter was a student at Alfred Tech University (Agriculture school in upstate New York) with ambition of becoming a veterinarian. His plans were cut short by his draft notice in 1943. He went to basic training in Miami Beach Florida and was housed at a commandeered (a hotel that was seized by the government for military purposes). He then attended mechanic air plane training school in Tulsa, Oklahoma and was transferred to Eagle Pass Army Air Force Base (EPAFF). For a boy from Brooklyn, it was a culture shock to be dropped in the middle of the brush country at Spofford, TX, 25 miles from EPAAF, a mere railroad crossing. Dust and brush replaced the sights of people and buildings. This culture shock would only continue as he settled in Eagle Pass. Before leaving Brooklyn for the Army Air Force, he had never met a non-Jewish person. While in the Army, Lloyd was exposed to new experiences and people.

Later he met his wife, Yolanda Schwartz at a Hanukkah Party hosted by her parents, Sam and Ellen Schwartz. Because he had the night shift at the base, he could never sleep because of the aircraft noise. He got permission from the base to go to his future in-laws house, the Schwartz's on 2nd Street to sleep and eat lunch during the day. At the same time Yolanda was working at the base at Zachry Construction. They married on May 19, 1946 after he was discharged. Lloyd lived in Eagle Pass until his death in 1989. He loved animals and was glad to live in a place where he was able to help with his father-in-law's ranch and family theater business.

MURRAY, CHARLES E.
Private, U.S. Army; administration clerk

MURRAY, WILLIAM H.
Tec4, U.S. Army, HQ Company, Army Service Forces Training Center; Army Specialist Training Program, classification specialist
Qualifications: Sharpshooter
Honors: Good Conduct Medal, Victory Medal, American Campaign Theater Medal
Private Garcia was inducted into the Army on June 1, 1943; Grand Island.

MUNOZ, ARTURO

MUNOZ, JOSE M.
Private First Class, U.S. Army, Company B, 126th Infantry; rifleman
Honors: Asiatic-Pacific Campaign Medal, Victory Medal

MUNOZ, MORTIMER

MUZQUIZ, FELIPE EULALIO
Staff Sergeant, U.S. Army Air Forces, 1030th Army Air Force Base Unit; airplane armorer gunner
Battles: Air Offensive Europe, Normandy
Honors: European-African-Middle Eastern Campaign Medal, Air Medal, Good Conduct Medal

NAVARRO, EDWARD J.

NEUMAN, MARCUS
Corporal, U.S. Army; infantry

Battles: New Guinea

Honors: Combat Infantryman Badge

As told by The Eagle Pass News Guide, "Marcus Neuman came to Eagle Pass in 1939 from Presov, Czechoslovakia. He had been living here only two years-was not yet a citizen- when he volunteered to go with the American fighting forces back to the war theater from which he had come. Three months after he entered the service in January (1942), Corporal Marcus Neuman was in Australia. Corporal Neuman said, "Life is the living of it, anyway so why worry?" "Marcus wired his paycheck to his brother, Nandor Neuman in Eagle Pass, as a gift to Nandor's little daughter. Nandor bought War Savings Bonds with it, in the hope that the war material will help Corporal Neuman in the drive of victory. We hope he comes back to enjoy the country he is fighting for".

NEY, MARSHALL N. "Nick"
Tec4, U.S. Army, 3326th Company; radio operator

Battles: Rome-Arno, Northern Apennines, PO Valley

Honors: European-African-Middle Eastern Campaign Medal, Good Conduct Medal, Combat Infantry Badge

Nick was a direct descendent of Marshall Ney, one of Napoleon Bonaparte's best generals. Marshall Ney was one of the original 18 Marshals of the Empire created by Napoleon. He was a French soldier and military commander during the French Revolution. Nick was also the brother in law of CV Lee who was lost on the U.S.S. Arizona at Pearl Harbor.

NUNCIO, ANACLETO
Private First Class, U.S. Army

A letter written by Brigadier General Jesse Auton praised PFC Nuncio by saying, "I desire to commend you for your part in the activities of your station against the enemy during the critical period of the invasion of France from June 6, 1944 to June 27, 1944. The success of this operation depended a great deal upon the support given by the aircraft of your group. You performed your duty in such as zealous manner, working many hours a day beyond your normal amount, that your aircraft gave maximum support to our ground forces & claim the destruction of 19 enemy planes and damaged 5." This letter was published in The Eagle Pass News Guide on August 3, 1944.

O'DONNELL, JAMES E.
Corporal, U.S. Army, 61st Field Artillery Battalion

Honors: Army of Occupation Medal Japan, Victory Medal

While serving in the occupation of Japan, he supervised, requisitioned, procured, and distributed ammunition. His unit also taught classes on ammunition, care and cleaning of equipment, and first aid. He was given a special assignment as a guard to the Emperor of Japan, Hirohito, on an auto and train tour of Japan after the war. The emperor was persuading his people to cooperate with the American occupation. His wife, Rosa related stories to the author that no weapons could be carried by the American soldiers detail on the tour because it could be implied that the Emperor was a prisoner. After

Cpl O'Donnell finished this extraordinary duty, the Emperor gave Cpl O'Donnell a cigar with the Imperial Chrysanthemum (seal around the cigar). Cpl O'Donnell took a snapshot of the Emperor's automobile. The Emperor is sitting in the back.

Cpl O'Donnell died in 2012.

OLDHAM, C.E. "Jack"
U.S. Navy

O'LEARY, WILLIAM JOSEPH
Private First Class, U.S. Marine Corps; heavy artillery crewman

Qualifications: Heavy Artillery Crewman

Battles: Saipan, Guam, Iwo Jima

PFC O'Leary served overseas and at sea from December 16, 1943-November 11, 1945. He served in the Asiatic-Pacific, Hawaiian Island, Iwo Jima, and Marinas Island.

OLIVARES, ADOLFO
Sergeant, U.S. Army, 96th Division, Company I, 383rd Infantry; rifleman

Battles: Southern Philippines, Ryukus

Honors: Asiatic-Pacific Campaign Medal, Purple Heart Medal with and oak leaf cluster (4/23/45 and 6/13/45), Combat Infantry Badge

OLIVARES Jr., MANUEL ROBERTO
Master Sergeant, U.S. Army Air Forces, 3rd Air Force, 316th Bomb Wing; military intelligence

Qualifications: Expert Carbine

Honors: American Campaign Medal, Asiatic-Pacific Campaign Medal. Good Conduct Medal, Victory Medal with 1 Service Stripe

Published in The Eagle Pass News Guide, February 17, 1944, MSgt Olivares was assigned to the film library in the intelligence section of the 3rd Air Force Headquarters.

OLIVO Jr., CRUZ L.
Private, U.S. Army, Company B, Infantry Advance Training Battalion Camp; cook

Qualifications: Marksman

OMANA, CARLOS E.
Private First Class, U.S. Army, Company A, 34th Infantry; rifleman

Battles: Southern Philippines, Luzon

Honors: Asiatic-Pacific Campaign Medal with 2 battle stars, Philippine Liberation Medal with 1 battle star, Good Conduct Medal, Distinguished Unit Badge, Victory Medal, 2 Overseas Service Bars, Combat Infantry Badge

ORTIZ, ALFREDO
U.S. Army

ORTIZ, CLAUDIO
Private, U.S. Army

ORTIZ, PEDRO

OSBORNE, HENRY

OSBORNE, JOHN
Tec4, U.S. Army, Battery A; gun mechanic

OLIVARES, MANUEL R.
Corporal, U.S. Army Air Force, 316th Bomb Wing, Military Intelligence; intelligence specialist
Honors: Asiatic-Pacific Campaign Medal, Good Conduct Medal, Victory Medal, 1 Service Stripe

OYERVIDES, EDULIO CANO
Private First Class, U.S. Marine Corps
Qualifications: Sharpshooter

OYERVIDES, FEDERICO
Corporal, U.S. Army, Company D, 317th Infantry Division; machine gunner
Battles: Northern France, Central Europe
Honors: Victory Medal, American Campaign Medal, European-African-Middle Eastern Campaign Medal with 2 battle stars, Good Conduct Medal

PANIAGIA, VICENTE R.
Tec5, 332nd Army Air Force Band; bandsman
Honors: Good Conduct Medal

PATILLO, ROBERT WALTON

PENA, EUGENIO CASTRO

PENA, LUIS T.

PENDELL, EDWARD
U.S. Army

PERALES, ANTONIO
Private First Class, U.S. Army, 84th Depot Supply Squadron; supply clerk

Qualifications: Rifle

Battles: Rome-Arno, Ardennes, Air Offensive Europe

Honors: European-African-Middle Eastern Campaign Medal with 3 battle stars, 2 Overseas Bars, Good Conduct Medal, Purple Heart Medal, Combat Infantryman Badge

PFC Perales was wounded in action in Italy on September 16, 1944.

PEREZ Jr., JUAN
Seaman First Class, U.S. Navy

PEREZ, JUAN
Private First Class, U.S. Army, Medical Detachment, 149th Infantry; medical aidman

Battles: Philippine Campaign

Honors: American Defense Service Medal, American Campaign Medal, Asiatic-Pacific Campaign Medal with 1 battle star, Philippine Liberation Medal with 1 battle star, Victory Medal, Purple Heart Medal

PFC Perez was wounded in action in Leyte, Philippines on December 5, 1944.

PEREZ, MANUEL H.
Private First Class, U.S. Army, 44th Troop Carrier Squadron, 316th Group; cook

Battles: Sicily, Naples-Foggia, Rome-Arno, Normandy, Northern France, Rhineland, Central Europe

Honors: European-African-Middle Eastern Campaign Medal with 7 battle stars, Good Conduct Medal, Distinguished Unit Badge with 1 Oak Leaf Cluster

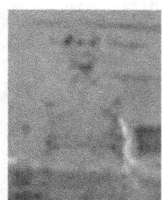

PEREZ, RAUL F.
Tec5, Medical Department, U.S. Army, Medical Department of the 165th Infantry Brigade, 27th Infantry Division

Tec5 Perez was killed in action in Shima, Okinawa on May 4, 1945. He was buried at the United States Armed Forces Cemetery in Okinawa, Ryukyus Islands. His remains were later repatriated by his parents to his final resting place in Eagle Pass.

PEREZ, SIMON
Private First Class, U.S. Army, Battery C, 965th Field Artillery Battalion; guard patrolman

Qualifications: Sharpshooter

Battles: Northern France, Rhineland

Honors: European-African-Middle Eastern Campaign Medal with 2 battle stars, Good Conduct Medal, Victory Medal

PERRY, BILLY MAURICE

Seaman Third Class, U.S. Navy; cook

Honors: European-African-Middle Eastern Campaign medal with 3 battle stars, Good Conduct Medal, Victory Medal, 3 Overseas Service Bars

Having enlisted on December 17, 1943, Seaman Perry reported to boot camp at the U.S. Naval Training Station in San Diego, California. He served 18 months overseas on several Tugboats - U.S.S. ATR87, U.S.S. PGM-31, and U.S.S. YMS-427 going to Honolulu, Johnson Island, Guam, Saipan, Philippines, Okinawa, and Shanghai.

In an interview on May 27, 2013 with Billy Perry:

Seaman Perry said that he had a choice between the army or the navy. He chose the navy because he wanted good food and a bed close by. He became a cook for the 3 officers plus 50 crewmen on a Tugboat. He obtained food supplies from other ships. Tug boats are small auxiliary ships that are the towing, diving, salvage and rescue ships of the U.S. Navy. They are equipped with defensive equipment, cannons and radar equipment to detect submarines. There were no doctors, no pharmacy, or no church services. If anyone died at sea, they had to throw the body overboard.

The tugboat was considered the workhorse of the Navy where they can maneuver ships or barges etc. in a crowed harbor or a narrow canal. Perry mentioned that his tugboat had to tow barges that carried high octane aviation fuel which is very explosive. When the Japanese started to attack their boat, his commanding officers ordered the crew to let the barge loose because it could explode. After the Japanese stopped the bombing, the tugboat went back and picked up the barge.

Sometimes his crew, aboard the tugboat, would travel alone or with a convoy of other ships. Toward the end of the war, the Japanese planes would conduct suicide missions by attacking the biggest ship in the convoy. Seaman Perry witnessed two suicide Japanese's planes flying towards the battleship New Mexico on January 6, 1945. The first suicide plane missed their target while the second plane hit the fantail of ship which killed the commanding officer, Captain Robert Fleming, British Lieutenant General Herbert Lumsden and 29 other crew members. Lt. General Herbert was part of a British mission to observe operations and was Winston Churchill's personal military representative to General Douglas MacArthur.

Later that year, in March 1945, the tugboat YMS-427 was assigned to the first Fleet serving in the assault and occupation of Okinawa. They were used during WWII for inshore sweeping to prepare the way for amphibious assaults. Okinawa harbor consisted of many caves at the side of the mountain. The Japanese would bury their dead, hide and booby trapped the caves. Small Japanese boats would cruise the harbor and would give smoke screens so the American ships could not see where they were going and could not bomb the caves. The Japanese would also drive some small suicide boats into the U.S. ships.

The atomic bomb was dropped when Perry was stationed in Okinawa and he heard that the war was over shortly thereafter. The ship Australia started to blow all its horns.

After the war was over, Perry and the rest of crew explored some of the caves. He said that they found deteriorated skeletons in vases. In one cave, Perry also found a Japanese rifle. Since the war was over and the ship had 40-50 boxes of M-1 rifles, the officers decided to give rifles away. The officers also gave the crew a choice whether to stay or go back to the United States. Perry decided to go home. On the transport back to the United States, the officers told them that if you have an M-1 rifle it may cause problems when entering the United States, so Seaman Perry turned his M-1 rifle in. However, it was okay to keep the Japanese rifle.

On the way back to the United States, the transport boat docked at Shanghai, China the mouth of the Yangtze River for shore leave. The pirates at the Yangtze River were still active, which Perry witnessed. Shanghai was an open city with no passport requirements where refuges all over the world came to live and visit, including German Jews escaping the Nazi regime and White Russians escaping the Soviet Union communists. Perry figured out that the Chinese liked butter and coffee and that he could trade them for other food and 'services' in Shanghai. Several times, a white Russians came on the ship, looking for work. Perry would trade food for the Russians to cook. Seaman Perry said that they were good bakers and he watched and learned how to bake from them.

During shore leave, Seaman Perry and his shipmates found a bar in the off-limits portion of Shanghai ran by an old German man. Perry fondly remembered meeting many Chinese girls and the good time they had there.

Seaman Perry lost some of his hearing during the war because of the loud noises from the bombing. After returning home after the war, Seaman Perry worked in a barbershop in Quemado and Eagle Pass, in real estate, as a farmer and he currently grows a Pecan Orchard in Quemado.

PERRY, CHARLES
U.S. Navy

PERRYMAN, MARK
Captain, 5th Cavalry

Captain Perryman originally served under General Patton at Ft. Clark and participated in the recapture of Manila. He was promoted to Captain from Master Sergeant on the battlefield during this battle.

PEUFFIUS, BENNY C.

PFRIMMER, ELVIN
Seaman Second Class, U.S. Navy

PFRIMMER, JOHNNY
U.S. Navy

PFRIMMER, LAWRENCE W.
Private First Class, U.S. Army, 349th Infantry; duty soldier

Battles: Rome-Arno, Northern Apennines, PO Valley

Honors: American Campaign Medal, Good Conduct Medal, Victory Medal, European- African- Middle Eastern Campaign Medal with 3 battle stars, 1 Service Stripe, 2 Overseas Service Bars, Badge, Combat Infantry Badge

PICAZO, ROBERTO L.
Seaman First Class, U.S. Navy

Seaman Picazo served 24 months of sea duty.

PICON, HIGINIO
Sergeant, U.S. Army, Battery C, 65th Anti-Aircraft Gun Battalion; observer height finder
Qualifications: M1 Rifle
Battles: Aleutian Islands
Honors: American Defense Service Medal, Distinguished Unit Badge, Asiatic-Pacific Campaign Medal with 1 battle star

PILGRIM, J.G. CHARLES
Lieutenant, U.S. Army

PINGENOT, BEN E.
Tec5, U.S. Army, 130th Station Hospital; clerk general
Honors: Army of Occupation Medal, Victory Medal

PIPER, WILLIAM BERNARD
Radarman Third Class, U.S. Navy

PLUMB, J.D.

POLENDO Jr., MANUEL
Aviation Boatswain's Mate Third Class, U.S. Navy,

PONCE, HOMERO L.
Private First Class, U.S. Army, 182nd Infantry Regiment

POLLAY, HARVEY
Ensign, U.S. Navy

According to The Eagle Pass News Guide, January 21, 1943, Ensign Pollay had been the recipient of the Simpson Memorial Award when he graduated from Eagle Pass High School. He went on to graduate from the University of Texas School with a degree in Journalism. In June 1941, Ensign Pollay worked at the San Antonio Light as a police reporter, market reporter, and covered reports on federal buildings and downtown hotels. Months before the attack on Pearl Harbor, Ensign Pollay submitted an application to enter the Naval Training School and was commissioned on April 17, 1942. He graduated from the Great Lakes Training Station in Chicago, Illinois in 1942 and was stationed and saw action on units of the Pacific fleet. On the way home to Eagle Pass, Ensign Pollay was killed in a Navy patrol bomber crash at Henley Field, Dallas, Texas on January 15, 1943. The bomber, which had arrived on a routine flight from San Diego, California, struck its nose on the runway of the station field and burned, killing all 7 men on board.

PORTER, PASQUAL E.
Private First Class, U.S. Army, 2nd Battalion, 508th Parachute Infantry; paratrooper

Battles: Central Europe, Aleutians Islands

Honors: European African Middle East Campaign Medal with 1 battle star, Asiatic-Pacific Campaign Medal with 1 battle star, Victory Medal, American Campaign Medal, Combat Infantry Badge

PFC Porter was with the 4th Infantry Regiment 1st Battalion that fought the Japanese in the Attu attack in 1942.

PORTER, RODOLFO
Private First Class, U.S. Army, Battery B, 225th Field Artillery; gunner, cannoneer

Qualifications: Deep diving with no equipment

Honors: American Defense Service Medal, Asiatic-Pacific Campaign Medal

PRICE, ALAN E.

RAMIREZ, GERARDO F. "Calulo"
Corporal, U.S. Army, Company F, 323th Infantry Regiment; heavy mortar crewman

Battles: Southern Philippines (Palau and Leyte), Western Pacific

Honors: American Campaign Medal, Asiatic-Pacific Campaign Medal with 2 battle stars, Philippine Liberation Medal with 1 battle star, Good Conduct Medal, Victory Medal, 1 Service Stripe, 3 Overseas Service Bars, Combat Infantryman Badge

In an interview with his son Rogelio Ramirez on April 16, 2001:

Corporal Ramirez remembered only too well the battles fought in the Philippines in the treacherous terrain and debilitating heat. "During the time of fighting," as he recalled, "you never slept. You just kept moving. We were in the front and the ones in the back had the task of picking up the dead bodies and the injured soldiers."

As a member of the 323rd Infantry Regiment he remembered enduring the unthinkable. He spent two years in the Philippines, came back home, then re- enlisted for one more year. He fought in battles in Palau, Philippines and in New Guinea. He considered himself lucky when bullets hailed past him; but his friend fighting beside him was not so lucky. He was struck in the head and killed.

It was on Christmas day that he vividly remembered hearing the loud sound of bombs going off, only to see hordes of naked Japanese men running out of the bushes with their hands up in the air. "Things had just settled down and we were about to enjoy our Christmas dinner. We had no idea they were there!"

What amazed Ramirez about the Japanese was that they lived in caves. "There were these huge caves like warehouses! They had everything down there....big tanks, artillery, ladders to get in and out, and even kitchens."

After taking the Japanese as prisoners he had the daunting experience of supervising them as they ended up with the task of picking up pieces of legs, arms, heads, and other body parts. They would wrap them up in blankets and then they would bury them in these large trenches.

Despite the horrendous moments he endured while fighting in the Pacific, there were some fond memories and comical experiences with other soldiers. He also recalled everyone being treated equally while in the service.

Ramirez came back to his hometown of Eagle Pass in 1946, after being honorably discharged from the army at Fort Sam Houston, San Antonio, Texas. He was married to his wife Virginia and fathered seven children, and many grandchildren and greatgrandchildren.

But his last words about the war were, "we had faith, no matter what, we always had faith. This was what kept us going despite everything we all endured during this time of tragedy."

RAMIREZ, JACINTO "EL CHINO"

Tec4, U.S. Army, HQ 3rd Battalion, 349th Infantry; cook

Battles: Naples-Foggia, Rome-Arno, North Apennines, PO Valley

Honors: Good Conduct Medal, European-African-Middle Eastern Campaign Medal with 4 battle stars, Purple Heart Medal

Tec4 Ramirez was wounded in battle on March 23, 1944 in the European-African-Middle Eastern Camp

RAMIREZ, JESUS NAVIDAD

RAMIREZ, MARIO J.

Private, U.S. Army; artillery engineer

Pvt Ramirez was stationed at Camp Polk, Louisiana on June 17, 1943. The Eagle Pass News Guide stated, "Rapid and startling changes have been made by the Army. Not the least of these has been the transformation of Orchestra Leader-Musician J. Ramirez of Piedras Negras into an Artillery Engineer."

RAMIREZ, MAXIMO F.

Tec5, U.S. Army, Coast Artillery Corps, Battery A, 547th Anti-Aircraft Artillery

Tec5 Ramirez died at the 59th Field Hospital on January 17, 1945 of an accidental gunshot wound. He was buried in Hama Luxembourg.

RAMIREZ, REYNALDO SALAS

RAMOS, CASIMIRO

RAMOS, DIEGO M.

Tec5, U.S. Army, 4264th Quartermaster Truck Company; truck driver

Qualifications: Marksman Rifle

Battles: Normandy, Northern France, Ardennes, Central Europe

Honors: Victory Medal, Good Conduct Medal, 3 Overseas Service Bars, American Campaign Medal, European African Middle Eastern Campaign Medal with 4 battle stars

RAMOS, FLORENTINO

Private First Class, U.S. Army, Battery B, 913th Field Artillery Battalion; cannoneer

Qualifications: Marksman

Battles: Rome-Arno, Apennines, PO Valley

Honors: American Campaign Medal, European-African-Middle Eastern Campaign Medal with 3 battle stars, Good Conduct Medal, Victory Medal

RAMOS, MANUEL
Private First Class, U.S. Army, 840th Quartermaster Gas Supply Company; truck driver

Qualifications: Sharpshooter

Battles: Normandy, Northern France, Ardennes, Rhineland, Central Europe

Honors: European-African-Middle Eastern Campaign Medal with 5 battle stars

RAMOS, SANTOS
Private, U.S. Army, Company H, 85th Battalion, 18th Group Army Service Forces Training; rodman and chainman surveying

Qualifications: Sharpshooter

Honors: American Defense Service Medal, Good Conduct Medal, Asiatic-Pacific Campaign Medal

RAU, CHARLES H.
Staff Sergeant, U.S. Army Air Force; armorer-gunner

Qualifications: Sharpshooter, pistol

Battles: Papua, New Guinea, New Britain, Admiralty Island Campaign

Honors: Distinguished Flying Cross, Asiatic-Pacific Campaign Medal with 3 battle stars, Air Medal, Good Conduct Medal, Purple Heart Medal

S/Sgt Rau was wounded at Simpson Harbor Rabaul, New Britain on November 2, 1944.

REBER, LLOYD L.

REYES, GEORGE V.
Private First Class, U.S. Army, 18th Medical General Laboratory; cooks helper

Honors: American Campaign Medal, Asiatic-Pacific Campaign Medal, Good Conduct Medal, Victory Medal

REYES, NAREUZO

REYES, RODOLFO "Fito"
Staff Sergeant, U.S. Army Air Forces, B17, 8th Air Force; aerial engineer

Honors: Air Medal, European Theater of Operations Medal, Good Conduct Medal, Purple Heart Medal

SSgt Reyes graduated from Eagle Pass High School in May of 1941. He enlisted in the Army Air Corps in September of 1941 and was trained as a mechanic.

Sergeant Rodolfo Reyes had the distinction of being a member of the U.S. Famed Eighth Air Force 352 Bombers Group. Flying over Nazi-occupied France, Sgt Reyes was shot, earning him the Purple Heart Medal for his bravery and shrapnel wounds sustained while in combat on January 3, 1943.

Reyes journey began in September of 1941 when he first joined the military and later became an aerial gunner with the Army Air Force. One of the famous planes he flew was the Buckeyed Blitz, which later went down in the Netherlands, killing all of its crew members.

He flew a total of seventeen missions leaving England and flying over Russia, Germany, and France where fighting was the heaviest. The English would bomb at night and the Americans would bomb during the day. As a flight engineer he sat behind the pilots. Flying at 30,000 feet with open air where the temperatures would reach at least 50 degrees below zero, he recalled that many of the pilots would end up with frostbitten feet. Because of the dampness and rainy weather in England they would end up with wet boots, consequently causing their feet to freeze at these altitudes.

Reyes will never forget January 3, 1943 when he was shot while flying one of his missions. The shrapnel spiraled into his back, tearing through his shoulder, and eventually landing in his chest. Lieutenant Donald Barnes later wrote a story about it. He took care of him during this tragic moment and safely landed the plane in England.

Reyes later was transferred to Laredo, TX as an aerial gunner instructor. He eventually left the military in 1953 and went to work in New York as an instrument repairman.

REYNA, RAUL O.
Private, U.S. Army

Private Reyna died in Trois-Viorger, Luxembourg of non-battle wounds sustained during a premature explosion while working in a demolition pit.

REYNOLDS, LOWELL G.
Tec4, U.S. Army, 237th Signal Service Company; telephone switchboard operator

Qualifications: Sharpshooter

Honors: European Theater Operation Medal

Prior to WWII, Tec4 Reynolds served in the U.S. Army for 3 years and with the National Guard for 1 year.

RHODES, JEREMIAH I.
Lieutenant J.G., U.S. Navy

Lieutenant Rhodes served on a destroyer under the command of Admiral William "Bull" Halsey. He later became rear gun mount commander and served in the Pacific from 1944 to 1945. He went on shore in Japan, 3 days after the surrender.

RICHARDS Jr., JOHN D.
Tec5, U.S. Army; sanitary technician

Qualifications: Marksman

Battles: Normandy, Northern France; Ardennes, Rhineland, Central Europe

Honors: American Campaign Medal, European-African-Middle Eastern Campaign Medal with 5 battle stars, Good Conduct Medal, Victory Medal

RICHARDSON, WEINERT
Ensign, U.S. Navy; pilot
Ensign Richardson attended Texas A&M and Texas University.

RIDDLE, LOYD
Tec4, U.S. Army, 135th Quartermaster Truck Company; cook
Qualifications: Marksman
Battles: Northern France, Ardennes, Rhineland, Central Europe
Honors: European-African-Middle Eastern Campaign Medal with 4 battle stars, American Defense Service Medal, Good Conduct Medal

RIDDLE, HENRY
Tec4, U.S. Army, HQ Detachment 1857th Service Command Unit; cook
Qualifications: Marksman
Battles: Northern France, Rhineland
Honors: Good Conduct Medal, European-African-Middle Eastern Campaign Medal with 2 battle stars, American Defense Service Medal, Purple Heart Medal
Tec4 Riddle was wounded at European Theater on September 12, 1944.

RILEY, JESSIE J.

RIOJAS, ELEVINIO

RIOJAS, GREGORIO G.
Tec4, U.S. Army; cook
Qualifications: Expert Carbine; attended bakery and cookery school
Battles: Normandy, Northern France, Rhineland, Central Europe
Honors: American Campaign Medal, European-African-Middle Eastern Campaign Medal with 4 battle stars, Good Conduct Medal, Victory Medal, 1 Service Stripe, 2 Overseas Bars
After the war, Tec4 Riojas opened and ran a bakery in Eagle Pass for years..

RIOJAS, GUILLERMO
Private First Class, U.S. Army, Battery B, 167th Anti-Aircraft Artillery Battalion; duty soldier
Qualifications: Sharpshooter
Battles: Normandy, Northern France, Rhineland
Honors: European-African-Middle Eastern Campaign Medal with 3 battle stars, Victory Medal, Good Conduct Medal, 4 Overseas Service Bars

RIOJAS, HECTOR ROLANDO

RIOJAS, RAUL

RIOS, ALFREDO F.
Private First Class, U.S. Army, Company M, 142nd Infantry; heavy mortar crewman

Battles: Rome-Arno, Southern France, Rhineland, Central Europe

Honors: Good Conduct Medal, Distinguished Unit Badge, European African Middle Eastern Campaign Medal with 4 battle stars, American Campaign Medal and 1 Bronze Arrowhead, 3 Overseas Service Bars, Victory Medal, Combat Infantryman Badge

RIOS, FEDERICO F.
Private First Class, U.S. Army, 259th Infantry, 65th Division; rifleman

Honors: European-African-Middle Eastern Campaign Medal, American Defense Service Medal, Combat Infantryman Badgee

RIOS, RODOLFO
Sergeant, U.S Army Air Forces, 93rd Air Depot Group; radio repairman

Honors: Victory Medal, American Campaign Medal, Asiatic-Pacific Campaign Medal, Good Conduct Medal

RISKIND, REUBEN
Technical Sergeant, U.S. Army Air Forces, 10th Air Force

It was his abilities to type and take shorthand dictation that landed SGT. Riskind in jobs as a clerk typist for several military officers throughout his army career. It was also his illustrious background as a top-seeded tennis player for the University of Texas, as well as the state of Texas, that opened doors for him to compete against high ranking officials, and in one case, against the son of a Chinese warlord.

The tennis coach, D.A. Pennick of the University of Texas tennis team recruited Reuben to play on the tennis team. He won the freshman tournament and became number one in the freshman team. He ranked at the top of squad in his Junior and Senior year and reached the finals of the SW Conference Championship twice.

Riskind's induction into the army in 1942 began first going to Brackettville, then El Paso, Texas for physicals. He was then sent to Sheppard Field, Wichita Falls, Texas for basic training. Rueben expected to go into combat. After basic training, he was in a room with hundreds of other men when a soldier came in and asked if anyone can type. Reuben raised his hand and he was assigned to the Third Air Force HQ Squadron in Tampa, Florida, the largest Air Force base in the country. He had pride in his work, so much so that he taught himself shorthand.

In Tampa, he played tennis at the Tennis Club and played in many Army and Civilian tournaments (singles, doubles, and mixed doubles). Rueben only lost one match in the entire three years while he was stationed in Tampa. He became known as the "Texas Tornado."

SGT. Riskind was later reassigned to Piardoba Air force Base, originally a B-29 base around 2 hours from Calcutta India. Because temperatures reached as high as 127 degrees in India, there were many engine fires and the B-29's were moved to Saipan. Once again, because of his clerical skills, he was assigned as a secretary for one of the members of the Chief of Staff. In Piardoba, they were housed in British styled barracks called Bashas. Each Basha had one to two young Indian boys assigned to do laundry and keep the barracks clean. It was so hot there that laundry could be returned in 20 minutes. The dress code was very laxed. Riskind wrote "Every Friday it would be announced that all Jewish men who wish to attend services in Calcutta would receive passes. I was anxious to get a look at the city; so did my friend, Fred Carpenter. Fred was a Catholic, but on Friday he became "Jewish."

He was then transferred to Kunming, China which is situated at the end of the Burma Road. Reuben's first time riding in an airplane was over the "Hump" in the Himalayas to the Kunming airport, the busiest airport in world at that time. His group flew in a C47, the workforce of the Air Force and sat on benches and blankets. Again on his off duty hours, he was playing tennis with military personnel. He also played tennis with General Li's son, a provincial War Lord at his Palace. Soon a match was arranged for Sgt Riskind to play against Yunnan, a provincial champ at one of the local schools. Riskind wrote "He was a pretty good player who made me sweat before beating him in straight sets." Since the Japanese Army was retreating, they had received orders to move to headquarters to Liuchow, China

When Reuben's unit was busy loading transports, a call was put to the General at headquarters to stop packing because the War was over. Rockets, small arms, whistles, bells, all sort of noise makers were creating a great din. All headquarter people were invited to the General's house for a celebration. The General brought in magicians, musicians, tumblers, and singers for their entertainment and liquor. At midnight the General decided that all soldiers had better return to quarters before they ran into trouble with his curfew order. The next day, they found out the war was not over and moved to the Liuchow airbase.

The City of Liuchow was completely destroyed during the severe fighting that forced the Japanese to withdrawal. There were tents with dirt floors-until everybody scrounged enough bricks to make floors. After 10 days in Liuchow, Rueben's unit was sent back to Kunming. Shortly, after being back in Kunming, the war ended quickly after 2 atomic bombs dropped on Hiroshima and Nagasaki and his unit was transferred to Shanghai for shore leave before going home. Before Ruben was transferred he came down with a severe case of hepatitis and the doctor said that he needed immediate hospitalization. His weight dropped to 109 pounds on his 6' frame.

While he was in the hospital, a fight broke out between the National Chinese and the Chinese's communist "with a rattle of machine guns and the thump of mortar rounds." After a truce was called, the soldiers were evacuated to a hospital in Calcutta, India. At Calcutta, the situation was not that much better in that riots broke out between the Hindus and the Moslems. Sgt. Riskind recalls when Mahatma Gandhi came to Calcutta and as if by magic, the killing and pillaging stopped.

Finally, on November 15, 1945 embarked for New York via Suez Canal in a hospital ship for 40 days, Reuben was moved to Letterman General Hospital in San Francisco where he remained for three months. He was given an honorable discharge from the service in March of 1946 at Fort MacArthur, California. He then returned to Eagle Pass, Texas to work in the family business. He continued to play tennis until he retired at age 82.

RITCHIE, Jr., EDWARD W.
Tec3, U.S. Army, 195th General Hospital; surgical technician
Qualifications: Expert Rifleman

Battle: Rhineland

Honors: American Campaign Medal, European-African-Middle Eastern Campaign Medal with 1 battle star, Good Conduct Medal, Victory Medal, 2 Overseas Service Bars

RIVAS, LUIS I.

Private, U.S. Army, HQ Squadron, 31st Service Group; guard patrolman

Battles: Air Offensive Japan, Western Pacific

Honors: American Campaign Medal, Asiatic-Pacific Campaign Medal with 2 battle stars, Good Conduct Medal, Victory Medal

RIVERA, ERNESTO

Seaman Second Class, U.S. Navy

RIVERA, MOISES P.

Private First Class, U.S. Army

RIVERA, SECUNDINO

Private First Class, U.S. Army, Company B, 264th Engineer Combat Battalion; utility repairman

Battles: Rhineland, Central Europe

Honors: European-African-Middle Eastern Campaign Medal with 2 battle stars, Good Conduct Medal, Victory Medal, 2 Overseas Service Bars

PFC Rivera graduated from the Ft. Crook Ordnance Automotive School in Ft. Crook, Nebraska. The course covered maintenance, repair and convoying of government vehicles ranging from the ever popular "jeep" to the large prime mover. (The Eagle Pass News Guide)

RIZLEY, CURTIS

RIZLEY, LEVERT LOWELL

ROBERTSON, JOHN CLIFTON

Apprentice Seaman, U.S. NAVY

ROBINSON, EMILIO

ROBLES, ELENO C.

Private First Class, U.S. Army, 3199th Signal Service Battalion; message center clerk

Qualifications: Sharpshooter

Battles: Central Burma, India Burma

Honors: American Campaign Medal, Asiatic-Pacific Campaign Medal with 2 battle stars, Victory Medal, Good Conduct Medal

RODRIGUEZ, ALEJANDRO
Private, U.S. Army, 1920th Service Command Unit; guard
Honors: Victory Medal

RODRIGUEZ, ALFREDO G.

RODRIGUEZ, Jr., AMADO
U.S. Army Air Force; military intelligence
Battles: Guadalcanal, Solomon Islands, Munda, New Guinea Islands, Pacific Campaign

As recalled in The Eagle Pass News Guide, "He experienced hundreds of air raids but this occasion he had a "well built" fox hole. He relates that when the Marines landed at Guadalcanal, the son of Premiere Tojo of Japan was supposedly killed on the 13th day of a certain month. During the months, Rodriguez was there, he says that every 13th day of the month at the exact hour, the Japs would bomb the land. Finally the raids ceased. The boys concluded that Tojo was finally tired of sending his bombers back on the anniversary of his son's death."

One of Rodriguez's experiences in Guadalcanal was meeting Mrs. Roosevelt during her Pacific tour. He said that her visit was a "great morale builder."

RODRIGUEZ, ANDRES M.
Private First Class, U.S. Army, 141st General Hospital; medical technician
Qualifications: Marksman
Honors: Good Conduct Medal, European-African-Middle Eastern Campaign Medal, Victory Medal

RODRIGUEZ, ANTONIO CARLOS
Private, U.S. Army, Tank Destroyer Replacement Training Center; duty soldier

RODRIGUEZ, ARSENIO CANALES

RODRIGUEZ, CHARLES P.
Sergeant, U.S. Army, 333rd Bomb Group; munitions worker
Qualifications: Marksman
Honors: American Campaign Medal, Asiatic-Pacific Campaign Medal, Good Conduct Medal, Victory Medal

RODRIGUEZ, ELIVERTO T.
Private First Class, U.S. Army, HQ and Service Company, 344th Engineer Regiment; cook's helper
Qualifications: Marksman
Battles: Naples-Foggia, Rome-Arno, Southern France, Rhineland, Central Europe

Honors: European-African-Middle Eastern Campaign Medal with 5 battle stars, and 1 bronze Arrowhead, Good Conduct Medal, Meritorious Unit Award, Victory Medal, 4 Overseas Service Bars

RODRIGUEZ, Jr., EMILIO
Tec5, U.S. Army, HQ Detachment, 761 Military Police Battalion; military policeman
Honors: Asiatic-Pacific Campaign Medal, Good Conduct Medal, Victory Medal

RODRIGUEZ, ENRIQUE G.

RODRIGUEZ, GREGORIO
Private, U.S. Army, Medical Detachment, 1811th Service Command Unit; hospital orderly
Honors: Victory Medal, American Theater Service Medal

RODRIGUEZ, GENARO
Fireman First Class, U.S. Navy

RODRIGUEZ, GUADALUPE
Private, U.S. Army, Tanks Parks Section, Motor Pool Detachment; tank crewman
Qualifications: Sharpshooter
Honors: Victory Medal

RODRIGUEZ, JOSE JESUS
Seaman Second Class, U.S. Navy

RODRIGUEZ, JOSE M.
Sergeant, U.S. Army, 29th Weather Squadron; weather observer
Qualifications: Expert carbine
Battles: Eastern Mandates, Western Pacific, Ryukyus
Honors: European-African-Middle Eastern Campaign Medal, Good Conduct Medal, Victory Medal

RODRIGUEZ, JOSE M. "La Pucha"
Private First Class, U.S. Army, 8th Infantry Regiment
Honors: European-African-Middle Eastern Campaign Medal

RODRIGUEZ, JOHNNY L.
Yeoman Third Class, U.S. Coast Guard Reserve
Twin brother of Pvt Amado Rodriguez Jr.

RODRIGUEZ, JUAN
Mailman Second Class, U.S. Navy

RODRIGUEZ, LEO
U.S. Navy, aircraft maintenance

RODRIGUEZ, MANUEL F.
Tec4, U.S. Army, Battery C, 695th Field Artillery Battalion; blacksmith

Qualifications: Expert Rifleman

Battle: Rhineland

Honors: European-African-Middle Eastern Campaign Medal with 1 battle star, American Campaign Medal, Asiatic-Pacific Campaign Medal, Good Conduct Medal, Victory Medal, 1 Service Stripe, 3 Overseas Service Bars

RODRIGUEZ, MATIAS
Tec5, U.S. Army, Company K, 321st Infantry; welder

Battles: Southern Philippines

Honors: American Campaign Medal, Asiatic-Pacific Campaign Medal with 1 battle star, Philippine Liberation Medal, Good Conduct Medal, Victory Medal, Combat Infantryman Badge

RODRIGUEZ, PATRICIO F.
Tec3, U.S. Army

Tec3 Rodriguez died of non-battle wounds.

RODRIGUEZ, RAUL M. "Peanuts"
Staff Sergeant, U.S. Army Air Forces, 2124th Army Air Force Base Unit; maintenance technician

Qualifications: Sharpshooter

Battles: East Indies, Papua, New Guinea

Honors: Asiatic-Pacific Campaign Medal with 3 battle stars, Good Conduct Medal, Distinguished Unit Badge

Wasting no time in getting overseas soon after joining the Army in February, 1942, S/Sgt Rodriguez landed in Australia 30 days after his enlistment and soon after that, embarked for front line airfields in New Guinea.

S/Sgt. Rodriguez bore the brunt of the Japanese air offensive, but remained in the Pacific to watch the aggressor's air power wane and to enjoy the comparative comfort and security of overwhelming U.S. air superiority.

"During the early days of "42," he said, "we were bombed and strafed 4 times a day, in addition to night raids. We couldn't give the Japs much opposition at that time and often our signal system didn't warn us in time of enemy planes headed our way. One time, we were warned of a raid only by the bombers overhead and the sight of falling bombs." S/Sgt Rodriguez recalled that the U.S. stopped taking it and started dishing it out to the enemy about middle of 1943.

After 3 years overseas, he was assigned to the Eagle Pass Army Air Field. S/Sgt said to The Eagle Pass News Guide, "It is difficult to get used to being so close to home."

RODRIGUEZ, RAUL H.

Corporal, U.S. Army Air Forces, 1379th Army Air Force Base Unit, 5th Air Force; crew chief

Battles: Rome-Arno, Naples-Foggia, Southern France, Normandy, Air Offensive Europe, Air Combat Balkans, Rhineland, Northern France, PO Valley, Northern Apennines

Honors: European-African-Middle Eastern Campaign Medal with 10 battle stars, Distinguished Unit Badge with 2 Oak Leaf Clusters, Good Conduct Medal

Cpl Rodriguez was a crew chief with a P-47 Thunderbolt Fighter unit.

RODRIGUEZ, RAFAEL CORTINAS

Tec5, U.S. Army, 425th, washer

Battles: Africa, Italy

Honors: European-African-Middle Eastern Campaign Medal, Good Conduct Medal

RODRIGUEZ, RAYMOND G.

RODRIGUEZ, REYNALDO LUIS

Tec5, U.S. Army; cook

Battles: Western Pacific

Honors: Good Conduct Medal, Asiatic-Pacific Campaign Medal

The Army told Luis (the former delivery boy for the Wipff Meat Market), they were going to give him a free sea voyage. The first thing he knew he was baking under the palm trees looking at the volcano and the hula girls in Hawaii. (The Eagle Pass News Guide) Tec5 Rodriguez (Private at that time) was trained as a medical assistant in the Medical Corps in Honolulu.

RODRIGUEZ, RODOLFO R.

Private, U.S. Army Air Force, 707th Bombardment Squadron, 446th Bombardment Group; aviation mechanic

Battles: Ardennes, Central Europe, Rhineland, Normandy, Northern France

Honors: European African Middle East Campaign Medal

Pvt. Rodriguez, member of the B-24 Liberator Squadron had the unique record of flying 68 missions without the loss of a man. He worked in the armament section of his squadron which had been credited by pilots and crews for what they had done, cleaning and maintaining the guns under the constant pressure of invasion. According to The Eagle Pass News Guide August 3, 1944, his squadron, led by Lt. Colonel Hugh C. Arnold had taken part in the all-out bombing offensive of Germany's continental fortress and in the Eighth Air Force's attack on the invasion of the coast of France. The

10 man combat crews had bombed Berlin, Brunswick and the other war production centers of Germany, the invasion coast and Nazi communication centers in France. Many of these missions were accomplished in the face of intense anti-aircraft fire and formidable enemy fighter opposition.

RODRIGUEZ, RUBEN G.

ROGERS, MAURICE FLOYD

ROMO, Jr., PABLO
Private First Class, U.S. Army, 38th Infantry; gunner

ROMAN, RODOLFO C.
Staff Sergeant, U.S. Army, HQ Company 1st Battalion, 7th Infantry; squad leader

Battles: Algerian French Morocco Campaign, Tunisian Campaign, Sicilian Campaign, Rome-Arno Campaign

Honors: European-African-Middle Eastern Campaign Medal with 4 battle stars, Purple Heart Medal, Good Conduct Medal, American Defense Service Medal, 3 Oversea Service Bars, Combat Infantryman's Badge

S/Sgt Roman received an artillery fire wound, right leg on March 3, 1944, Anzio beachhead, Italy, resulting in surgical amputation.

Before the war, Rodolfo used to be Pitcher Roman, a star player with the "Ocampas" "Texas Fire Chiefs," "La Consolidada" baseball teams in and around Eagle Pass.

In a letter to his father Pvt Roman stated, "The fighting in North Africa is already 2 weeks gone, but life hasn't changed much for us. The sun's still hot, the days are long, and bugs still bite hard. Most of our trucks have acquired names. British drivers go for sentimental names reminding them of the girls back home. America drivers like names such as "Buck Rogers," or "Hitler Hearse." Those newspaper stories about all the prisoners we took in Tunisia, are true. You should have seen that long chain on German and Italian trucks, miles of them, puffing their way around these sharp African curves on the way to prison camps. Many of the enemy drove themselves to prison camps and they weren't unhappy either. Many, especially the Italians were smiling and singing." We landed on the Atlantic Coast of French Morocco in a town by the name of Fedala. From Fedala we moved to Casa Blanca where we really had some fun after we took the town. The people went for us in a big way. Those first letters I wrote were from cities there. Then we moved to Algeria and had a swim in the Mediterranean Sea. When things were really getting hot in Tunisia, we moved in the back door and the first Germans we saw were either dead or prisoners. There isn't a soldier in Africa who doesn't respect the Nazis as mighty tough customers."

(This letter was published in The Eagle Pass News Guide on July 8, 1943.)

ROSALES, FEDERICO
Private First Class, U.S. Army, 895th Chemical Company; truck driver

Qualifications: Marksman

Battles: Luzon, Southern Philippines Liberation

Honors: American Campaign Medal, Asiatic-Pacific Campaign Medal with 1 battle star, Philippine Liberation Medal, Good Conduct Medal, Victory Medal, 1 Overseas Service Bar

ROSALES, GILBERT OSBORN
Private, U.S. Army, Battery C, 339th Field Artillery Battalion; field lineman

Battles: Italian Campaign

Honors: Good Conduct Medal, European-African-Middle Eastern Campaign Medal, Purple Heart Medal

Pvt Rosales was wounded in action near Minturro, Italy on April 15, 1944.

ROSALES, HERMAN
Tec5, U.S. Army, 1468th Combat Engineer Maintenance; truck driver

Qualifications: Sharpshooter

Battle: Rhineland, Central Europe

Honors: American Campaign Medal, European-African-Middle Eastern Campaign Medal with 2 battle stars, Good Conduct Medal, Victory Medal

ROSALES Jr., PETE OSBORN
Private First Class, U.S. Army, 2nd Division, Engineer Corps

On February 2, 1941, PFC Rosales was killed in an automobile accident in which an Army truck collided with an automobile carrying 5 Eagle Pass youths about 20 miles from Eagle Pass on the Spofford Highway. WWII had already began in Europe.

ROSSI Jr., PETE
Staff Sergeant, U.S. Army Air Forces, 123rd Army Air Force Base Unit; message center clerk

Qualifications: Rifle Carbine

Honors: American Defense Service Medal, 1 Service Stripe, Good Conduct Medal

SSgt Rossi enlisted at Ft. Sam Houston on October 8, 1940 and was assigned to the 2nd Engineers Battalion. In August 1941, he was transferred to the Air Corps at Kelly Field for technical training in Instrument Flying. As reported in The Eagle Pass News Guide, November 2, 1944, "The modern airplane has so many electrical gadgets on the instrument board, it looks like Broadway on a Saturday night. SSgt Peter Rossi Jr's job is to teach cadet pilots how to read the instruments on the board in connections with long flights and night flying."

RUBIO, JESUS RAMIRO
Pharmacist's Mate Third Class, U.S. Navy

Jesus Rubio enlisted in the U.S. Navy at the age of 17 as a medical corpsman. He served aboard the U.S.S. Colorado and saw action at Tinian, Saipan, Leyte, and Okinawa.

In 1943, Rubio was in Mexico City studying to be a bull fighter when his draft papers arrived in Eagle Pass, Texas. He quit high school to join the Navy. Upon joining the U.S.

Navy, he had no idea of the danger that awaited him, and the courage he would need to muster, to carry him through those horrendous years during WWII.

After several weeks at boot camp in San Diego, California, he was trained as a naval medical corpsman at the navy hospital in San Francisco's Treasure Island Hospital. He finished High School on Treasure Island. After completion of school, he was sent off to war for twenty-two months on the battleship U.S.S. Colorado.

On May 5, 1944, the U.S.S. Colorado joined the Allied forces in preparing for the Marianas Campaign. Rubio's first battle was off the island near Tinian in the Marianas Campaign. Rubio was stationed on "top side" (deck). If a sailor becomes wounded, Rubio would apply first aid and then take them down to the sick bay, if needed. One day, he remembered going down to sick bay and he heard, "I've been hit! I've been hit! from an injured Dr. Brown, who was head of the medical staff, which suddenly brought about pandemonium to the ship and sent all the young medical corpsmen scurrying to take on the duties as physician and other medical staff. But the horrors brought on by the war were just beginning. To this day, Rubio vividly remembers one of his first experiences of having to amputate the leg of a sailor with a saw at the tender age of seventeen. He also saw three sailors who were sitting on chains of the ship when the Japanese bombed, the three disappeared. The U.S.S. Colorado was hit 22 times by the Japanese. Rubio said that they lost around 300 sailors.

After the U.S.S. Colorado went to the Admiralty Island to disembark wounded sailors to hospital ships, the U.S.S. Colorado sailed back to San Francisco for refitting and repairs of the battle damages. By chance he ran into another Eagle Pass sailor, Efrain Lozano, who recounted to him a bizarre story. As Lozano worked in the mailroom, he saw the lists of casualties from Tinian with Jesus Rubio on it. He was about to call Rubio's mother when this chance encounter occurred. Lozano said "You are not a causality" and Rubio looked down and said "No, I am not." While the battleship was being repaired, Rubio had a chance to go home. On the return flight to go back to San Francisco, his plane crashed, however he was not hurt.

In November 1944, the Colorado arrived in Leyte, Philippines providing naval gunfire support for the Allied troops. On November 27, two Japanese kamikazes (suicide) hit the U.S.S. Colorado, killing 19 sailors and wounding 72. Rubio said that most of the kamikaze attacks were early in the morning around 4-5:00 and did not let up until daybreak. Rubio remembers one day while taking a tray of spam sandwiches to the gunners on deck, as he opened the hatch to the compartment, he saw a kamikaze plane coming straight at him. Luckily for all of them, the plane veered off and their lives were spared.

Rubio also mentioned that he saw General McArthur land in the Leyte Gulf.

The next battle, Rubio recalled was in Okinawa from March until May 22, 1945. They spent 63 days bombarding the island prior to the Allied invasion. After the bombardment they left for Leyte Gulf. On August 6, 1945 they returned to Okinawa, right before the two atomic bombs landed over Japan. Shortly thereafter, Japan surrendered.

The U.S.S. Colorado was then assigned to Tokyo, Japan for the Occupation of Japan. After the mine sweepers cleared the channel, the U.S.S. Colorado entered Tokyo Bay. The Japanese had draped their cannons with white sheets as an indicator to the Americans not to fire at them. The Americans were also told not to shoot at the Japanese.

But it was when the U.S.S. Colorado arrived near the shoreline in Tokyo, Japan that he witnessed one of the saddest moments of his life. American POW'S suffering from beriberi were being released. Elated at the sight of the American ships, many began swimming desperately towards the ships, despite the command from the highest officials to stop. The sailors on the ships watched in horror, as many, unable to swim the distance, began slowly going underwater. Many of the POW'S drowned needlessly that day.

Rubio aboard the U.S.S. Colorado witnessed the Japan delegation going toward the U.S.S. Missouri to sign the surrender document on September 2, 1945. He said they were around two football fields away from the U.S.S. Missouri and the sailors had to use binoculars to get a glimpse of the signing. After the surrender ceremony, Rubio said that there were thousands of United States planes flying overhead, covering the sky. This was to demonstrate to Japan the futility of continued fighting.

The U.S.S. Colorado final assignment was to take part in transporting American servicemen home called Operation Magic Carpet. The battleship made three voyages from the Pacific to Pearl Harbor to transport the servicemen. Rubio remembered a prank that they pulled on the servicemen on the voyage. They told the servicemen that mail will be delivered, however since they are out to sea there was no delivery of mail.

Laughing, he recalled a soldier from Eagle Pass who after taking his basic training at Fort Sam Houston and was sent away to an unnamed destination. Waking up the next morning he had no idea of his whereabouts. Upon gazing out and overlooking across the desolate area, he immediately wrote to his mother that he was stationed in North Africa.

"Bruto!" someone told him. "You're in Eagle Pass, Texas! "

To this day, he still remembers that this poor, young man was the brunt of the joke of many.

Mr. Rubio eventually received an honorable discharge in Houston, Texas on December 15, 1945. He returned to Eagle Pass where he later married and had three children, along with several grandchildren. Mr. Rubio became a distinguished high school English teacher and later high school principal.

Adding to this story, Rubio later said, "Had it not been for the atomic bomb, we would've lost many more men in the war. But one of the things we need to understand from all of this, is that we need to treat each other as human beings."

RUIZ, CLEOFAS G.

RUIZ, EPIFANIO

RUIZ, JUAN

Private First Class, U.S. Army, 4th Air Supply Squadron; truck driver
Honors: Victory Medal, Philippine Independence Medal

RYAN, KEY WESLEY

Lieutenant, U.S. Army; airport engineer

Lt Ryan entered the Army at Camp Wolter, Texas on March 22, 1943. He graduated from Engineer Officer Candidate School at Ft. Belvoir, Virginia on October 27, 1943.

SAIZ, ARTURO M.
Private First Class, U.S. Army, HQ Battery 459th Anti-Aircraft Battalion; telephone operator

Battles: Normandy, Northern France, Ardennes, Rhineland, Central Europe

Honors: European-African-Middle Eastern Campaign Medal with 5 battle stars, Good Conduct Medal, Bronze Star Medal

SAIZ, JESUS
Fireman First Class, U.S. Navy

SALAZAR, FRANCISCO L.
Corporal, U.S. Army, 2518th Army Air Force Base Unit; medical laboratory technician

Honors: American Campaign Medal, Good Conduct Medal, Victory Medal

SALAZAR, SATURNINO L.

SALDANA, EPIFANIO MENDOZA
Corporal, U.S. Marine Corps

Qualifications: Amphibian Tractor Crewman

Battles: Asiatic-Pacific, Hawaiian Island, Volcano Island, Iwo Jima

SALISBURY, HOWARD GRAVES

SALAS, ESTANISLADO Z.
Private, U.S. Army Air Forces, Squadron A, 233rd Army Air Force Base Unit; duty soldier

Honors: Good Conduct Medal, American Campaign Medal, Victory Medal

SANCHEZ, ARMANDO
Seaman Second Class, U.S. Navy

Seaman Sanchez entered active duty service on December 17, 1943 served aboard the U.S.S. Mississippi for 23 months of sea duty.

SANCHEZ, CONCEPCION
Tec5, U.S. Army, Company D, 366th Medical Battalion; messenger

Qualifications: Sharpshooter

Battles: Normandy, Northern France, Ardennes, Rhineland, Central Europe

Honors: American Campaign Medal, Good Conduct Medal, Victory Medal, European-African- Middle Eastern Campaign Medal with 5 battle stars, Purple Heart Medal (June 14, 1944))

SANCHEZ, DIEGO
Private, U.S. Army, Company G, 130th Infantry Regiment, 33rd Division; rifleman

Battle: Luzon

Honors: Asiatic-Pacific Campaign Medal, Philippine Liberation Medal, Good Conduct Medal, Victory Medal

SANCHEZ, FEDERICO J.
Private, U.S. Army

SANCHEZ, JESUS R.
Private First Class, U.S. Army, 4005th Area Service Unit; military police

Honors: Victory Medal

SANCHEZ, JOSE BERNAL
Private First Class, U.S. Army, 81st Reconnaissance Battalion, 1st Army Armored Division "Old Ironsides"; radio operator/car crewman

The following letter is from Jose Sanchez when he was in the POW camp in Germany to his mother, Mrs. Lorenza B. Sanchez on May 10, 1944:

To you, dear Mother, who taught me to receive whatever comes, good or bad, as a part of life, and not to reject trouble as though it were an intruder but respond to it, rejoice in its valiantly and thus transform tragedy into triumph for happiness come not from avoiding hard situations but from overcoming them. I dedicate this Mother's Day even though we may be far apart, my thoughts, clean living and unselfish services become a living and shining memorial to you. Life is all too short to grumble at every misfortune. If we cannot change the circumstances that surround our lives, at least we may be master of them. There'll be better Mother's Day yet to come; when you and I again shall meet and God rewards us for what we suffered. Regards to all, Love & Kisses Jose

SANCHEZ, LINOS M.
Staff Sergeant, U.S. Army, Company F, 1st Infantry; squad leader

Battles: New Guinea, Papua, Luzon

Honors: Good Conduct Medal, Bronze Star, American Defense Service Medal, American Campaign Medal, Asiatic-Pacific Campaign Medal with 2 battle stars and 1 Bronze Arrowhead, Victory Medal, Philippine Liberation Medal with 1 battle star, 4 Overseas Bars, Combat Infantryman Badge

SANCHEZ, MANUEL R.

Staff Sergeant, U.S. Army Airforce, 451st Bombing Group, 726th Bombardment Squadron, airplane armorer/ball gunner B-24 liberator

Qualifications: MKM Pistol

Battles: Rome-Arno, Air Offensive over Europe, Northern France

Honors: European-African-Middle Eastern Campaign Medal with 2 battle stars, Good Conduct Medal, Distinguished Unit Badge with Oak Leaf Cluster, Silver Star Medal, Air Medal, Purple Heart Medal

SSGT. Manuel Sanchez at 19 years old became a hero on his very first combat mission while in route to Vienna, Austria. He was awarded one of the highest medals, the Silver Star, which is the second highest military decoration for valor that can be awarded to any person serving in any capacity with the United States Armed Forces. The medal is awarded for gallantry in action against an enemy of the United States.

The following story entitled "Eight Came Back" was written by Flight Officer Chester A. Ennis to a cousin who had it re-printed in the Fort Belvoir newspaper.

His first mission was a bombing raid over Markersdorf Aerodrome in Vienna, Austria. His squadron was leading the 15th Air Force and was in the number 5 position in the squadron formation. Just before they arrived at their target, 65 German fighters attacked the plane and damaged the hydraulic system in the bomb bay and the hydraulic fluid was spurting all over. It was a fight to control the plane. The pilot immediately realized that they were in serious trouble and started to turn south. Since there was no navigator and the bombardier was his first mission, they did not know their position. Since they still had the bombs, Flight Officer Chester A. Ennis pulled the emergency bomb salvo handle. It was supposed to open the doors and drop the bombs however he pulled too hard and all it did was drop the bomb, fused and the 120 pound fragmentation bombs laid on the doors. Finally the doors were opened. The bombardier had been hit in the hand by a shell fragment.

There were explosions in the back of the plane and the ammunition for the 50 caliber guns were burning and popping off. Two 20 millimeter shells had hit Sanchez's left foot, blowing it off, except for the tendon at the heel. Sanchez had managed to get himself out of the turret and into the fuselage of the plane where he sat down and applied a tourniquet to his thigh. Another gunner helped him apply a tourniquet to his knee where he noticed that one of the waist window gunners had been hit and a gun was unattended. Sanchez took over the gun, and by kneeling and handling the gun with one hand was able to fight off two attacking fighters. He probably destroyed or at least seriously damaged both of them. Through all of this, more German fighters were attacking the plane in an attempt to finish them off and there were continuous explosions under the floor of the rear compartment. The ammunition was burning and popping. The plane was barely flying above stalling speed and they were down to one good engine. Eventually, they made it over the Alps and could see the Adriatic Sea, but had very little idea of where they were. All the maps showed the countryside as German occupation. Since they were losing altitude, as soon as they flew over land the pilot told the engineer to tell everyone to bail out of the plane. Sanchez had to bail out of the plane without even a bandage to protect his wound. Sanchez said that "just before he hit the ground, he had pulled his legs up so he landed on his back, then he just laid there yelling until someone found him. In order for them to bandage his leg, he had taken his pocket knife and cut the tendon that was holding his foot on. He exhibited more courage in those few days than most men are called upon to show in their entire lives.

The Yugoslavia underground- Partisans discovered the 8 crewman and hid them in one location. Mike, a middle age man acted as their interpreter during most of their stay. He asked Flight Officer Ennis if he wanted to send a few words to General Twining, Commanding General of the 15th Air Force and gave him their aircraft number and the number of known wounded men. Mike told the Partisans that he had a small radio set on the island that was in touch with the British on the Isle of Vis, so that his message could be relayed. They wouldn't take Ennis to the radio, since they were always on the move and it would be too dangerous. There were Germans all over the island looking for the Americans. They spent the next two nights in the little valley, guarded all the time by the partisan patrol. Each meal time, one man and his wife would arrive with their back packs loaded with china dishes, silverware, and good food. The meat and chicken was reserved for the crewman and the Partisans ate the soup out of tin cups.

Flight Officer Chester A. Ennis said that his biggest worry was to keep Sanchez alive. He knew that he needed a blood transfusion. He remembered reading that salt water was good to replace blood, so had Mike obtain a lot of salt, made up some strong brine, and had Sanchez drink that and a lot of red wine that the Yugoslavians gave them. He also tried to keep him doped up on morphine. A Yugoslav doctor arrived one day. He had walked 15 miles because he had heard that there were some wounded men there. When he was changing the bandage on Sanchez, Ennis handed him a package of sulfur powder. The doctor sprinkled it on the wound, in which Ennis started using it on Sanchez daily. Sanchez was improving.

During their stay, they had many visitors, among them, the daughter of the mayor of a nearby village. She was 19 years old and had been living in the forest for four years. She had killed 5 Germans with a knife, and carried a year old wound in a shoulder when a German had shot her. Most of the people that visited had been in hiding all during the war. The man who fed them hadn't slept in his own house in four years because the Germans had him on their list. He would go home daily to clean up and change clothes while his wife stood guard, but he slept on the ground hidden in the trees, and never twice in the same place. He was also their source of Italian cigarettes.

On the fourth day the Partisans reported that a Catalina flying boat with three P-38s (fighter planes) for escort will pick them up around the large bay. The wounded men were transported by rowboats which were 4-5 miles, while the rest walked 15 miles. Sanchez went to a hospital in Foggia. On the sixth day since the plane crashed, a Catalina flying boat with three P-38s (fighter planes) for escort picked them up and flew them to Foggia Main Airport. All the 8 crewmen were rushed to the large General Hospital, which were only 2 miles away from the airport.

Later, it was learned that the 451st had lost 9 airplanes, carrying approximately 85 men. Of those 85, only eight came back. The group had shot down 36 known fighter planes before the escort showed up and had a field day. Markersdorf Aerodrome received heavy damage from the bombers that reached the target, and the 451st received a Presidential Unit Citation for that mission. They had broken the back of the German Air Force in Vienna area.

Corporal Sanchez was promoted to Staff Sergeant and was awarded the Silver Star for shooting down the two aircrafts after he should have been completely out of action. The Silver Star was one of the highest decorations ever bestowed upon an airman for a first combat mission and he was one of five soldiers from Eagle Pass who were decorated the Silver Star. He was also awarded the Purple Heart Medal.

Flight Officer Ennis wrote "somewhere in the world today are eight of us who came back, partially through the nerve of a 19 year old boy named Sanchez. I know I will never forget him, and I feel sure none of the other seven will either."

After the war, Staff Sergeant Sanchez opened the Sunset Inn, a bar on Main Street in Eagle Pass where many WWII veterans shared their memories and problems.

SANCHEZ, PLUTARCO B.
Private First Class, U.S. Army, Army Service Forces Training Center

SANCHEZ, REYES

SANCHEZ, SALVADOR
Private First Class, U.S. Army, Company F, 1467th Station Complement Unit, Adjutant General Schools; military police
Honors: American Campaign Medal, Good Conduct Medal, Victory Medal

SANFORD, JOHN R.

SANTOS, BERNARDO R.
Private First Class, U.S. Army, Company E, 129th Infantry Regiment, 37th Division; automatic rifleman
Battles: Northern Solomon, Luzon
Honors: Philippine Liberation Medal with 1 star, Asiatic-Pacific Campaign Medal, Victory Medal, American Campaign Medal, Good Conduct Medal, Combat Infantryman Badge
PFC Santos was wounded on January 29, 1945 at the Asiatic Pacific Theater.

SANTOS, FRANK F.
Sergeant, U.S. Army, Troop H, 12 Cavalry; squad leader
Battles: Bismarck Archipelago, Luzon, Southern Philippines, New Guinea
Honors: Good Conduct Medal, Bronze Star Medal, American Defense Service Medal, Asiatic-Pacific Campaign Medal, Philippine Liberation Medal, Purple Heart Medal, Combat Infantryman Badge
Sgt Santos was wounded at Leyte on November 30, 1944.

SAN MIGUEL, FRED
Staff Sergeant, U.S. Army, U.S. Army Signal Corps; radio operator

SAN MIGUEL, GEORGE
Private First Class, U.S. Army, HQ Company, 10th Infantry; field lineman
Qualifications: Marksman Carbine
Battles: Central Europe
Honors: Good Conduct Medal, European-African-Middle Eastern Campaign Medal, Combat Infantryman Badge

SAN MIGUEL, JOSE ANDRADE
Private First Class, U.S. Army, Battery D, 440th Coast Artillery Battalion; intelligence observer

Qualifications: Marksman Rifle

Battles: Normandy, Northern France, Ardennes, Rhineland, Central Europe

Honors: European-African-Middle Eastern Campaign Medal with 5 battle stars, Good Conduct Medal, 1 Service Stripe, 3 Overseas Service Bars

SAUCEDO, LUCIANO
Private First Class, U.S. Army, Military Police Detachment; rifleman

Battles: Normandy, Northern France, Rhineland, Central Europe

Honors: Air Medal, Purple Heart Medal, American Campaign Medal, European-African-Middle Eastern Campaign Medal, Good Conduct Medal, Victory Medal, Combat Infantryman Badge

SAVAGE, HARRY G.
Sergeant, U.S. Army Air Forces, 1522nd Army Air Force Base; cook

Honors: Good Conduct Medal

SCHMERBER, JUAN
Seaman First Class, U.S. Navy

SCHMERBER, TEODORO N.

SCHMIDT Jr., EDWARD HERMAN "Schmidty"
Staff Sergeant, U.S. Army Air Forces, 253rd Army Air Force Base Unit; administrative specialist

Honors: American Campaign Medal, Victory Medal, Good Conduct Medal

SCHOFIELD, EZRA ELLIS
Lieutenant, U.S. Army, Engineer Corps

Lt Schofield attended Officer's Training School at Camp Leonard Wood, Missouri in August of 1942.

SCHROEDER, CARLOS ANTONIO
Tec4, U.S. Army

The Eagle Pass News Guide, dated September 3, 1942, reported, "Technician 4th Grade Carlos Antonio Schroeder was among 42 soldiers who became citizens of the United States recently at the first naturalization ceremony held at Camp Barkley, Texas." At the same time he changed his name to Carl Anthony Schroeder. A native of Mexico, Schroeder was assigned to the 37th Station Hospital at Camp Barkley. He was inducted May 8, 1942.

SCHWARTZ, ARNOLD I. "The Horn"
Tec5, U.S. Army, Company C, 748th Railway Operating Battalion; locomotive engineer
Qualifications: Marksman
Battles: India Burma

Honors: American Campaign Medal, Asiatic-Pacific Campaign Medal, Good Conduct Medal, Victory Medal, 1 Service Stripe, 3 Overseas Service Bars

Arnold graduated high school from Peacock Military School in San Antonio, TX. He trained horses in Eagle Pass, the most famous being his trick horse, "Coaly." On August 5, 1943 The Eagle Pass News Guide mentioned that while he was in the Army on leave, he would often delight spectators with his horse Coaly at Fort Duncan Park Arena.

In the words of author Bill Munter, Arnold's nephew: "One time we were at a coffee shop in Del Rio, Texas and I ordered pancakes for breakfast. Arnold told me that when he was in the army in India, he only ate pancakes for breakfast, lunch and dinner and after the war, he swore he would never eat another pancake in his life. Arnold also mentioned that India was very hot and it was not unusual to reach 115 degrees in temperature. He said that as a train engineer he ran the steam engine fueled by coal-fire and the engine room's temperature would became even higher. Arnold also told Bill that he remembered when his train was strafed by the Japanese "zeros'. His small finger was injured and he could never straightened it. When Arnold came home from the war, he suffered from severe dysentery."

Arnold grew up in the movie theater business at the Aztec Theater. He went to work with his father, Sam Schwartz, and his brother-in-law Lloyd Munter, in the movie theater business and ranching after the war ended. Per the box Office Magazine, June 23, 1951, Arnold Schwartz during his army days (World War II) saved the government thousands of dollars in reclaiming and repairing projectors and sound systems, both 35mm and 16mm. Arnold and J.M. Schwartz were brothers. Since J.M. graduated from University of Texas in Austin, Arnold became an avid "Long Horn."

SCHWARTZ, JOSEPH M. "J.M."
1st Lieutenant, U.S. Army, 32nd Quartermaster Company, 32nd Division

Lt Schwartz was a member of the Red Arrow Division which participated in the New Guinea and Southern Philippines Campaigns.

Before the war, J.M. graduated from The University of Texas in 1940 as a business administration major. He met his wife, Cecilia Stein at college and was married after graduation in 1940. J.M. was also an accomplished polo player and a Mason. After graduation, J.M. worked for the U.S. Consulate in Piedras Negras, Mexico. Since he worked for the United States government he was exempt from the draft. However, in 1942 he volunteered to serve in the Army. He took basic training at Ft. Bliss, Texas and thereafter went to the Quartermaster Officer Candidate School at Ft. Lee, Virginia. Upon graduation, he was commissioned Second Lieutenant and was assigned to Ft. Sam Houston, Texas. In October 1944, he was transferred to the Philippines to the 32nd Infantry Division where he served in the Quartermaster Corp.

In early January 1945, JM was diagnosed with Poliomyelitis and died a few days later on January 17, 1945 at the 126th Field Hospital at Palo, Leyte, Philippines. J.M. was Arnold Schwartz older brother.

SCOTT, LEE WILLIAM

SCOTT, LOUIE LEWIS

SEGUIN, JUAN MANUEL
Seaman Second Class, U.S. Navy

Seaman Seguin served over 10 months of sea duty aboard the U.S.S. Arkansas and U.S.S. Wainwright.

SELLERS, LENN
Machinist Third Class, U.S. Navy

Sellers participated in amphibious landings at Attu, Kiska, Tarawa, Saipan, Tinian, Kwajalein, and Leyte.

SEPULVEDA, JESUS VARGAS
Private, U.S. Army, HQ Company, 2nd Battalion, 4th Infantry

Battles: Asiatic-Pacific Campaign

Honors: Asiatic-Pacific Campaign Medal with 1 battle star, 2 overseas Service Bars, Good Conduct Medal

SEPULVEDA, RAUL
Private, U.S. Army, Company I, 381st Infantry, 96th Division; rifleman

Battles: South Philippines Liberation

Honors: American Campaign Medal, Asiatic-Pacific Campaign Medal with 1 battle star, Philippine Liberation Medal with 2 battle stars, Good Conduct Medal, Victory Medal, Combat Infantryman Badge

SERRATO, ELIAS
Private, U.S. Army, Company C, 4th Cavalry Recon Squadron, 87th Infantry Division.

PFC Serrato was killed in action from internal injuries on March 31, 1945 in Laasphe, Germany.

SERVERA, FELIPE
Tec5, U.S. Army, Service Company, 382nd Infantry; truck driver

Battles: Philippines, Ryukyus

Honors: Victory Medal, American Campaign Medal, Asiatic-Pacific Campaign Medal, Philippine Liberation Medal, Good Conduct Medal, Meritorious Unit Medal, Bronze Arrowhead Medal, Combat Infantryman Badge

SHAMBURGER, MYLEN V.
Private, U.S. Army

Pvt. Shamburger was killed in action.

SHANNON, WILLIAM R. "Bill"
Major, U.S. Army Air Forces, 15th Army Air Force; navigator B-24 liberator

Battles: Central Europe

Honors: Distinguished Flying Cross

Major Shannon flew missions over Germany, France Romania, Hungary, and Austria. He received his training at Hondo Army Air Force Base navigation school.

Major Shannon met Rosalie Dowe of Eagle Pass at an afternoon tea dance sponsored by Our Lady of the Lake University for AAF cadets at the Gunter Hotel in San Antonio, TX.

SHELL, EARLE NEIL

SHOFNER, BUELL EARL
Master Sergeant, U.S. Army, 3rd Photo Reconnaissance Squadron; crew chief

Battles: Air Offensive Japan, Guam, Saipan

Honors: American Campaign Medal, Asiatic-Pacific Campaign Medal with 2 battle stars, Good Conduct Medal, Victory Medal, 1 Service Stripe, 2 Overseas Service Bars

SHOFNER, EARL BUELL
US Army

Earl Shofner is the twin brother of MSgt Buell Shofner.

SIEFERT, CHARLES GEORGE

SIFUENTES, TRINIDAD A.
Private First Class, U.S. Army, Company C, 121st Medical Battalion; medical aidman

Battles: New Guinea, Luzon

Honors: American Campaign Medal, Asiatic-Pacific Campaign Medal, Philippine Liberation Medal, Victory Medal

SILMAN, JAMES BENJAMIN
Major, U.S. Army; assistant corps quartermaster

Honors: Bronze Star, Distinguished Unit Badge

Major Silman enlisted in the Army, October 1940. A year later, he was commissioned as an officer. The Eagle Pass News Guide reported, "The Guinea moon cuts one the No. 10 tin can footlights as officers of the unit put on a musical extravaganza for the other officers and men of headquarters in a hillside amphitheater. Major Silman was in charge of stage management for men in Papuan campaign in the Hollandia Operation which cut off Japanese 18th Army and the Biak action."

SILVA, FIDENCIO
Seaman Apprentice, U.S. Navy

Seaman Silva served aboard the U.S.S. LSM and U.S.S. Platte.

SILVA, GUADALUPE
Private, U.S. Army, 342nd Harbor Craft Company; anti-tank gun crewman
Honors: Asiatic-Pacific Campaign Medal, Victory Medal

SILVA, MANUEL
Tec5, U.S. Army, HQ Camp Army Ground Forces Replacement Depot #2; supply clerk
Honors: Victory Medal

SILVA, RAYMUNDO
Corporal, U.S. Army Air Forces, 4505th Army Air Force Base Unit; duty NCO
Honors: Asiatic-Pacific Campaign Medal, American Campaign Medal, Victory Medal

SKELLEY, GREGORY CLINE
Tec4, U.S. Army, 8th Engineer Squadron; welder
Qualifications: Marksman
Battles: New Guinea, Bismarck Archipelago, Southern Philippines, Luzon
Honors: Asiatic-Pacific Campaign Medal with 4 battle stars, Good Conduct Medal, Philippine Liberation Medal with 2 battle stars

SMITH, HAROLD
Staff Sergeant, U.S. Army, Company B, 58th Signal Battalion; radio operator
Battles: Philippines Liberation, Asiatic-Pacific Campaign
Honors: Asiatic-Pacific Campaign Medal, Philippine Liberation Medal, Good Conduct Medal, Victory Medal, Meritorious Unit Award

SMITH, LOCKHART
U.S. Navy

SMITH, WILLIAM A.
Private, U.S. Army, 459th Coast Artillery Battalion; chauffeur
Battles: Normandy, Northern France, Ardennes, Rhineland, Central Europe
Honors: European-African-Middle Eastern Campaign Medal with 5 battle stars, Good Conduct Medal

SOTO, BENIGNO A.
Private First Class, U.S. Army, 314th Quartermaster Battery Company; automatic rifleman
Qualifications: Sharpshooter Carbine
Battles: New Guinea, Battle on Peleliu Island
Honors: Asiatic-Pacific Campaign Medal, Purple Heart Medal, Combat Infantryman Badge PFC Soto was wounded in Peleliu in the Pacific on October 19, 1944.

SOUTHALL, DONALD

SPENCE, JOSEPH WALTON
Aviation Storekeeper Third Class, U.S. Navy

SPENCE, WALTER EARNEST
Storekeeper Second Class, U.S. Navy
Honors: Asiatic-Pacific Campaign Medal with 1 battle star, American Campaign Medal, Good Conduct Medal, Victory Medal
Spence served aboard the U.S.S. Dixie.

SPENCER Jr., JAMES NEWTON "Lefty"
U.S. Army, field artillery

STAGGS, OBIE GARROT
Fireman First Class, U.S. Navy
Staggs served 14 months of sea duty aboard the U.S.S. Alchiba and U.S.S. Comstock.

STAGGS, JOHN
Sergeant, U.S. Army Air Forces; B-24 crewman
After the war ended, in 1946 Sgt Staggs became County Commissioner.

STATEN, CHARLES EWIN

STATEN, HENRY JEFFREY
Sergeant, U.S. Army Air Forces; aerial engineer
Qualifications: Army Air Force Technical Badge
Honors: European-African-Middle Eastern Campaign Medal, 1 Service Stripe, 2 Overseas Service Bars, Good Conduct Medal, Victory Medal, American Defense Service Medal, American Campaign Medal

STEEL, PAUL
Colonel, U.S. Army
Col Steel commanded a regiment in Italy.
After the WWII, Col Steel conducted leadership training at the high school and also became an elected judge.

STEPHENSON, EARL E.
Pharmacist's Mate Second Class, U.S. Navy
Stephenson served 14 months of sea duty aboard the U.S.S. Flint

STEPHENSON, JERRELL MILFORD, Jr.

STEVENSON Jr., THOMAS ALEXANDER
Staff Sergeant. U.S. Army
SSgt Stevenson assisted with the establishment of a African American pilot training school in Tuskegee, Alabama, home of the famed Tuskegee Airmen in July 1942.

STEWART, CLYDE
Private First Class, U.S. Army

STEWART, WORTH ALLEN

STEWART, VERNON
Private First Class, U.S. Marine Corps
PFC Stewart was killed in action at Iwo Jima.

STILL, FELDER WILLIAM

STROBEL, OSCAR

STROMAN, FRED WILLIAM
Tec4, U.S. Army, 3634th Quartermaster Truck Company; auto mechanic

Battles: Naples-Foggia, Rhineland, Central Europe

Honors: European-African-Middle Eastern Campaign Medal with 5 battle stars, American Defense Service Medal, Good Conduct Medal, Combat Infantryman Badge

Before entering active service as one of the first draftees from Maverick County, Stroman work with his father in the well drilling business.

STROMAN, LEROY JOSHUA
Chief Metalsmith Third Class, U.S. Navy

As reported in The Eagle Pass News Guide, Stroman stated, "I am in Hawaii now and love it very much. As a matter of fact the Huisache tress, prickly pear and various brush remind me of home and the weather is ideal."

STONE, CARLOS B.
Private, U.S. Army, 520th Engineer Maintenance Company; truck driver

SURITA, TRINIDAD F.
Sergeant, U.S. Army, 519th Ordnance Heavy Maintenance Company; assistant squad leader

Battles: Rhineland, Central Europe

Honors: American Defense Service Medal, American Theater Campaign Medal, European African Middle Eastern Campaign Medal with 2 battle stars, Good Conduct Medal, Victory Medal, Combat Infantryman Badge

THOMAS Jr., ADALBERTO C.
U.S. Army

Thomas went to the Engineer Replacement Training Center for intensive training in military engineering. He was trained in the use of tools and equipment that could build fixed and floating bridges, demolitions, and the construction of roads and obstacles.

THOMAS, CHARLEY LAWRENCE

THOMAS, HENRY GARCIA

THOMPSON, ALBERTO VARGAS
Seaman Third Class, U.S. Navy

THOMPSON, ANSEL

THOMPSON, DONALD W.
Captain, U.S. Army Air Forces, 460th Bomb Group; pilot (B-24)

Battles: Rome-Arno, Southern France

Honors: European-African-Middle Eastern Campaign Medal with 2 battle stars, Distinguished Flying Cross, Air Medal with 3 Oak Leaf Clusters

TINAJERO, DOMINGO B.

TORRALBA, HUMBERTO
Specialist Second Class, U.S. Navy

TORRES, FRUCTOSO R.
Private, Army Air Force, Squadron I, 3702 Air Force Base Unit Buckley Field, Colorado

Honors: American Campaign Medal, Victory Medal

TORRES, JESUS
Sergeant, U.S. Army, Submarine Detachment, #3 Medical Detachment; dental technician

Honors: American Campaign Medal, Asiatic-Pacific Campaign Medal, Good Conduct Medal, Victory Medal

TORRES, JOSE L.
Private First Class, U.S. Army, Pacific Division; clerk

Honors: American Campaign Medal, Asiatic-Pacific Campaign Medal, Good Conduct Medal, Victory Medal

TORRES-MUNOZ, JOSE LUIS
Sergeant, U.S. Army

SGT Torres entered the armed forces at 17 years old in 1941.

TORRES, LUZ R.
Private First Class, U.S. Army Air Forces, 742nd Air Maintenance Squadron, 500th Air Service Group; duty soldier/truck driver

Battles: Normandy, Northern Rhineland, Central Europe

Honors: European-African-Middle Eastern Campaign Medal with 4 battle stars, Good Conduct Medal

TORRES-MUNOZ, MANUEL MARIO
Seaman First Class, U.S. Navy

TORRES, PETE

TORRES, SANTIAGO DE LEON

TORRES, MARIO

TORREZ, CELESTINO
Private First Class, U.S. Army, HQ Company 2nd Battalion, 515th Parachute Infantry; rifleman

Battles: Normandy, Ardennes, Rhineland

Honors: European-African-Middle East Campaign Medal with 3 battle stars, American Campaign Medal, Good Conduct Medal, Victory Medal, Distinguished Unit Badge, 3 Overseas Service Bars, Purple Heart Medal, Combat Infantryman Badge

TORREZ, FRANCISCO
Private, U.S. Army

TOVAR, EUGENIO G.
Private, U.S. Army, 3813th Quartermaster Gasoline Supply Company; truck driver

Qualifications: Sharpshooter

Battles: Northern France, Normandy, Ardennes, Rhineland, Central Europe

Honors: American Campaign Medal, European-African-Middle Eastern Campaign Medal with 5 battle stars, Victory Medal

TOVAR, GREGORIO
Private, U.S. Army, Infantry; gunner

Honors: Purple Heart Medal

Mrs. Maria Tovar, mother of Pvt Tovar received the Purple Heart Medal posthumously on behalf for her son, who was killed in action in France on July 17, 1944. In addition to the Purple Heart Medal, Mrs. Tovar received a Presidential Citation which reads "In Grateful Memory of Private Gregorio Tovar, who died in the service of his country in the European Area, July 17, 1944, He stands in the unbroken line of patriots who have dared to die that freedom might live and grow, and increase its blessing." (The Eagle Pass News Guide)

TOVAR, REYNALDO L.
Corporal, U.S. Army, HQ Company, 3rd Battalion, 41st Armored Infantry

Honors: American Defense Service Medal, Purple Heart Medal, European-African-Middle Eastern Campaign Medal

TOVAR, TEODORO L.
Private, U.S. Army, Company B, 117th Infantry Battalion, 30th Division; military police

Honors: American Campaign Medal, Good Conduct Medal, European-African-Middle Eastern Campaign Medal, Victory Medal

TOWNS, DAVID P.
Second Lieutenant, U.S. Army; 207th Engineer Combat Battalion; combat engineer

2nd LT. Towns was an Eagle Pass native who had a brilliant future ahead of him; but unfortunately because of the war his life was cut short. So it was while he was attending The University of Texas at Austin to become an architect that WWII broke loose, and after Pearl Harbor was attacked he joined the army and was commissioned on February 14, 1942.

After attending basic training Towns was sent to Hawaii to train as a medic for eight months. While stationed there he decided to participate in a quiz for a local radio station which he ended up winning. Unbeknownst to him, a general was listening and was quite impressed with his answers. The general recommended that he be sent to officer's candidate school. Towns was then sent to Fort Bell, Virginia where he graduated three months later as 2nd Lieutenant. He was then moved to Camp Swift, Texas and assigned to the 207th Engineer Combat Battalion under the command of Colonel John Burdening. It was in 1943 that he also married his high school sweetheart, Lilia Martinez. In December of that same year he received his orders to be transferred to England. He went by rail from Texas to Camp Shanks in New York. But before he left, his wife went to see him in San Antonio to bid him farewell, not knowing that this would be the last time she would ever see him alive.

Towns left to England on the Queen Mary. He was to become a part of the great invasion force. Unfortunately he was killed in action in France a two days after D-Day on June 8, 1944. His wife was notified via Western Union while at San Juan Plaza in Eagle Pass as she was walking with their infant son, David Towns, Jr., who later became a prominent medical doctor.

TOWNS, PEDRO P.

Lieutenant Commander, U.S. Merchant Marines Battles: North Africa, New Guinea

Honors: Purple Heart Medal

Lt Commander Towns transported vital supplies, food and equipment to the troops. He survived a torpedoed blast aboard a ship which sunk in the White Sea near Russia.

After graduating Eagle Pass High School in 1941, he enlisted as a Cadet Midshipman at the U.S. Merchant Marine Cadet Basic School at San Mateo, California and held the distinction of having the second highest grades in his class. David and Pedro Towns were brothers.

TOWNSEND, RAYMOND H.

First Lieutenant, U.S. Army; B-24 Liberator pilot

Honors: Air Medal with an Oak Leaf Cluster

Lt Townsend graduated from pilot training at Ellington Field, Texas. He reported as "missing in action" at the age of 28 on April 8, 1944 over Germany following his 22nd bombing mission.

TOWNSEND, W. M.

First Lieutenant, U.S. Army, 489th Bomb Group, 845th Bomb Squadron; navigator, bombardier

Honors: American Campaign Medal, European-African-Middle Eastern Campaign Medal with 4 battle stars, Good Conduct Medal, 1 Service Stripe, 3 Overseas Service Bars, Victory Medal

TREVINO, ANTONIO D.

Corporal, U.S. Army, 1294th Military Police Company; military police

Battles: Normandy, Northern France, Rhineland, Central Europe

Honors: European-African-Middle Eastern Campaign Medal, Good Conduct Medal

TREVINO, CARLOS C.
Pharmacist Mate Third Class, U.S. Navy
Seaman Trevino was valedictorian of his Eagle Pass High School graduating class.

TREVINO, EDUARDO

TREVINO, JOSE M.
Tec5, U.S. Army, 1983rd Service Command Unit; long shoreman
Battles: Papua, New Guinea
Honors: Asiatic-Pacific Campaign Medal, Good Conduct Medal, Meritorious Unit Award

TREVINO, GUADALUPE

TREVINO, MANUEL
U.S. Army
Battles: Normandy
Medals: Bronze Star Medal, 2 Purple Heart Medals

TREVINO Jr., MAURO
Coxswain, U.S. Navy

TREVINO, RAUL S.

TREVINO, REFUGIO
Apprentice Seaman, U.S. Navy

TUCKER, ELMO F.
Private, U.S. Army; truck driver

TURNER, THOMAS EDWARD

URBINA, ARMANDO
Seaman Second Class, U.S. Navy
Seaman Urbina served on the U.S.S. Auriga, U.S.S. Jupiter, and U.S.S. Linewald

URBINA, LUIS ROGELIO
Seaman First Class, U.S. Navy

VALDEZ, CHARLIE
U.S. Navy

Battles: Sicily, Makin Island, Gilbert Island

Honors: American Campaign Medal, European-African-Middle Eastern Campaign Medal with 1 battle star, Asiatic-Pacific Campaign Medal with 1 Silver Star, Philippine Liberation Medal Presidential Unit Citation-Philippine

Valdez served on the U.S.S. Leonard Wood. He participated in the amphibious invasion of the southern coast of the Island of Sicily between the Acate River and Svoglitti, July 10-12, 1943. He also participated in the naval amphibious invasion of Makin Island and the Gilbert island Group, November 20-24, 1943.

VALDEZ, ELIAS
Private First Class, U.S. Army; infantry

Honors: Purple Heart Medal

PFC Valdez was wounded on December 15, 1943 in San Pedro, Italy.

VALDEZ, VALERIANO

VALLEJO, ALFONSO B.

VAQUEZ, VICTORIANO E.
Tec5, U.S. Army, 248th General Hospital; cook

Battles: New Guinea; Luzon

Honors: American Campaign Medal, Asiatic-Pacific Campaign Medal with 2 battle stars, Philippine Liberation Medal with 1 battle star, Good Conduct Medal, Meritorious Unit Award, Victory Medal, 1 Service Stripe, 4 Overseas Bars

VALENZUELA, ALFONSO HERRERA

VAN DALSEM, ARTHYETA
Major, Women Army Corps, 4020th Army Air Force Base Unit; administrative officer

Major Van Dalsem was the second highest officer, next to Col. Oveta Culp Hobby. The headquarters for the Women Army Corps (WAC) was located at Waco, Texas. After the war, Major Van Dalsem lived in El Indio for approximately 40 years until 1992, until she moved from the area.

VANEGAS, ENRIQUE G

Private First Class, U.S. Army, 1927th Ordinance Ammunition Company; munitions worker

Battles: Northern France, Rhineland, Central Europe

Honors: American Campaign Medal, European-African-Middle Eastern Campaign Medal with 3 battle stars, Victory Medal, Meritorious Unit Award

VANEGAS, JOE L.

Private First Class, U.S. Army, 312th Field Artillery Battalion; cannoneer

Qualifications: Marksman

Battles: Normandy, Northern France, Rhineland, Central Europe

Honors: American Campaign Medal, European-African-Middle Eastern Campaign Medal with 4 battle stars, Good Conduct Medal, Victory Medal

VARGAS, ALFREDO Z.

Private First Class, U.S. Army Air Forces, 418th Training Group

VASQUEZ, GERONIMO

Private

VASQUEZ, VICTOR E.

Tec5, U.S. Army, 248th General Hospital; cook

Battles: New Guinea, Luzon

Honors: American Campaign Medal, Asiatic-Pacific Campaign Medal with 2 battle stars, Philippine Liberation Medal with 1 battle star, Good Conduct Medal, Meritorious Unit Award, Victory Medal, 1 Service Stripe, 4 Overseas Bars

VAUGHN, ROSWELL F.

Captain

VELEZ, MARCELO

Private, U.S. Army, Company B, 1st Battalion, 27th Infantry Regiment; rifleman

Honors: Victory Medal, Army of Occupation (Japan) Medal

VELEZ, RAUL S.

Private First Class, U.S. Army, Troop C, 116th Cavalry Reconnaissance Squadron

Battles: Rhineland, Central Europe

Honors: European-African-Middle Eastern Campaign Medal with 2 battle stars, Good Conduct Medal, 1 Overseas Bars, 1 Service Stripe

VIELMA, COXSWAIN JUAN VARGAS

U.S. Navy

VILLA, FRANCISCO
Tec5, U.S. Army, 184th Infantry Regiment; tank driver
Qualifications: Sharpshooter
Honors: Asiatic-Pacific Campaign Medal, Army of Occupation Medal, Victory Medal

VILLANUEVA, DAVID V.
Private First Class, U.S. Army, 894th Chemical Company; duty soldier
Battles: Bismarck Archipelago, New Guinea, Southern Philippines, Luzon, Western Pacific
Honors: Asiatic-Pacific Campaign Medal with 5 battle stars, Philippine Liberation Medal with 1 battle star, Good Conduct Medal, Victory Medal, 4 Overseas Bars

VILLANUEVA, SANTOS F.

VILLARREAL, GERONIMO
Private, U.S. Army, Company D, 4th Armored Replacement Battalion

VILLARREAL, VALENTIN G.
Private First Class, U.S. Army, Company C, 350th Regiment, 88th Infantry Division PFC Villarreal was killed in action on July 19, 1944 at Vic Castelialfi, Italy.

VILLASENOR, GUILLERMO
Private First Class, U.S. Army, Battery C, 459th Anti-Aircraft Artillery Battalion; telephone operator
Battles: Normandy, Northern France, Ardennes, Rhineland, Central Europe
Honors: European-African-Middle Eastern Campaign Medal with 5 battle stars, Good Conduct Medal

VILLASENOR, MANUEL
Private First Class, U.S. Army, 64th General Hospital; duty soldier
Battles: Rome-Arno, PO Valley
Honors: European-African-Middle Eastern Campaign Medal with 2 battle stars, Good Conduct Medal, 1 Service Stripe, 4 Overseas Service Bars, Victory Medal

VILLASENOR, OSCAR
Private First Class, U.S. Army; military police
Honors: Japan Occupation Medal, Victory Medal

PFC Villasenor was a military policemen on occupation duty in Okinawa after the war. The commander of the base had reports from the mess hall that the food supply was disappearing. The military police finally figured out that some Japanese soldiers who were still living in the caves, did not realize that the Japan had surrendered and they were pilfering the food to eat. PFC Villasenor was part of a unit that had to convince

the Japanese soldiers that the war was over and to surrender. After surrendering to the Americans they would ship the Japanese soldiers to Japan.

The picture of the 3 WWII soldiers is of PFC Villasenor on the far right, next to him is PFC Vargas, father of Jesus Vargas, an attorney in San Antonio and personal friend of the authors and the other soldier is unknown. In a chance meeting in an airport in Hawaii by PFC Villasenor son Hector Villasenor and Jesus Vargas' sister, they discovered that their fathers were army buddies in WWII some over 60 years ago. Jesus Vargas, son of PFC Vargas had framed and hung this picture in his law office. I, Bill Munter, when visiting Jesus at his office asked him about this picture and was told of this story. Hector, a medical doctor and Jesus's law office is 5 blocks from each other in downtown San Antonio, Texas.

VIVIAN, GEORGE EDWARD

Corporal, U.S. Army Air Forces, 79th Fighter Group, 20th Fighter Squadron; armor airplane bomber

Battles: Northern France, Normandy, Ardennes, Rhineland, Central Europe

Honors: European-African-Middle Eastern Campaign Medal with 6 battle stars, Good Conduct Medal, Distinguished Unit Badge

VOCHAM, E. HUBEN

VOSS, PAUL

U.S. Navy, Construction Battalion, Seabees

Battles: Iwo Jima

WALTON, FRANK

Captain, U.S. Army

After WWII, Captain Walton became a rancher in Quemado.

WARD, REDFORD M.

Private First Class, U.S. Army, Battery C, 459th Coast Artillery Anti-Aircraft; machine gunner

Honors: European-African-Middle Eastern Campaign Medal with 4 battle stars, Good Conduct Medal

WATKINS Jr., EDWARD MENEFEE

First Lieutenant, U.S. Army, Photo Recon Group, 32nd Tactical Recon Squadron; pilot

Lt Watkins was the first soldier from Maverick County to graduate from the U.S. Military Academy at West Point in June 1943. While at West Point, he excelled in both academics and athletics, earning four athletic letters while earning the "Flying Rings" honors in gymnastics. (The Eagle Pass News Guide)

Lt Watkins was killed in action when a torpedo hit his ship in the Mediterranean Sea on April 20, 1944 before his 24th birthday.

WATKINS, ROSS

WATTS, JOSE RIVERA
Seaman Second Class, U.S. Navy

Seaman Watts served on the U.S.S. Magvoketa. The U.S.S. Magvoketa had a dangerous task of transporting gasoline to warships in the fleet and to the remote Navy stations. It supplied gasoline to ships in the Marshall Islands on May 23, 1945 for 3 months, then sailed to Okinawa and then to support the occupation forces in Japan after the war ended for 14 months.

WEBSTER, ROBERT
U.S. Navy

WESTERFIELD, ANTONIO
Private, U.S. Army, Company C, 44th Engineer Battalion; construction worker

Battles: Normandy, Northern France, Ardennes, Rhineland, Central Europe

Honors: European-African-Middle Eastern Campaign Medal with 5 battle stars, American Campaign Medal, Good Conduct Medal

WEISSHEIMER, JOHN W.
Second Lieutenant, U.S. Army; statistical control officer

Lt Weissheimer graduated from the Miami Beach Army Air Base Class of 43G at Soldier Field School as a Statistical Officers. He died of non-battle wounds.

WHITE, JIMMY B.
Staff Sergeant, U.S. Army Air Forces, 3701st Army Air Force Base Unit; supply clerk

Honors: Good Conduct Medal

Sgt. White sat next to Sgt. Jerry Denike when they both went home on their furloughs.

WHITLEY, C.B.

WHITEWATER, GEORGE

WILLIAMS, DAVID O. Jr.
Second Lieutenant, US Army Air force, 10th Fighter Squadron, 50th Fighter Group; pilot P-40 and P-47

After Williams graduated from Eagle Pass High School in 1942, he attended the Agricultural and Mechanical College of Texas (Texas A&M University) and the University of Hawaii. He obtained a bachelor's degree in military science.

He entered the Army Air Forces as an aviation cadet in May 1943 and graduated from the pilot training P-40 and P47 fighter training at the Advanced Flying Training School at Aloe Army Airfield, Texas. He was released from active duty in December 1945, however he re-enlisted in September 1946.

He served in the United States Airforce for over 30 years. He flew over 100 combat missions over North Korea in an F-84E aircraft. He was also a graduate of the Air Command and Staff College, 1959, and the Air War College, 1966. David Williams's military decorations and awards included the Silver Star, Legion of Merit with two oak leaf clusters, Distinguished Flying Cross, Bronze Star Medal, Air Medal with 9 oak leaf clusters and Air Force Commendation Medal. He was a command pilot with more than 5,300 flying hours, of which most are in a jet fighter aircraft. David Williams advanced to Brigadier General on March 24, 1973. (U.S. Air Force)

WILLIAMS, JOE D.
Tec3, U.S. Army

WILLARS, JESUS
Corporal, U.S. Army Air Forces, 2126th Army Air Force Battalion; clerk
Honors: Good Conduct Medal

WILSON, JOSEPH R.
Private First Class, U.S. Army, Battery A, 601st Field Artillery Battalion; driver
Battles: Rome-Arno, Rhineland, Central Europe, Aleutian Islands
Honors: American Defense Service Medal, European-African-Middle Eastern Campaign Medal with 3 battle stars, Asiatic-Pacific Campaign Medal, 1 Service Stripe, 2 Overseas Service Bars

WILSON, THOMAS ANTHONY
Carpenter's Mate Third Class, U.S. Navy
Wilson served 27 months of sea duty.

WIMBERLEY, HOOVER

WIPFF, CYRILL, LEON
Private First Class, U.S. Army, Medical Regiment

Before WWII, Pfc Cyrill spent 2 years at A&M College learning to ranch the modern way. He came back home and raised cattle before joining the Army.

In a letter Pfc Wipff said, "Imagine a country boy like me passing through Chicago, Philadelphia, Pittsburg, and New York City all on one trip. Before this war is won, I'll probably go around the world. I gave a good start." (Eagle Pass Guide August 13, 1942)

Later in The Eagle Pass News Guide, Pfc Wipff was quoted as saying, "We did a lot of traveling all over Tunisia (places as Lebessa, Ferriana, Sauk Ahras, Mateur and Tunis). The towns are mostly small and many of them have been pretty well shot up, especially Mateur. Have seen many prisoners go by some of them singing. When I was working at the hospital several wounded prisoners came through. One, Czech, said he was forced to fight and was glad to hear that German cities were being bombed."

WOOTEN, JAMES ENNIS

WOOTEN, WINFRED B.

WRIGLEY, JAMES EDWIN
Seaman First Class, U.S. Navy
Seaman Wrigley served 14 1/2 months of sea duty aboard the U.S.S. St. Louis.

WUESTE, ADOLPH
Private First Class, U.S. Army
Honors: European- African- Middle Eastern Campaign Medal, American Campaign Medal, Good Conduct Medal, Victory Medal, Bronze Star

WUESTE, CHARLES GEORGE
Sergeant, US Army, 90th fighter Squadron; clerk, typist
Honors: American Defense Service Medal, American Campaign Medal, Asiatic-Pacific Campaign Medal, Good Conduct Medal, Victory Medal, 3 Overseas Service Bars, 1 Service Stripe

WUESTE Jr., DANIEL ERNEST
Private First Class, U.S. Army Air Forces, 434th Fighter Control Squadron; information center operator
Battles: Rhineland
Honors: European-African-Middle Eastern Campaign Medal with 1 battle star, Good Conduct Medal, 3 Overseas Service Bars, 1 Service Stripe

WUESTE, ERNEST D.
Private, U.S. Army, 12th Field Artillery Battalion; cannoneer, driver
Qualifications: Marksman
Honors: American Defense Service Medal, European-African-Middle Eastern Campaign Medal

WUESTE, OSCAR
Private First Class, U.S. Army, 90th Infantry Division, 359 Infantry
Honors: European-African-Middle Eastern Campaign Medal, American Campaign Medal, Good Conduct Medal, Victory Medal, Purple Heart Medal
PFC Wueste landed at Normandy Beach in France on D Day. His brother, Adolph landed there the next day. Oscar Wueste was killed about 30 days later while trying to cut off a German division from reaching the coast on July 5, 1944.

WUESTE, ROBERT A.
Seaman First Class, U.S. Navy

WUTEN, WINFORD B.

YBARRA, FRANCISCO M.
Private, U.S. Army, 235th Quartermaster Salvage Collection Company; truck driver

Battles: Normandy, Northern France, Ardennes, Rhineland, Central Europe

Honors: European-African-Middle Eastern Campaign Medal with 5 battle stars, 4 Overseas Service Barsrs

YEAGER, CALVIN HOMER
Tec4, U.S. Army, 554th Signal Aircraft Warning Battalion; radar repairman

Honors: Good Conduct Medal, American Campaign Medal

YZQUIERDO, ARNULFO
Private First Class, U.S. Army, 163rd Infantry Regiment, 41st Infantry Division; rifleman

Honors: American Campaign Medal, Asiatic-Pacific Campaign Medal, Victory Medal, 3 Overseas Service Bars

YZQUIERDO, JESUS
Tec5, U.S. Army, Company B, 271st Engineer Combat Battalion, 71st Infantry Division

Honors: European-African-Middle Eastern Campaign Medal with 2 battle stars

Tec5 Yzquierdo's unit commanded by General George S. Patton crossed into Germany through the Siegfried Line. His division liberated the Sien labor concentration camp (Straubing Concentration Camp) that held Hungarian Jews. He fed the victims, gave them medical help and buried the dead. After he came back to Eagle Pass after the war, he suffered nightmares.

Pvt Yzquierdo was a liberator of one of the camps of the Holocaust. His story is included the Holocaust section of this book.

YZQUIERDO, RAMON
Private First Class, U.S. Army, 922nd Enlisted Transit Detachment; automatic weapons crewman

Qualifications: Marksman

Honors: American Campaign Medal, European-African-Middle Eastern Campaign Medal, Good Conduct Medal, Victory Medal, 1 Service Stripe

YZQUIERDO, RAUL

ZAMARRIPA, AURELIO
Sergeant, U.S. Army Air Forces, 215th Army Air Force Base Unit; airplane engine mechanic

Qualifications: Marksman

Battles: Air Offensive Japan, New Guinea, Western Pacific

Honors: Asiatic-Pacific Campaign Medal, Good Conduct Medal, Air Medal with 6 Oak Leaf Clusters, Distinguished Flying Cross

ZAMARRIPA, HUMBERTO C.
Seaman Second Class, U.S. Navy

ZERR, JOHN
Major. U.S. Army

Battles: Normandy, Ardennes

ZUNIGA, RUBEN R.
Corporal, U.S. Army, 158th Army Airways System; airplane control power operator

Honors: American Campaign Medal, Asiatic-Pacific Campaign Medal with 2 battle stars, Meritorious Unit Award, Good Conduct Medal, Victory Medal

U.S.S Arizona Memorial at Pearl Harbor

The picture shown below is the U.S.S. Arizona right after the Japanese bombed her deck and detonated a 14-inch powder magazine which caused a massive explosion. Over 1,100 Americans, including CV Lee and Ralph Campa, lost their lives that day on the U.S.S Arizona on December 7, 1941.

Ralph Campa   C.V. Lee

Lloyd Munter, back row 2nd from the left

Milton Adams

Albert Garza, 1st on the left

Ferdinand Herring, 2nd on the left

Percy Bingham

Herbert Herring

Leroy Arquette, 2nd from the left

Oscar Villasenor, 3rd from the left

The Adams' Brothers

In the Philippines, courtesy of Rodrigo Garcia

E.V. Guillot served on the destroyer U.S.S. Gheradi, stationed offshore of Normandy Beach in France on D-Day, June 6, 1944

Armando Daniel-left-Solomon Islands 1943

Gregorio Riojas　　Charles Backus　　Billy Perry　　Ramon Johnston

Enrique Castro and his Unit-101st Airborne Division

Arthur Backus　　Joe Frank Barksdale　　Buell and Earl Shofner

Roland Blair, front row, center in Iwo Jima

Scootie Carver with his crew members, front row, 3rd from the left

Edulio Cano

Charlie Valdez in Sicily

SS Keosanqua (Sam Michaels ship)

Sam Michaels in Eniwetok Atoll

William Edward Masters

Carlos Guerrero

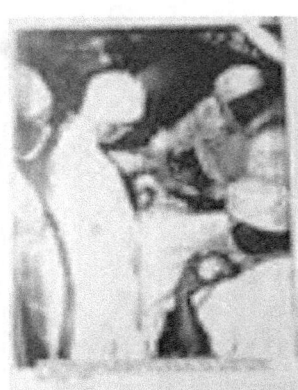
Jesus Rubio, assisting in surgery on the U.S.S. Colorado

Calvin Yeager visiting with Jack Demsey, Heavy Weight Champion

Efrain Lozano in New Caledonida

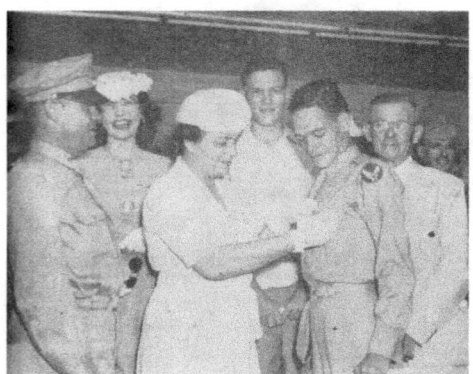
Harry Mathis earned Silver Wings, presented by his mother, Jan Mathis at EPAAF

Arthyeta Van Dalsem, 3rd from the left

Alberto Gil, 1st from the left

Herberto Maldonado

Charles Helms, Iwo Jima

Oscar Wueste, burial site located in France
(picture taken by grandniece Margaret Wueste Lesesne)

Emperor of Japan (rear seat)

James O'Donnell, guard of Emperor of Japan

Monday nite

Dearest Family-

Well- I have spent a pleasant week-end studying my head off! I have never liked anything quite so much as I do this flying. We are going on our fourth trip tomorrow and I don't even have an instructor - so keep your fingers crossed.

I flew my last mission at 20 thousand feet and about an hour before we got in I got sick as a dog - I guess it was from lack of oxygen - but I got a failing grade on the flight but I wasn't the only one that got sick - 42 out of 102 liked to died.

Don't worry about me having any money - 'cause I do. I have $80. I intended to send it home but I lent it to a boy yesterday to go home on. His wife was killed yesterday and he got a 10 day furlough to go to her funeral - and he didn't have a darned cent - so I lent him $60. I still have about $28 left thou (sp?) and we signed the payroll last Sat. so I imagine we will be paid again in a few days.

I am going to wait a few weeks and make sure I am going to get thru and then I am going to start buying my uniforms - unless you need the money for anything - if you do write and I will send it to you. Mama - if you are sick and want to see me you just write and I will come a- running.

Navigation is No. 1 now in the air-corps. If we wash out of this we can take pilot training and get a 1st Lt. commission if we wash-out after 9 weeks. But I   a commission in this 'cause you really learn so much more and you get to know how to manipulate the plane and every thing.

Jimmy Stewart is stationed here at the field- and is he unmilitary. He runs around with his hand in his pockets all the time and salutes like a marine.

Max Bear was out here the other day and came in our barracks and talked to us - he is one hell of a big fellow. He owns a big ranch just a little way from the field and he has invited a few of us out next Sunday. He told me he had a string of good roping horses and about 30 good calves. So - I guess we will rope a few - he is a really a Texas lover.

I love you all,
Scootie

Papa keep your fingers crossed and your son will try to make up for all the trouble he has caused you and mama.

Scootie Carver Letter to Family

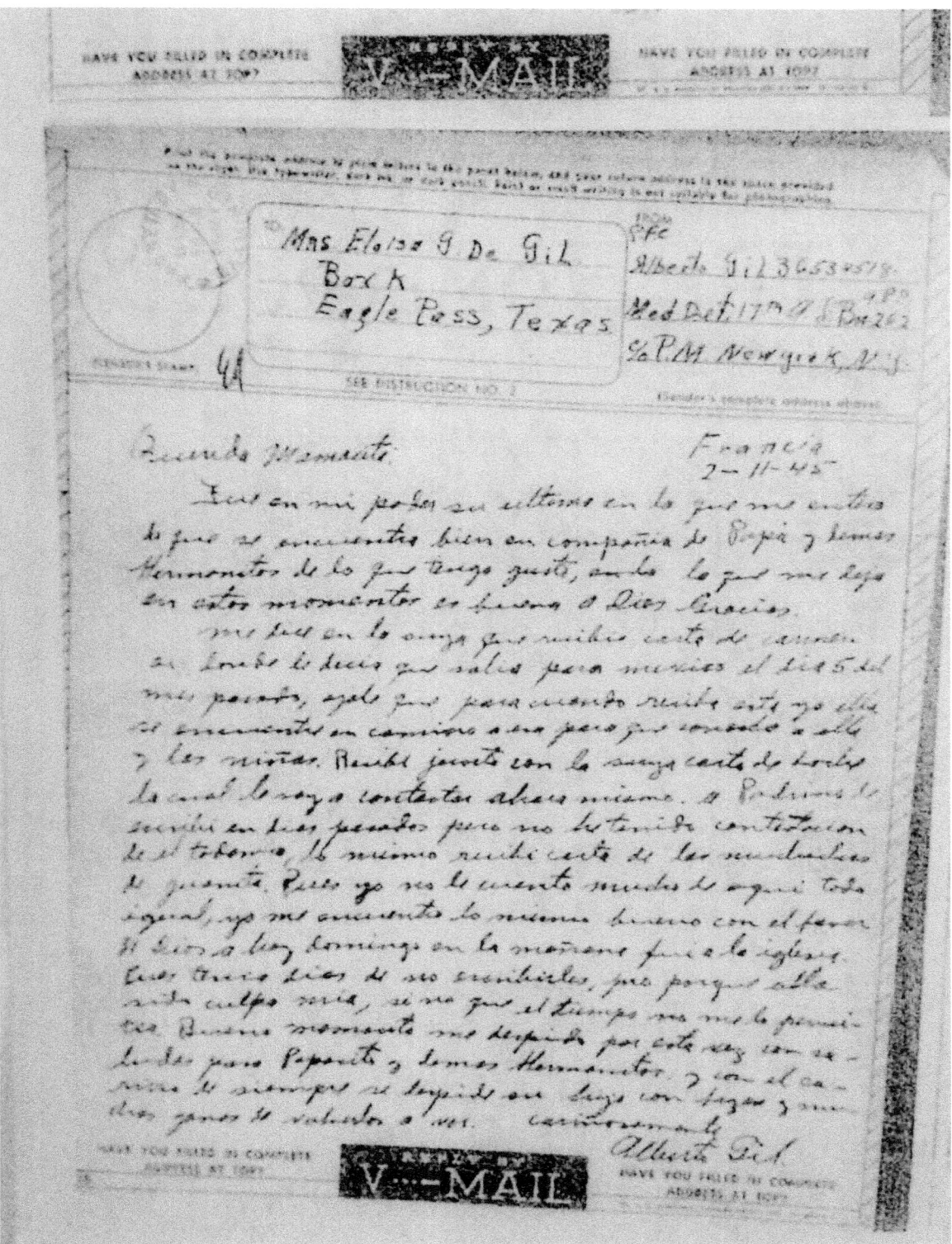

Alberto Gil Letter to his family.

THE HOMEFRONT

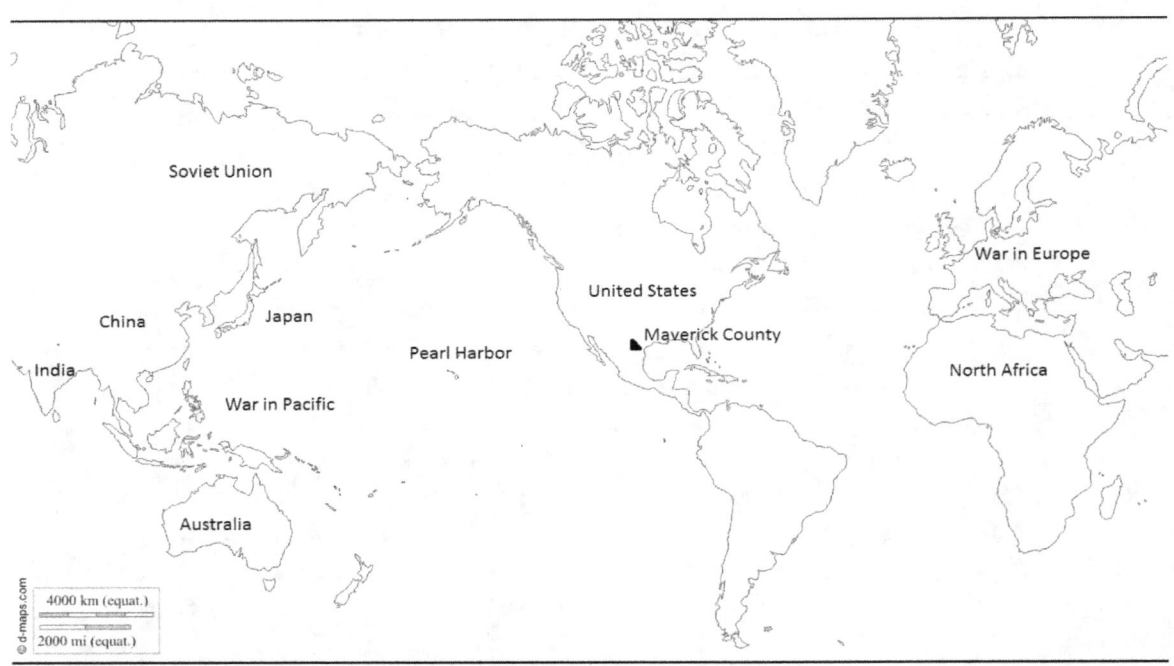

History of Maverick County

Maverick County, located in southwest Texas, was carved out from McKinney County in 1856. Finalized in 1871, the triangular shaped county contains 1,287 square miles. Maverick County was named for Samuel Maverick, a lawyer, politician and a rancher. He served as representative to the Congress of the Republic of Texas, Chief Justice of Bexar County, and then mayor of San Antonio. He was also one of the signers of the Texas Declaration of Independence. As a rancher, Sam Maverick was notorious for refusing to brand his cattle.

According to historian John Stockley, ranches around the area would round up cattle and Maverick would claim that all non-branded cattle belonged to him. In 1867, the term "Maverick" became synonymous with "independently minded." After a brief illness, Samuel Maverick died on September 2, 1870.

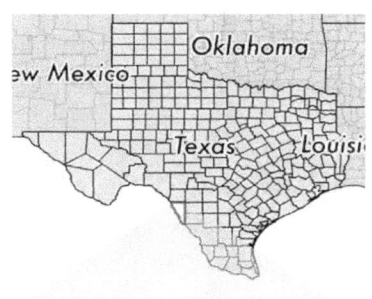

Before the 1700's, Maverick County was inhabited by prehistoric hunter-gatherers. Later bands of Coahuiltecan and Lipan Apache Indians roamed the area. This area became known as El Paso del Aguila (Pass of the Eagle), named after the Mexican eagles that frequently flew across into Mexico. Soldier Jessie Sumpter stated in his 1849 memoirs that for many years, an eagle's nest could be seen in a huge, old pecan tree where Rio Escondido empties into the Rio Grande.

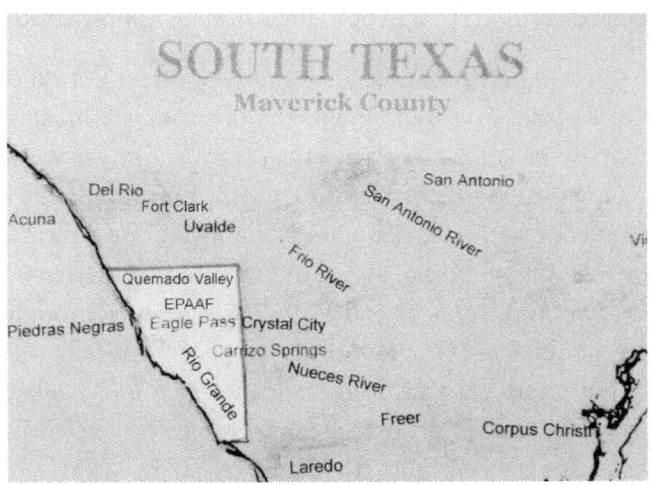

According to the Texas State Historical Association, after the Mexican-American War of 1846, the United States launched temporary posts along the Rio Grande River to establish boundaries between United States and Mexico. The United States believed the border should be located at the Rio Grande River, while Mexico believed it should be at the Nueces River. A temporary post named Camp Eagle Pass was established. In 1849, Fort Duncan named after a Mexican War hero, James Duncan was established a few miles from Camp Eagle Pass. Enlisted men and hired workers constructed a storehouse, two magazines (buildings that stored guns), a hospital, four officer's quarters, and enlisted men's quarters.

On February 2, 1849, the Treaty of Guadalupe Hidalgo was signed establishing the Rio Grande as the border between United States and Northern Mexico. The military contracted Frederick W. Groos to haul supplies. Groos was able to convince 70 Mexican families to live near Ft. Duncan in support of the freighting business. At the same time, many families, traveling west through Eagle Pass in pursuit of the riches of the California Gold Rush, established a post with tents and wagons known as California Camp. Henry Matson, a member of the California convoys, borrowed a soldier's tent and with two kegs of liquor, opened the first saloon in the area. With this growth of population and economy, the town of Eagle Pass was born.

In 1851, the first post office was built, a stage coach line was established, and the Lady of Refuge Catholic Church was erected. Eagle Pass was becoming a thriving settlement town. Piedras Negras, a town across the Rio Grande, established in 1850, became a haven for outlaws and fugitive slaves. Frederick Law Olmsted, a landscape architect, visited Eagle Pass in 1854 and noted the many slave hunters and runaway slaves resided in Piedras Negras. He also mentioned the many saloons and gambling houses, which catered to Fort Duncan's soldiers and other "unsavory characters." Years later, Olmsted designed Central Park in New York City and Prospect Park in Brooklyn. By 1860, the estimated population of Eagle Pass was 726.

Before the Civil War, farmers in the South exported cotton to Great Britain. In 1861, the early years of the Civil War, the policy of the newly created Confederate States of America believed that an informal embargo on cotton would push Great Britain to recognize the Confederacy. As the only port capable of exporting cotton, Eagle Pass became an essential location for the Confederacy. Friedrich Groos, seeing an opportunity, switched from the merchandise and freight business to shipping cotton to Matamoros, Mexico where the cotton was shipped to Great Britain. Enormous amounts of cotton passed through Eagle Pass by 1864. Cotton bales could be seen lined from the river to the edge of town on a regular basis. During the Civil War, a party of renegades crossed from Piedras Negras into Eagle Pass, attacking the Confederate troops who were housed at Fort Duncan. The townsmen defended Eagle Pass behind a barricade of cotton bales and successfully drove their assailants away.

When the Civil War ended in 1865, Joseph Shelby, a Confederate major general, was not ready to surrender to the Union. He encouraged his men to continue the fight in Mexico under Emperor Maximilian. On June 1, 1865, the Shelby Expedition marched from Corsicana through Waco,

Austin, and San Antonio to Eagle Pass. While crossing the Rio Grande at Eagle Pass into Mexico, a ceremony was held to bury the last flag to fly over the Confederate troops in the river.

According to the Texas State Historical Association, in 1871 Mike Wipff and his nephews, Joseph and Theo, established a cattle ranch in the Quemado Valley, approximately eighteen miles northwest of Eagle Pass. Quemado Valley, meaning "burned valley," was named by Spanish explorers who believed that the area was "parched by volcanic eruption." Farmers who were escaping the drought from the Texas panhandle moved into Quemado shortly afterwards.

The Galveston, Harrisburg, and San Antonio Railroad branch from Spofford to Eagle Pass was finished in the late 1882. This connected Maverick County to the rest of the world.

In 1885, Patrick W. Thompson, a Scottish-born rancher, conceived an idea of using water from the Rio Grande to create a gravity-flow irrigation system. In 1904, rancher Louis Dolch, began the irrigation of fig and onion crops with water pumped from the Rio Grande. The Maverick County Canal System, in full operation by April 1932, became the largest gravity irrigation system in the state at that time. This spurred a substantial increase in farming activity in the Quemado Valley and El Indio in the south as farmers grew greater amounts of corn, cotton, and hay. Farmers also introduced the cultivation of spinach, pecans, and tomatoes during this time. By the beginning of WWII, as many as 34,500 acres were sustained by gravity irrigation.

Quemado had five grocery stores, three filling stations, a post office, a tourist camp, a community canning plant, a tile plant, a vegetable-loading platform, and a school. The community served a diverse populace of ranches and farms. Eagle Pass, where three-fourths of the county's population was located, became the center of commercial activities. By this time, Maverick County, as a whole, reported over 10,000 residents.

EAGLE PASS ARMY AIR FORCE BASE (EPAAF)

On December 8, 1941, after the United States declared war on Japan, President Roosevelt issued a radio address to the American public through his "fireside chat." "Every citizen, in every walk of life, shares this same responsibility. The lives of our soldiers and sailors- the whole future of this Nation—depend upon the manner in which each and every one of us fulfills his obligation to our country." The United States, including Maverick County, went from not wanting to get involved in the war to "What can I do, as an individual, to help win this war and bring home the soldiers?"

The United States needed to quickly train and supply soldiers with uniforms, guns, cannons, tanks, airplanes, and other war-time equipment. Many airfields were constructed in Texas, including Maverick County, due to its excellent year-round weather. The location proved ideal for training soldiers to be pilots.

The Eagle Pass Army Air Force Base (EPAAF) was built approximately 10 miles north of Eagle Pass in 1942. The facilities vital to the training mission were constructed first, which took about six months. Buildings were constructed of wood, tar, paper, and non-masonry siding. The use of concrete and steel was limited due to critical need elsewhere. With no air-conditioning, heating, or insulation, most buildings were very hot and dusty in the summers and very cold in the winters. The airfield consisted of three 5,500-foot, concrete runways, along with four large hangars, support buildings, barracks, a street network, electric, sewer, and water lines. It also controlled 3 auxiliary fields. One of the hangars is still in use today as offices and a maintenance shop for the Maverick County Water Control and Improvement District #1.

Nearly 5,000 airmen, officers, enlisted men, Brazilian cadets, Women Army Corp (WAC) and Women Air force Service Pilots (WASP) were stationed in Eagle Pass. The airbase functioned as a small city. EPAAF had hangars, barracks, fire department, warehouses, hospitals, dental clinics, dining halls, and maintenance shops. There were libraries, social clubs for officers and enlisted men, a general store, a bowling alley, and a movie theatre. Other forms of entertainment on the base consisted of boxing matches and dance lessons from Madam La Zonga to learn the two-step and tango. Classical music hour, Spanish classes, and bingo could also be enjoyed. The American Association of University Women would give coffee and cake to airmen from 3:00-5:00 every Sunday. Protestant, Catholic, and Jewish religious services were also made available on base.

After the war the air base was returned to Maverick County and eventually became the Maverick County International Airport.

Colonel John Bundy left his post at Kelly Field, San Antonio, Texas on June 1, 1942 to take command of EPAAF, which was still under construction. Under his supervision, the field was developed rapidly. In November 1942, six months after Bundy's arrival, the first class of aviation cadets (Class 43 A) began advanced training. Cadets earned their wings and commission 10 weeks later. (The Eagle Pass International Guide April 19, 1945).

Col. Bundy would host benefit rodeos for all enlisted servicemen and women. One of the rodeo events was "bull riding." A sport where a rider attempts to stay mounted on the back of a bull while the animal tries ferociously to throw him off. According to John Stockley, Bundy would pay enlisted men $1 for every second they were able to stay on the bull. He would also tie a $20 bill to a bull's horn. If an airman was able to catch the bull, he would receive the $20. Colonel Bundy was known to always wear his cowboy boots even in his uniform. His reputation was well known throughout Maverick County, so much so that Eagle Pass Army Air Force Base was referred to as Bundy's Ranch.

General Gustavo A. Salinas, Chief of the Mexican Air Force is shown exchanging a "Good Neighbor" handclasp with Colonel John H. Bundy. Also pictured are General de Brigada, Juan Barrazon, Chief of the Mexico Artillery and Brigadier General Arthur H. Harris, U.S. Military Attaché from Mexico City.

Col. Bundy with Tito the Steer, mascot of the base. Tito was part Brahma and part Longhorn.

Colonel John H. Bundy

CADET TRAINING

After Air Corp Basic Training, there were four training phases. These phases consisted of ground school, pre-flight school, basic flying school, and finally advanced flying school. Each phase was 10 weeks long, with a total of 40 weeks of training to become a pilot.

EPAAF became an Advanced Fighter Training School for single-engine planes from 1942 to 1944. It was assigned to the Central Flying Training Command (CFTC), under the jurisdiction of the 57th Basic Flying Training Group, 33d Flying Training Wing. This is where cadets completed the advanced flight training. Upon graduation, they were commissioned as Second Lieutenants

P-40 on the tarmac at EPAAF: note the letters SNAFU above the numbers, a common acronym meaning "Situation Normal All Fouled Up."

Low Altitude Flyby of AT6 Texans over EPAAF, date unknown

Brazilian Cadets

Major Blake explained that many times other airplanes flew to EPAAP, as shown by the picture above, from other airbases to protect these airplanes from a storm from their home base. Note the P-39 Air Cobra in foreground with tricycle landing gear.

African American Soldiers

Air School Barracks

and assigned to an operation unit within a Numbered Air Force. EPAAF graduated 3,800 Second Lieutenants from November 1942 to November 1944.

Major Ray Blake, stationed at EPAAF in 1944, graduating in the class of '44, mentioned that each instructor had five students. Training would alternate daily between ground instruction in the morning and pilot training in the afternoon and vice versa.

Ground Instruction consisted of navigation, plane and ship identification, army combat tactics, and basic mechanical repairs. Students would learn by sitting in a grounded plane equipped with guns loaded with live ammunition. They would practice aerial warfare by shooting at stationary targets. The flying portion of training consisted of a cross-county solo flight from Eagle Pass to various bases in surrounding areas, typically in a triangular pattern. There was instruction in aerobatics such as loops, slow rolls, fast rolls, and snap rolls. The students would also learn air-to-air combat tactics and how to fly at high altitudes. The aircraft AT-6 Texan was used for training. The P-40 was used for more advanced training. According to PFC Lloyd Munter, two mechanics were assigned for every plane. Mechanics would conduct repairs at night.

On November 23, 1944, the base was converted to a basic flying school, which provided flight training on the P-17 to cadets with little or no previous flight training.

A year later, after Major Ray Blake graduated from the Advance Training School Class of 1944, he returned as an instructor at the basic flying school.

Major Ray Blake (second from left) as instructor at EPAAF with 3 of his aviation cadet students when he returned to EPAAF in February 1945.

Cadet training at EPAAF. Courtesy of Scootie Carver's family.

BRAZILIAN CADETS

Brazilian Air Force officers were also trained at EPAAF. They were trained to fly reconnaissance missions over the Atlantic Ocean in search of German U-Boats that were threatening to sink Naval and merchant ships.

AFRICAN AMERICAN SOLDIERS

According to Dr. Dan Hauman of the Air Force University at Maxwell Air Force Base, Alabama, the 354th Aviation Squadron located at EPAAF specialized in engineering. Their duty was to keep the runways in good condition. Captain Charles Maltz was the squadron commander.

UNITED STATES NAVY FIELD CENSORSHIP STATION, EAGLE PASS, TEXAS

The United States Navy had a Field Censorship Station in Eagle Pass. The station monitored wartime information, deciding whether information should be censored or released to the public. The post office would send all letters to and from Mexico for screening at the Censorship Station. The test as to whether information should be published or suppressed by the censor would lie in the question: "Will this news aid the enemy in his war against us?" *(Department of the Navy Field Manual)*.

Women in WWII

WOMEN'S ROLE BEFORE THE WAR

The typical woman of the 1930s had a husband who, although employed, had probably taken a pay cut to keep his job. If a man lost his job, his family often had the resources to survive without going on relief or losing all of their possessions. Still, Eleanor Roosevelt noted, "Practically every woman, whether she is rich or poor, is facing today a reduction of income." In 1935–1936 the median annual family income was $1,160, which translated into $20–$25 a week to cover all living expenses, to include food, shelter, clothing, and perhaps an occasional treat like going to the movies. Women "made do" by substituting their own labor for something that previously had been bought with cash or by practicing petty economies like buying day-old bread or warming several dishes in the oven at a time to save gas. (National History of Woman)

Many woman were forced into the workforce in order to make ends meet, however; they were met with heavy discrimination and social criticism. At the time, the majority of society felt woman were taking jobs from men. In reality, women entered the work force in low-paying, traditionally female jobs, such as manufacturing, domestic service, and clerical work. Another popular criticism of women workers was the perception that they were abandoning their families in a time of extreme need. The media rallied against working mothers. All the while failing to recognize that a large number of married women who entered the Depression-era labor force did so out of the absolute necessity to save their families from starvation and homelessness.

When Norman Cousins (1915 –1990) an American political journalist, author, professor, and world peace advocate, realized the number of gainfully employed women in 1939 was almost equal to the national unemployment rate. He offered this flippant remedy: "Simply fire the women, who shouldn't be working anyway, and hire the men. Presto! No unemployment. No relief rolls. No depression."

WOMEN DURING THE WAR

From 1940 to 1945, the number of women in the workforce increased from 25% to 35%. Betty Adams Shofner, from Quemado, reminisced of when her five brothers joined the armed forces.

Their family raised crops for a living. Before the war, the entire family worked on the farm. When Betty's brothers left to join the war effort, the family was unable to harvest as many crops, which reduced the family income.

To help their family while away, the five Adams brothers sent home a portion of their paychecks.

Betty remembered when her mother started to work as a seamstress for several families to help with the family income.

During the war, an aggressive media campaign featuring "Rosie the Riveter," urged more than 6 million women to take over jobs so men could join the armed forces. Many learned new skills in banking, retail, industry, and factories. By proving they were capable of doing "men's work," they were able to create an entirely new image of women in American society. This set the stage for the advancements of women's right for the upcoming generations.

"Rosie the Riveter"

Women not only stepped up in the workforce and at home, but also in support of the war effort. While general public opinion and Armed Forces leadership initially opposed women serving in uniform, the shortage of men necessitated a new policy.

WOMEN'S ARMY AUXILIARY CORPS (WAAC)
(Renamed Women's Army Corps (WAC))

The Women's Army Auxiliary Corps (WAAC), was created on May 15, 1942 to enable women to serve in noncombat positions as an auxiliary unit. Members of the WAAC were the first women to serve in the army, other than nurses.

The WAAC organization was coordinated by Lt. Col. Gilman C. Mudgett. He had to discard nearly all of his original plans before going into operation because he expected 11,000 volunteers, but over 150,000 women volunteered. Anglo, Hispanic, African American, and even Japanese-American women, some of whose family members were confined in government relocation camps, served their county with pride. Maria Estela Leyva, a Hispanic, was the first WAC from Maverick County.

Although WAACs were desperately needed overseas, the Army could not offer them the same protection as male soldiers if captured nor the same benefits if injured. The war on the Eastern front and in the Pacific required a larger army, with more jobs than men to fill them.

Establishment of the Women's Army Corps (WAC) with the same benefits as their male counterparts such as pay, privileges, and equal protection, was seen as a partial solution to the Army's problem. On July 1, 1943, President Franklin Roosevelt signed a bill, converting the

Women's Army Auxiliary Corps (WAAC) to the Women's Army Corp (WAC). Colonel Oveta Culp Hobby, a Texan, became its first director. Major Arthyeta Van Dalsem from El Indio, 17 miles southwest from Eagle Pass, was the second highest ranking WAC officer next to Col. Hobby.

Because WACs were not expected to go into combat, basic training was abbreviated. A physical training manual was published by the War Department in July 1943. The manual begins by naming the responsibility of the women: "Your Job: To Replace Men. Be Ready To Take Over." One section of the manual satirized a national recruit named "Josephine Jerk" who does not participate wholeheartedly: "Josephine Jerk is a limp number in every outfit who dives into her daily dozen with the crisp vitality of a damp mop."

According to the Army Heritage Center Foundation, the WACs served with the Army Air Forces (AAF), Army Ground Forces (AGF), and the Army Service Forces (ASF). As the war progressed, the job opportunities expanded. The AAF assigned WACs as weather observers and forecasters, electrical specialists, sheet metal workers, flight-simulator instructors, control tower specialists, airplane mechanics, photo-laboratory technicians, and photo interpreters. The AGF assigned WACs to Armor and Cavalry Schools and as radio mechanics. They took care of records and requisitions involving radio equipment, and repaired and installed radios in tanks and other vehicles – both in camps and in the field. They also trained women in field artillery and the coding and decoding of messages. Over 100 women worked as parachute riggers at Fort Benning, Georgia's Parachute School. The Signal Corps assigned women as telephone operators, radio operators, teletype operators, and photographic experts. The Technical Service employed WACs in the Transportation Corps to assist in processing troops and mail. Women served in the Medical Department as medical and surgical technicians. The Adjutant General's Corps, Chemical Warfare Service, Quartermaster Corps, Finance Department, Provost Marshal, and Corps of Chaplains all used WACs for administrative services. One of the most important projects WAC units were assigned to was the atomic bomb program, "Manhattan Project."

While most women served stateside, some went to various places around the world, to include Europe, North Africa, and New Guinea. In July, 1944, WACs landed on Normandy Beach just a few weeks after the initial invasion.

General Douglas MacArthur called the WACs "my best soldiers," adding that they worked harder, complained less, and were better disciplined than men. Many generals wanted more of them and proposed to draft women, but it was realized that this "would provoke considerable public outcry and Congressional opposition." So, the War Department declined to take such a drastic step. Those 150,000 women that did serve released the equivalent of seven divisions of men for combat. General Dwight D. Eisenhower said "their contributions in efficiency, skill, spirit, and determination are immeasurable.""

WAACS/WACS AT EPAAF

The week of May 20, 1943, the first contingent of WACs arrived at the EPAAF. Second Officer Bernice R. Peachy, of Massachusetts served as the company commander, and Third Officer Bertha Breskin of Miami, Florida, as the executive officer. The WACS were assigned duties in the motor pool, administrative, personnel sections, and as cooks and bakers.

One of the WACs assigned to Eagle Pass Air Force Base was Joan De Munbran. The following story was reported from the Army News Service, June 25, 2013.

"By the time she was 20, De Munbrun had started her own beauty store under the marquee of a theater, two blocks from the "wealthy district" in Minneapolis. Those were the only people who could afford a hairdresser," De Munbrun said. She said at the time "I didn't have more than an eighth-grade education." Instead, she learned from her customers, most of them teachers, professors and other professionals. It wasn't until later, while in the Army, that she would earn a high school diploma.

"On December 7th, 1941, the whole world changed; that was the day the war began," De Munbrun said, her voice dropping low. "My patrons all had husbands and brothers, and they all left, all of them left." The fiancée of one of her friends left shortly after the war started. He was among the first casualties in the first two weeks of the war, two weeks before his wedding. "After that, it was one after another. Most of the boys who went in first were casualties," De Munbrun said. "You can imagine what that did to me. The girls were so upset that I just couldn't take it. As soon as I heard that they were going to take women, I signed up." She was among the first women to do so.

For nine months, women were accepted into the Woman's Auxiliary Army Corps. After that initial nine months, they were officially sworn in as part of the Army, where De Munbrun served for three years. "I was never out of uniform, and I was only home once," she said. Her time in the service was not easy. "The casualty list would come out, not only one or two, but 500 or 1,000 boys," she said. More than 410,000 American service members died in World War II."

De Munbrun was sent initially to Eagle Pass Army Airfield in Texas, near the Mexican border. She, unlike the other women, requested to work "in the field," where she served as a photographer for 18 months. As a photographer for the Army during that time, De Munbrun said she was aware of many that did not make it home to their families.

"We had to take the picture of the crashed planes, send the serial number to Washington so they could write the plane off. Then, when the boys were causalities, and there were many, we had taken their picture when they came on the field, and I'd have to go pull the picture, pull the negative, and develop it for their families," she said. "Can you imagine what that meant? Nine men died every 13 weeks. You felt a loss."

After Texas, she was transferred to Denver, Colorado, where for 18 months she taught the operation and mechanics of aerial cameras to service members."

WAAC's marching at EPAAF

WOMAN AIR FORCE SERVICE PILOTS (WASPS)

"Fifinella" aka "Fifi" was designed by Walt Disney Studios for a proposed film "The Gremlins." During WWII, the WASP asked permission to use "Fifi" as the official mascot..

In 1939, Jacqueline "Jackie" Cochran, after sending a letter to the First Lady, Eleanor Roosevelt outlining her vision that a women's air corps could handle almost any non-combat duty, approached General Hap Arnold with the plan of using women as pilots. This would allow for more male pilots to serve in combat duty overseas. The plan was rejected, however in 1941 General Hap Arnold asked Ms. Cochran to organize 25 women pilots to fly to England to study the women pilots of the Royal Air Force. Cochran stayed in England, assisting General Arnold with arrival of the America's 8th Air Force. Upon the realization of a severe shortage of trained pilots, Gen Arnold asked Cochran to return to the United States and to train women pilots to assist in the war effort. The Woman Air Force Service Pilots (WASP) was formed on September 15, 1942. (National WASP World War II Museum).

Of the 25,000 young women who applied, only 1,830 were accepted. Ultimately a total of 1,074 trainees graduated. Unlike the male cadets who learned to become pilots during training, the WASPs were required to have pilot training before applying. On November 16, 1942, 150 women started their 23-week training program, under the direction of Jackie Cochran, based at the Municipal Airport in Houston, Texas. Three months later, the training was moved to Avenger Field in Sweetwater, Texas. WASPs flew more that 60 million miles for their country, in every type of aircraft, and on every type of non-combat mission that male AAF pilots flew. The WASPs were stationed at 120 Army Air Bases all over the United States, including EPAAF.

In the summer of 1944, Lieutenant Colonel Paul Tibbets was in charge of training pilots to fly the B-29 Super Fortress bomber. Male pilots were reluctant to fly the B-29 because of the reputation of the plane's engine catching fire. Tibbets decided that if he could enlist a couple of WASP's to fly the B-29 without incident then he could convince the male pilots to fly the B-29 Bomber. Tibbets never told his 2 recruits, Dora Dougherty and Dorothea Moorman, of the plane's flaw. The plan worked and the two WASP pilots flew the bomber without incident and the male pilots stopped complaining about flying the B-29.

Some other duties of the WASPs included ferrying planes, towing target racks for ground-to-air or air-to-air gunnery practice, transporting personnel and cargo, simulated strafing, training navigators and bombardiers, smoke laying, flying night tracking missions, drones, and slow timing engines. They also took over the positions as engineer test pilots and instrument instructors.

African-American females were not allowed into the WASPs, although a number of qualified applicants applied. One Native American (an Oglala Sioux from Pine Ridge Indian Reservation, South Dakota), Ola Mildred Rexroat "Rexy," was stationed in Eagle Pass. Her job was the dangerous task of towing targets for aerial gunnery students at EPAAF. When the war ended, Ola joined the Air Force and served for almost ten years.

Thirty-eight WASPs lost their lives while serving their country. Since the WASP was not considered part of Air Force, WASPs were not granted the same rights as their male counterparts. Their bodies were sent home in cheap pine boxes to be buried at the expense of their families or classmates. The WASPs would "pass the hat" around, collecting donations to help pay for the body to be shipped home. American flags were not allowed to cover their coffins and gold stars not permitted in their parents' windows.

On December 20, 1944, the WASPs were disbanded without any benefits or official recognition. Because the WASPs were not considered as part the Army Air Force, they had to pay their own way home. Dorothy Kocher, a WASP, wrote in response of the deactivation, "I would be happy to fly for any Allied country for any length of time, and under any conditions... I would only like to be assured of this: That my services are needed, and wanted, and the fact that I am a woman will not be used against me."

WASPs assigned to Eagle Pass:

Susanne Bane (Armstrong)
Patricia Blackburn (Bonansings)
Martha Blair (Gaunce)
Margaret Chamberlain (Tamplin)
Margaret Cox (Stegall)
Margaret Helburn (Kocher)
Kathleen Hilbrandt
Dorothy Hoover
Mary Jershin (O'Rourke)
Ann Karlson (Kenney)

Virginia Knapp (Healy)
Muriel Martin (Kiester)
Virginia Mullen
Anne Noggle
Ola Mildred Rexroat
Edith Smith (Beal)
Dorothy Sorensen (Van Valkenburg)
Esther Stahr (Cuddington)
Kathryn Stark (Gunderson)

WASPs stationed at the EPAAF
(Courtesy of John Stockley and Ft. Duncan Museum)

The commander of the gunnery school at EPAAF decided to "use WASPs exclusively for target towing because the men often strayed into Mexico air space." The WASPs would fly overhead, towing aerial targets: simulating enemy aircraft. Anti-aircraft gunnery trainees fired live ammunition at them.

In 1975, Colonel Bruce Arnold, son of General "Hap" Arnold, began lobbying the U.S. Congress for WASP pilots to be recognized as veterans. They were eventually successful. In 1977, with the support of Senator and former ferry pilot, Barry Goldwater, President Jimmy Carter signed the G. I. Bill Improvement Act which granted WASP pilots full military status. Seven years later, their medals came in the mail. On March 10, 2010, Congress awarded the WASP the Congressional Gold Medal, the highest civilian honor Congress can bestow. The ceremony was held in Emancipation Hall in the Capital of the United States.

Photo on left: WASP Deannie Parrish accepting the Congressional Gold Medal from House Minority Leader, John Boehner, Senator Harry Reid, Speaker of the House Nancy Pelosi and Senator Mitch McConnell. Photo on right: President Obama on July 1, 2009, signed into law, the bill to award the Congressional Gold Medal to the Women Airforce Service Pilots (WASP).

CADETS AND SOLDIERS KILLED DURING TRAINING

Over 30 cadets and soldiers were killed in accidents while stationed at EPAAF. The accidents were triggered by poor aircraft and component design, inadequate training, carelessness, bad weather, improper maintenance, and sometimes just plain, bad luck. In fact, according to the Fatal Army Air Forces Aviation Accidents in the United States, 1941-1945 by Anthony J. Mireles, U.S. Air Force General Curtis E. LeMay said, "the fatality rate in the Boeing B-29 training program late in the war exceeded the fatality rate in combat." Mireles further stated, "By the end of 1943, AAF aircraft accidents were occurring with an appalling frequency, alarming and angering some AAF pilots and commanders." It is interesting to point out that the AAF lost over 4,500 aircraft in actual combat against Japan, at the same time, losing over 7,100 aircraft stateside while moving them and teaching people how to fly.

Information on the fatal crashes was obtained from airforceaccidents.com, Fatal Army Air Forces Aviation Accidents in the United States, 1941-1945 by Anthony J. Mireles, *The Eagle Pass News Guide*, and *The Eagle Eye* base newspaper. The following is the list of cadets killed on training missions based at EPAAF and surrounding areas:

DECEMBER 24, 1942:
2Lt. Donald W. Pittsley, pilot

2Lt. William L. Jones, navigator instructor

A/C James A. Hiller, student navigator

While flying a Beech AT-7 from Hondo Air Force Base on a navigation training exercise over Maverick County, the plane crashed 16 miles northeast from Eagle Pass.

JANUARY 31, 1943:
January 31, 1943:

A/C Phillip C. Crowther

Soon after take-off from EPAAF, the AT-6C training aircraft dove into the ground 13 miles northwest of Eagle Pass, where it exploded into flames upon impact.

MARCH 5, 1943:
2Lt. Herbert I. Sullivan, pilot

The North American AT-6C crashed five miles east of the EPAAF while returning to the field after completing a night flight. The pilot flew the airplane into the ground with the landing gear extended while on a straight-in approach to the active runway. Passenger, F/O Charles Phippen, who informed the pilot that the plane was flying too low, was seriously injured.

MARCH 18, 1943:
A/C Raymond H. Allen, pilot

The Curtis P-36C was taking off to the southwest on Runway 21 and appeared to have engine trouble. He was attempting to gain altitude when the plane suddenly dove into the ground and erupted into flames. Investigation revealed engine problems.

JUNE 11, 1943:
A/C Verl Chamberlain, pilot

A/C Frederick M. Carrington, pilot

The North American AT-6C was flying two miles east of Spofford Road, 10 miles north of EPAAF, when it veered to the right and crashed into a bank. It was reported that the plane exceeded 45 degrees and was travelling at high speeds.

JULY 25, 1943:
A/C Raymond J. Pech, pilot

Two Curtis P-40F airplanes collided in mid-air three miles north of EPAAF. Cadet A/C Junior G. O'Nell, the other pilot, stated that he was flying at 11,000 feet and noticed a P-40 flying some miles away. Cadet O'Neill pulled up to let the other P-40 pass under him. While pulling up, Cadet O'Nell stalled the airplane and the starboard wing dropped. The port wing of P-40, piloted by Cadet Pech, collided with the starboard wing of Cadet O'Nell's P-40. Cadet Pech's airplane was seen entering a steep, high-speed dive straight to the ground, where it exploded into flames upon impact. Cadet O'Nell was able to land his seriously damaged plane and miraculously, walked away without injury.

AUGUST 22, 1943:
A/C Luther N. Sparkman, pilot

Upon investigation, the engine of the Bell P-35N started sputtering when it approached approximately 500 feet. The pilot made a turn to the right while trying to gain altitude. Two pieces dropped from the plane, the engine failed completely. Flames burst from the cockpit as the plan dove straight into the ground, exploding on impact.

AUGUST 27, 1943:
A/C Harold C. Milligan, pilot

The North American AT-6C collided in mid-air 20 miles north of Eagle Pass with another AT-6C. The pilot, A/C John Maxell, was able to parachute to safety, receiving minor injuries. The planes were part of a four-airplane flight on a gunnery mission. Cadet Milligan was warned, after his second pass on the tow target, he was flying too close to Cadet Maxwell. On the third pass, Cadet Milligan flew into the rear of Cadet's Maxwell's plane. Cadet Milligan and his plane crashed to ground, immediately bursting into flames.

SEPTEMBER 30, 1943:
A/C William S. Gorman, pilot

The Curtiss P-40E crashed 12 miles east of EPAAF. The airplane had taken off from EPAAF and failed to return. Two instructors found it crashed later that evening, but personnel could not get to the site until the next day. Investigation revealed the airplane dove into the ground vertically at high speed and exploded upon impact.

OCTOBER 13, 1943:
A/C Bernard G. Baebler, pilot

Two AT-6C collided in mid-air, 32 miles east of EPAAF. The airplanes were part of the three ship Lufbury Circle (defensive air combat tactic) to the left, at an altitude of 7,200 feet. One cadet flew out of the maneuver because his plane was suffering engine trouble. Moments later, he saw Cadet Baebler's port wing strike the starboard wing of A/C Wehmfoefer's airplane. A/C Baebler was unable to parachute to safety and crashed with the plane. A/C Wehmhoefer stated that his airplane "entered an inverted attitude just after the collision and immediately entered a spin." He parachuted to safety and landed near the crash site, which smashed to the earth within one-half mile of each other.

OCTOBER 26, 1943:
A/C Robert L. Torgeson, pilot

The AT-6D, along with instructor 2Lt. Melville V. Keeton, was on a training mission when it collided with another AT-6C, with instructor Lt. James E. Faull and student A/C Harry Wilkerson, who were on an instrument training mission. Lt. Faull took control and dove to the left to avoid the collision with Torgeson's plane, but was unsuccessful. Torgeson's airplane was seriously damaged, losing the starboard wing, and spinning out of control to the ground. Investigators speculated that the separating wing struck Lt. Torgeson as it rolled over the fuselage, rendering him unconscious. His instructor, Lt. Keeton, parachuted to safety, receiving minor injuries. Lt. Faull and Harry Wilkerson were uninjured and able to land at EPAAF.

NOVEMBER 25, 1943:

A/C John E. Goodson, pilot

The North American AT-6C crashed 25 miles southeast of the EPAAF. He was on an authorized night navigation flight to Carrizo Springs, Texas via Rock Springs, Texas and was to return to EPAAF. He crashed about 10 minutes before he was due back to EPAAF.

JANUARY 27, 1944:

A/C Charles A. Taylor, pilot

The Curtis P-40N, on a transition flight, crashed five miles southeast of the EPAAF. The airplane exploded into flames upon impact, killing Cadet Taylor instantly. Investigators could not determine why the airplane crashed.

MARCH 4, 1944:

A/C James Walker

A North American AT-6D crashed five miles east of the EPAAF, killing A/C James Walker and seriously injuring A/C Kenneth L. Vaughn. The plane took off from EPAAF on an instrument training flight. A/C Vaughn was under the hood on instruments and A/C Walker was flying as the safety pilot. The students completed the instrument flight and A/C Walker took the controls and headed toward the field. The plane, which was observed to be flying around 3,000 feet, entered a spiral and crashed into the ground.

MARCH 5, 1944:

2Lt. Theodore V. Affinito; pilot

While taking off from EPAAF, flight leader, 1Lt. Elbert M. Brown, mistakenly took three planes for take-off on Runway 30. The control tower noticed the mistake and ordered the planes to stop. All students' "ships" were to take off at the Southeast runway. A/C Warren F. Aderholt, the student in ship #3, didn't hear the order, and continued down the runway, colliding with Lt. Brown's ship, sending them both out of control. The A/C Anderholt's propeller collided with the cockpit where 2Lt. Affinito was sitting, killing him instantly. The instructor, 1Lt Elbert M. Brown, received serious injuries. A/C Warren was left unscathed.

MARCH 20, 1944:

A/C William J. Brown, pilot

The North American AT-6C crashed one-half mile north the AAF Auxiliary Airfield near Eagle Pass. Investigators stated, "A/C Brown was making his initial approach for a landing at the auxiliary field. As he was making his turn from the base leg to his approach leg, at an altitude of approximately 700 feet above the ground, his plan stalled. As a result, he turned one and half spins to the right prior to impact with the ground. The aircraft was demolished and it exploded upon striking the ground."

APRIL 1, 1944:

1 Lt. Marilo W. Truax, pilot

A/C Patrick D. Seals

The P-40N took off from EPAAF on a transition flight and collided midair, approximately two miles away, with a North American AT-6D plane. Student A/C Patrick D. Seals and instructor Arthur V. Stevens, had just completed an instrument training flight. At that moment, Lt. Steven's plane took a sharp nose dive. Lt. Stevens immediately opened his canopy, unfastened his seatbelt, parachuted successfully, and was uninjured. Unfortunately, A/C Patrick D. Seals and A/C Marilo W. Truax were both killed in the crash.

APRIL 28, 1944:

2Lt. Robert A. Kelly

2Lt. Clyde J. Cagle

The North American AT-6D took off from EPAAF on an instructor training flight. The plane was observed executing a series of dives and steep pullouts. 12 miles northeast of the EPAAF, as it pulled out of a dive, two civilians observed two pieces fall from the plane before it dove into the ground and exploded. Both instructors were killed instantly.

MAY 17, 1944:

A/C Woodruff W. Watkins, pilot

The AT-6D crashed four miles west of the municipal airport at Pawnee, Texas. The airplane took off from EPAAF on a student night training mission. It was one of several student airplanes practicing landings at the airport. The airplane smashed into the ground in a vertical position; trees in the area of the crash were undamaged. Several witnesses observed the crash and explosion, but were unable to locate the crash site because the fire had died down. The wreckage was found by a civilian pilot during daylight hours. Investigators speculated that the pilot had lost the horizon while turning away the field.

A military funeral for A/C Watkins, youngest of a famous fighting family of seven soldiers, was held at Arlington National Cemetery, Washington, D.C.

Cadet Watkins, the third member of his family to sacrifice his life in this war, was to have been commissioned to 2Lt. and awarded silver wings during graduation a week after his death. His father, Col. Dudley W. Watkins, an active Command pilot and Deputy Commander at the Air Forces Proving Ground Command at Eglin Field, Florida, and his brother, Maj. John C.A. Watkins, holder of the Distinguished Flying Cross and the Air Medal with twelve oak leaf clusters, planned to fly to Eagle Pass for the graduation.

MAY 24, 1944:

2Lt. Earl E. Plummer, pilot

The North American AT-6C crashed at Cuevas Auxiliary Airfield #1, 10 miles north of Eagle Pass. Lt. Plummer had been in transition gunnery training following his graduation with the class of 44C. Lt. Plummer was survived by his wife, Marjorie, a temporary residence of Eagle Pass. Investigators stated, "Lt. Plummer, a member of a flight of airplanes was making 'dry runs' on ground targets preparatory to firing on these targets. This flight was using a right-hand traffic pattern. Lt. Plummer was noticed by students, who were on the ground, to be making fairly steep and fast pull-ups in his first few passes at the targets. On his last pass at the target, the airplane rolled to the right and stopped in the inverted position. It was then seen by witnesses that Lt. Plummer attempted to initiate a recovery by rolling the airplane back to an upright attitude. The airplane at this time nosed down and struck the ground in an almost inverted position. The right wing and engine struck the ground first, almost simultaneously. The airplane exploded on impact, but did not burn."

JUNE 30, 1944:

A/C Freddie Seagle

A/C Charles Funk

Two North American AT-6C airplanes collided midair 12 miles east of the EPAAF. They were part of a five-ship formation on a training flight. The formation was turning to the left, with A/C Funk leading, when he turned inside the formation and collided with A/C Seagle's airplane. The starboard wing of A/C Seagle's airplane was sheared off and he fell out of control, smashing to the ground. A/C Seagle made no attempt to leave his airplane and it was speculated that he was killed or knocked unconscious in the collision. A/C Funk descended to the ground in his parachute, but was apparently killed when he hit the ground on his head.

JULY 3, 1944:

Pvt. John R. Chitwood

Pvt. Chitwood, an armorer whose job was loading ammunition into the guns on the aircrafts, was accidentally shot and fatally wounded at the airplane machine gun range. His death was the first fatality to an enlisted man in the performance of duty at EPAAF. He was stationed in Eagle Pass for 20 months.

JULY 12, 1944:

2Lt. Alva McEwen, Jr.

The AT-6D took off from EPAAF on a night cross-country navigation flight to Hondo, Texas, then onto Laredo, Texas. About 10 minutes after take-off, the plan burst into flames upon impact, killing 2Lt McEwan instantly. It was later speculated that he had probably lost the horizon, causing him to lose control of the plane.

JULY 13, 1944:
A/C Ernest M. Buzzard, pilot

The AT-6C crashed 10 miles east of EPAAF. It had taken off from EPAAF on a night cross-country navigation flight to Laredo, Texas, then onto Hondo, Texas, and back to EPAAF. The student flew around aimlessly for some time before making contact with two cadets in the air. Both cadets gave the student the correct coordinate to return to EPAAF. He headed for the field in an attempted to complete the flight. The plane ran out of fuel and the student attempted an emergency forced landing. He lost control of the plane as it struck a stand of mesquite trees in a port wing low and nose-down altitude. The airplane did not burn, but was completely destroyed.

APRIL 2, 1945:
A/C Luke V. Dean, Jr., pilot

The AT-6D crashed 16 miles north-northwest of EPAAF. It had just taken off from Auxiliary Airfield #3 in preparation to perform student night landing practice. The plane failed to return to the field and was not found until daylight hours the next day. It apparently flew into the ground about one mile east of Auxiliary Airfield #3. Investigators speculated that the student had set his altimeter incorrectly or had suffered from vertigo, causing him to inadvertently fly the plane into the ground. It did not burn, but was utterly destroyed.

APRIL 15, 1945:
2Lt. Percy Bingham

2Lt Bingham graduated from Advanced Single Engine Pilot School at EPAAF in February 1944, Class 44B. Investigators noted that the pilot flew the previous day and was allowed to stay overnight at his parents' home at Quemado.

2Lt Bingham was invited, by the base commander, to participate in a fly-by aerial review being conducted for Memorial Services for President Franklin D. Roosevelt in celebration of the final graduating class from EPAAF. His parents and two brothers, Benson and Edmond Bingham, were in the stands watching the celebration.

He was instructed to fly by the reviewing stand, perform 180 degree turn, and then fly past the reviewing stand a second time. Investigators stated, "Lt. Bingham took off, circled south of the field until he received the signal to come in, and then climbed to an altitude of approximately 5,000 feet. He made a diving turn toward the field from the south end of the ramp, leveled out at about 75 feet, and flew across the ramp heading north at estimated airspeed of 450 mph or more. About 200 yards north of the reviewing stand, he attempted to execute a steep pull-up straight ahead, and when he had attained a nose-up altitude of about 45 degrees and an altitude of 100 to 200 feet, both wings failed almost simultaneously and became detached. The tail section and empennage became detached immediately after the wings due to the tail being struck by the right wing. The fuselage continued to rise for about 400 feet, revolving to the right, and then tumbled to the ground about 1,000 yards from the spot where the wings became detached. The engine and fuselage caught fire upon contact with the ground. The left wing and the right wing tank were found on Runway 8, about 50 to 100 yards north of the spot where they became detached. The right wing, the right landing wheel, and the tail section were scattered about 50 yards further north. Numerous small pieces of metal and fabric were also found in that area. The remainder of the aircraft was 600 to 700 yards further north, outside the boundary of the field."

(See the Roll of Honor list for 2Lt Percy Bingham's story in WWII)

MILITARY INFLUENCE ON EAGLE PASS AND MAVERICK COUNTY

According to the Texas Almanac, the census of 1940 reported 10,071 people living in Maverick County. The Eagle Pass Army Air Force Base (EPAAF), with over 5,000 troops training at the base at any given time, was constructed in 1942. The population of Maverick County increased by almost 50% within the first 6 months of EPAAF opening. Upon opening in 1942, EPAAF transformed the economy and the culture of Maverick County: more eligible single men, more diverse culture, and extra money to stimulate the economy.

SERVICEMAN CLUBS

FT. DUNCAN OFFICER'S CLUB

In 1942, the mayor of Eagle Pass offered Ft. Duncan for military use during World War II. Ft. Duncan became a temporary headquarters for Col. Bundy until EPAAF was finished. Six months after construction of EPAAF was completed, Ft. Duncan became the "Officer's Club."

Major Blake said when he graduated from EPAAF as a 19 year-old, 2Lt, his father came to Eagle Pass from West Virginia. Upon graduation, all graduates were invited to the Officer's Club at Ft. Duncan. Major Blake was nervous because it was his first time drinking liquor in front of his father. After a couple of drinks, neither of them cared.

AFRICAN-AMERICAN'S USO

The Armed Forces of the United States segregated African American service members from white service members. The African American's USO opened on February 27, 1944. This was located at the 100 block of Commercial Street.

SOCIAL INFLUENCE

ELIGIBLE, SINGLE MEN

Dances were often held at EPAAF. Enlisted men and young Maverick County women would mingle. Some soldiers married local women, like author Bill Munter's mother, Yolanda Schwartz. "It was said that the women of Eagle Pass never had it so good. The lucky ones were the soldiers who married Eagle Pass women." said Elby Beard, one of the local women who married Lt. Ralph Beard, an engineer officer at EPAAF.

EVENTS

Social events, sponsored by EPAAF were held in Eagle Pass. Frequently, the Army Air Force Band would play at San Juan Plaza.

WEEKEND PASSES

Weekend passes were given to officers, cadets, and enlisted men. Soldiers would frequently visit the USO, Aztec Theater, Victory Club, Ft. Duncan Officer's Club, Cadet Club (Main and Commercial Street in Eagle Pass) and the Moderno Restaurant and Nightclub in Piedras Negras, Mexico. According to Mr. Riddle and the late Julio Santos Coy, a Piedras Negras historian, the basement of the Moderno Restaurant was a "Cuban style" casino with card tables, craps tables, and a roulette wheel. As legend has it, there were topless dancers who would put on a Cuban style show. Army Air Force officers and wealthy Mexican ranchers would frequently visit the casino.

Soldiers were permitted to travel to Mexico while on a weekend pass. They were required to follow rules such as, stay on paved roads, go with another soldier, and to remain in uniform at all times.

Before WWII, Salomon Abraham, grandfather of Carmen Abraham, a long-time resident of Eagle Pass and Piedras Negras, opened the first curio store in Piedras Negras across from the Moderno Restaurant. He stated that "because of the influx of soldiers visiting Mexico during WWII, his Mexican curio store had the best business in the history of the store."

BIRTH OF THE NACHO

One day in 1943, twelve wives of officers stationed at EPAAF decided to go shopping in Piedras Negras, Mexico and stopped at the Victory Club to eat. The restaurant had already closed for the day and the chef had already gone home. With no chef available, the maître'd, Ignacio "Nacho" Anaya, invented a new snack for them with what little he had available in the kitchen: tortillas and cheese sauce. Anaya cut the tortillas into triangles, added shredded cheddar cheese, quickly heated them, and added sliced jalapeño peppers. He served the dish, calling it "nachos especiales - meaning "special nachos" in Spanish. (Huffington Post 5/15/2012)

Anaya went on to work at the Moderno Restaurant in Piedras Negras and later opened his own restaurant, "Nacho's Restaurant." Anaya's original recipe was printed in the 1954 "St. Anne's Cookbook."

The popularity of the dish swiftly spread throughout Texas. The first known appearance of the word "nachos" in English, dates to 1949, from the cookbook "A Taste of Texas." Carmen Rocha, a waitress from San Antonio, introduced the dish to El Cholo Mexican Restaurant in Los Angeles in 1959.

A modified version of the dish, with permanently soft cheese and pre-made tortilla chips was marketed in 1976 by a man named Frank Liberto, owner of Rico's Products. Liberto began selling nachos at sporting events at Arlington Stadium in Arlington, Texas. During a Monday night football game, sportscaster Howard Cosell, would mention the dish "nachos," introducing it to a whole new audience.

Ignacio Anaya died in 1975. In his honor, a bronze plaque was erected in Piedras Negras. Every year in October, Piedras Negras celebrates the International Nacho Fest. For years, Anaya's son, Ignacio Anaya Jr., served as a judge for the Annual Nacho Competition.

FINANCIAL INFLUENCES

BLACK MARKET

When I first met my wife Judy, I was invited to dinner by her sister's future father and mother-in-law, Lester and Anne Copland. After the customary introduction and interrogation, Lester asked me where I was from and of course I mentioned Eagle Pass. He then asked me if I knew Sam Schwartz. I was shocked! After a pause, I said, "Yes. He was my grandfather." I asked how he knew him. It was then revealed that Lester was stationed at EPAAF and met my grandfather at one of the many parties my grandparents threw for the soldiers.

Once married to Judy, I listened to many of Lester's stories. During the war, he had a little black market operation in Eagle Pass and Piedras Negras, Mexico. Because France was occupied by Germany, imports of French perfume were forbidden by United States Customs laws. Lester would buy imported French perfume in Mexico and transport it to his hometown of Houston, Texas to sell it. He would also buy and sell women's nylon stockings, which were also nonexistent during the war.

One of the most tragic stories Lester told was of when he was a sergeant in AAF working as a mechanic. One of the pilots of the plane he was working on wanted him to go on a "check out flight" with him. This way, if the plane had any mechanical issues, Lester could correct the problem. Lester agreed and during the flight, the plane crashed in Mexico. The pilot was killed and Lester suffered a broken back. He was rescued the next day and spent the remainder of the war at Brooke Army Hospital at Ft. Sam Houston in San Antonio, Texas.

WAR BONDS AND STAMPS

To help pay for the war, the people of the United States saw an increase in Federal Income Tax and the sale of "War Stamps " and "War Bonds," a certificate issued by the government in an attempt to remove currency from circulation to reduce inflation. The "Victory Tax" of 1942 sharply raised Income Tax rates and allowed, for the first time in our nation's history, taxes to be withheld from paychecks.

According to the September 10, 1942 article of The Guide, "One of 94 theatres in Texas to be selected for the honor (The Aztec Theater), became an official sales agency for War Savings Bonds. Sam Schwartz, owner of the Aztec, had a special booth built on the east side of the foyer where patrons and pedestrians could buy bonds of any denomination. Members of the Women's Motor Corps in uniform, attended to the booth at night."

In fact, during the month of July of 1943, JC Penny's held a July War Bond Campaign. Their advertisement stated, "Families of Service men are being asked to bring their boys pictures to the store. The pictures will be used in the show windows during the month and then returned to owners."

The National WWII Museum, in Orleans, explained the purchase of War Bonds as the following: "You could purchase a $25 War Bond for $18.75. The government would take that money to help pay for tanks, planes, ships, uniforms, weapons, medicine, food, and everything else the military needed to fight and win. That's the investment in your country. Ten years from the time you purchased your War Bond you could redeem it and get $25. That's the investment you made in your own financial future. Now, $6.25 may not sound like a lot, but most Americans bought more than just $18.75 worth of War Bonds."

War stamps were issued by the United States Post Office, with the lowest domination for 10 cents. When the stamps totaled $18.75, the stamps could be redeemed to purchase war bonds.

REAL ESTATE ISSUES

To be near the service members, many families came to live in Eagle Pass. Housing and apartment complexes became full. In fact, rental space was scarce and new construction began. According to The Guide, March 4, 1943, a civilian housing project constructed 148 dormitory units, 94 dormitory apartments, 150 family units and 100 trailers. 20 of the family units were created solely for rent to migrate workers of the EP Flying School. The units were rented for $30 to $39 a month.

LABOR SHORTAGES AND BOOM

Young men of Maverick County held many jobs before the war started. Primarily, they worked in fields for the agriculture sector. These same young men volunteered or were drafted to join the war. This caused a shortage of workers to the agricuture sector as well as to the private sector. To fill the void, women and children joined the workforce.

EPAAF helped relieve the town's unemployment by creating jobs for local residents. Yolanda Schwartz Munter wanted to help with the war effort. She worked at the First National Bank in Eagle Pass and later, on base, for H.B. Zachary Construction. Henry Gonzales, a 14 year old from Eagle Pass, worked as a "pin boy" for the bowling alley on the base.

According to John Stockley, WWII also helped boost Quemado's economy. During WWII, Quemado farmers and ranchers sold milk and truck crops such as tomatoes, cabbage, and cauliflower to the base.

RATIONING

Ill prepared for WWII, all aspects of Americans lives were focused on winning the war. In order for the United States to succeed, all raw materials were needed to help manufacture war machinery. Food and consumer goods had to be diverted to support soldiers engaged in war efforts. Because certain foods and materials were in short supply on the home front, the government introduced "rationing" to ensure everyone got their fair share. War Ration Books and tokens were issued to each American family, dictating how much gasoline, tires, sugar, meat, silk, shoes, nylons, and other items any one person could buy.

Food was in short supply. Much of the processed and canned foods were reserved for shipping overseas to our military and Allies. Due to the transport of soldiers and war supplies, gasoline and transportation of fresh foods to the communities around the states became scarce. Foods, like coffee and sugar, were limited due to the restriction of imports from other countries.

The first non-food item rationed was rubber. The Japanese had seized plantations in the Dutch East Indies that produced 90% of America's raw rubber. President Roosevelt called on citizens to help by contributing scrap rubber to be recycled- old tires, old rubber raincoats, garden hoses, rubber shoes, and bathing caps.

The Guide on July 1943, listed rationing reminders on meat, cheese, butter, fats, canned fish, processed fruits and vegetables, sugar, coffee, gasoline, and shoes.

Yolanda Schwartz Munter mentioned that along the border, Americans, including her family, would drive across the Rio Grande into Piedras Negras to fill their tanks with Mexican gas. The Guide on December 10, 1942 stated that even though filling your cars with gas was done legally, "most of the gas at the stations in Mexican border cities was low grade, and did not work well in high compression cars. However, ingenious motorists were able to get around this by dropping moth balls into their gas tanks at the ratio of three to the gallon."

VICTORY GARDENS

Because the government rationed many foods, labor and transportation shortages made it hard to harvest and transport fruits and vegetables to market, the government encouraged citizens to plant "Victory Gardens" to help prevent food shortages. They wanted individuals to provide their own fruits and vegetables. Nearly 20 million Americans planted gardens in backyards and empty lots. Neighbors pooled their resources, planted different kinds of foods, and formed cooperatives.

By 1944, Victory Gardens were responsible for producing 40% of all vegetables grown in the United States. Collectively, more than one million tons of vegetables were grown in Victory Gardens during the war.

Farm families around Eagle Pass and Quemado had been planting gardens and preserving produce for generations. Now in the name of patriotism, their urban cousins followed suit.

OTHER COMMUNITY INVOLVEMENT

THE RIO GRANDE COMMANDOS

In 1941, Texas Congress authorized the Texas Defense Guard, a civilian army. The name was changed to the Texas State Guard in May 1943. The Handbook of Texas stated that The Texas State Guard organized 50 battalions throughout Texas, including Eagle Pass, "to protect public utilities, transportation arteries, and war plants; to maintain law and order; to suppress subversive activities; and to repel invasion if necessary." The state, counties, and cities of Texas, as well as individuals and civic clubs, supported the Guard. The "Commander-in-Chief" was the governor of Texas, while the administrative head was Adjutant-General, who was appointed by the Governor. At the beginning of the war, men aged 18 to 60 were eligible to volunteer to serve in the Guard for a term of three years. Later, the minimum age for service was dropped to 16 years, with parental consent. All members, except for enlisted soldiers, were unpaid volunteers.

Maverick County had a contingent of 76 men of all ages, which formed "Company E" of the 20th Battalion, later dubbed "The Rio Grande Commandos." WWI veterans, P.L. Harper, J.D. Plumb, and T.J. Jones, organized the civilian army. Harper was commissioned as captain. Plumb was commissioned as 1st Lieutenant, and Jones as 2nd Lieutenant. On July 10, 1942, Company E was officially recognized by the State Adjutant-General. Captain Harper's daughter, Nina Louise Harper from the Chamber of Commerce, began to recruit men.

Every Tuesday night, at an open field near Eagle Pass High school, The Commandos were trained by SGT R.W. Brown and Corporal William Garrett from EPAAF. According to The Guide, "at the beginning, there was some laughing and sarcasm at the unit, but it quickly became an organized, close knit drill unit."

The Commandos of the Rio Grande at attention with their wooden rifles
(Picture courtesy of the Eagle Pass News Guide)

NON-COMMISSIONED OFFICERS:

First Sergeant Bruce Thomson
Supply Sergeant Fred Thompson
Mess Sergeant H.A. Seymour
Platoon Sergeant C. M. Benavides
Platoon Sergeant Fred F. Weyrich
Sergeant William Lyall
Sergeant Donald Southall
Company Clerk A. Boubel

Corporal F. G. Aldridge,
Corporal Armando Antchagno
H. T. Dickson
Manuel Nieto
Archie D. Prestridge
George W. Stephenson

PRIVATES:

Juan C. Alvarado
E.J. Baron
Charles Backus
J.A. "Dudey" Bonnet
R.A. Braithwaite
W. H. "Billy" Brown
Enrique F. Cortinas
W.C. Butler, Jr.
Daniel Valentin
Homero A. de los Santos
Marciano F. Dovalina
Andrew H. Evans
Juan Daniel Flores
Walter O. Fitch
Alejandro C. Flores
Douglas J. Fletcher
Robert L. Forche
J. E. Funderburk
Jones G. Galan
O.C. Gilliland
T. H. Gonzalez
Ted Greenberg (later joined the Army)
Arnulfo C. Guedea
C.F. Hedrick
Calvin C. Huffman
S. Lloyd Jeffers
George A. Koudsi
James G. Lane

William Lyall
Rodolfo L. Marquez
William Masters, Jr.
Pete Mathiwos
O. D. Montgomery
Van Haile McFarland
Nandor Neuman
Manuel Nieto
Bill J. O'Leary
Antonio R. Pena
Hawley M. Pettit
Albert Riskind
Morris S. Riskind
Joe C. Rivas
Jose M. Rodriquez (later joined the Navy)
Leonel C. Rodriguez
Bruno Salazar
Plutarco B. Sanchez (later joined the Navy)
Emanuel Schwartz
Clayton B. Shofner
Earl Buell Shofner (later joined the Army)
Earl E. Stephenson
Harold D. Stewart
J. M. Watson
Harold C. Wood
Thomas A. Wilson
Edward Wueste
Leo M. Wueste

WOMEN'S MOTOR CORP (WMC)

The Women's Motor Corp (WMC) was a service organization designed to support benevolent, charitable, patriotic, and educational undertaking. The goal was to have an organized, trained group of women available and willing to act on behalf of our National Defense for any disaster. WMC organized and maintained emergency First Aid Stations for the benefit of the populace of Eagle Pass and lent aid and assistance to the personnel of the Advanced Flying School stationed at EPAAF. Mrs. Ben Spiegel, while attending a program given by the local chapter of the American Association of University Women, heard Mr. Conger Jones discussing the activities of the Women's Motor Corp of Texas. She didn't wait for someone else to bring this organization to Eagle Pass. Instead, Mrs. Spiegel visited the state offices in San Antonio, learned how to organize a local unit, and appealed to the civic-minded women of Eagle Pass to assist her in the task of creating a local chapter. The first meeting was held on May 19, 1942. Twenty-eight officers were elected and the local unit was organized. (Eagle Pass News Guide)

THE OFFICERS OF WOMEN'S MOTOR CORP

Commanding Officer and Chairman of Board of Directors: Mrs. Ben Spiegel
Executive Officer: Mary Reed Simpson
Recording and Corresponding Secretary: Miss Cecil Scarborough
Finance Officer: Mrs. Ward Wueste
Public Relations and Publicity Officer: Mrs. David Davies
Assistant Publicity Officer: Miss Rosella Riskind

Other charter members included:

Mrs. R.F. Abbot	Mrs. Leo Wueste
Mrs. William Boyd	Mrs. Kathleen Stanley
Mrs. A.V. Bonnet	Nellie May Glass
Mrs. Ernest Clark	Florence Neale
Mrs. Max Grossenbacher	Evelyn Perry
Mrs. Horace Hardt	Maria Riddle
Mrs. Bernice Hyatt	Rita Rodriguez
Mrs. William Lyall	Grace Scarbourgh
Mrs. Marvin Melson	Mary Williams
Mrs. John Sanford Jr.	Alma Pat Zeller
Mrs. Fred Weyrich	

Members who later joined:

Mrs. John Buckley Frances Robertson
Mrs. E.H. Schmidt Sr.
Frances Small
Eddie Wueste
Sybil Brown
L.P. Beck
Mary Backus Lopez
Vera de Leon

Virginia Nourse
Emma Cortinas
Josephine Rodriguez
Cynthia Lee
Mercedes Galan
Mary Jean Gunnarson (Joined the Navy WAVES)

Women who had a genuine interest in assisting, but were unable to actively participate in all of its phases became "honorary" members or "sponsors." Honorary members and sponsors:

Mrs. A.H. Evans
Mrs. W.A. Hewatt
Mrs. George Hollis
Mrs. O.C. Meyer
Mrs. John Sanford
Mrs. S.P. Simpson

Mrs. F.O. Weprich
Mrs. Roswell Vaughan
Mrs. Thomas Franks
Mrs. C.O. Ostrom
Mrs. Dena Kelso Graves
Mrs. F.L. Norris

As the membership list grew, the Women's Motor Corps began sponsoring a number of worthy projects and entertainments. First of these being the Army Emergency Relief Show, "Sound Off," presented by the 112th Cavalry Band of Fort Clark. Aware of the need for First Aid Stations in Eagle Pass, the organizations voted to equip stations using its own donations. According to the Eagle Pass News Guide, July 1943: 10,000 surgical dressings, made by 62 Eagle Pass women, were sent to the medical depot in Pueblo, Colorado. They spent more than 521 hours making the surgical dressings. Another project was to obtain every piece of scrap metal in Maverick County and sent it to the U.S. Army.

Mrs. Rosalie Spiegel

Women's Motor Corp standing at attention

EAGLE PASS FIRE DEPARTMENT

Eagle Pass' Volunteer Fire Department was the nucleus of Eagle Pass' Defense Organization of World War II. Even before the war broke out, this group of citizen-firemen were preparing for any eventuality. Selected members already had taken special courses from Texas A&M College in basic and advanced First Aid, methods of controlling inflammable bombs, clearing danger zones, and organizing auxiliary firing squads. Because most the physicians of the country were being called to military service, it was imperative that at least one person in every home should know First Aid, so that in the case of an accident or war injury, life can be maintained until a doctor arrives. Through the combined solicitation of the Woman's Motor Corps and the Fire Department, the city's first Emergency First Aid Station, complete with two fire trucks, stretchers, bandages, and medicines, was set up at the Fire Hall. (The Special Victory Edition of the Guide)

Discrimination & Racism

EAGLE PASS

Decorated soldier, Rodolfo Reyes, recounted a story of when he played basketball at Eagle Pass High School before the war. The team played against another basketball team from Sabinal, Texas. After the game, the team went to eat hamburgers at a restaurant in Sabinal. Before they ordered, the owner told the captain of the team, Richmond Harper, that Reyes would have to eat outside the restaurant because he was "Mexican." Reyes told Harper that it would be okay and that he will eat in the car. Harper immediately told the owner that "we will all go in or no one will go in."

After the war, Reyes visited the same restaurant in Sabinal. Dressed in full military uniform, complete with a Purple Heart Medal, the owner of the restaurant still refused his entry.

INTERNMENT CAMP

Internment Camps were a huge injustice in American history. Americans, out of fear, condemned groups of people because of their heritage. Japanese, Italians, and Germans were forced to leave their homes and live in internment camps for the sake of public safety. The Immigration and Naturalization Service (INS), under the authority of Department of Justice, operated over 20 camps, three of which were located in Texas-Seagoville, Kennedy, and Crystal City.

As of January 1941, all "Enemy Aliens" were required to register at local post offices, where they were fingerprinted, photographed, and required to carry photo-bearing "Enemy Alien Registration Cards" at all times. When Japan bombed Pearl Harbor on December 7, 1941, the FBI began arresting "Enemy Aliens" currently residing in America. Over 127,000 United States citizens were imprisoned during World War II. Their crime? Being of Japanese, German, and Italian ancestry.

The United States went beyond their borders. Around 3,000 Japanese, Germans, and Italians, residing in 12 different Latin-American countries, were turned over to United States authorities and placed in Texas camps. Seventy percent of the prisoners from Peru were of Japanese heritage. The official reason for their deportations was to secure the Western Hemisphere from internal sabotage and to provide bartering pawns to use in exchange of Americans captured by Japan.

However, most Axis nationals were deported as a result of racial prejudice, not because of actual security threats.

CRYSTAL CITY INTERNMENT CAMP
(Approximately 30 miles from Eagle Pass)

In the fall of 1942, on the outskirts of Crystal City, the INS acquired a piece of the migratory farmworker's camp from the Farm Security Administration. The INS spent more than $1M to construct more than 500 buildings. The INS faced an increasing number of requests from those volunteering to be interned to stay with their spouses. Crystal City Family Internment Camp was the only INS camp established specifically for families. Housing was built, surrounded by a 10-foot tall, barbed wire fence. It contained six guard towers, one located on each corner and two located half-way down the west-to-east side. Armed guards patrolled the fence line and an internal security force patrolled the Japanese and German sections of camp.

On December 12, 1942, the camp's first internees to arrive were German-Americans and German "Enemy Aliens." Soon after, in February 1943, Germans who were deported from Costa Rica arrived. On March 17, 1943 Japanese-American internees began to arrive. The Crystal City Family Internment Camp, consisting of Issei (first generation) Japanese immigrants, Nisei (second generation) Japanese-Americans, German-Americans, German nationals, Italian nationals, Latin Japanese, and a small group of Indonesian sailors. The population of the Crystal City camp peaked at 3,326 in May 1945. Languages spoken at Crystal City included Japanese, German, Italian, Spanish, and English, while the ages of the internees ranged from newborn to elderly.

Within the fenced compound, the INS granted internees a considerable degree of freedom. In part, to demonstrate to an outside observer that it adhered to international laws and protocols.

The INS divided internee activities into three categories:

The first was continuing education, such as "hobby shops" for men and "home economics"— cooking, sewing, flower arrangement, and rug weaving, for women. The camp also offered courses in agriculture, accounting, English, German, Japanese, Spanish, and French languages.

The second category concerned maintenance work, for which the INS paid internees 10 cents an hour up to a maximum of $4 per week. This payment was due to the Third Geneva Convention– Relative to the Treatment of Prisoners of War (1929), which stipulated that no internee had to perform manual labor against their will. These activities included laundry, carpentry, shoe repair, garbage collection, and ice and milk delivery. According to Historian John Stockley, several Japanese internees from Crystal City who were skilled in carpentry, helped build the Border Patrol office building and three houses for Border Patrol agents in Quemado.

The third category concerned communal recreation such as board games, boy and girl scouts, a swimming pool, and athletics like soccer, baseball, football, basketball, tennis, ping pong, and wrestling.

One of most beneficial programs established was an accredited education program. Robert Clyde "Cy" Tate, supervisor of the camp's school system, established three types of schools: the American (Federal) School, the Japanese School, and the German School. Each school provided an elementary, junior high, and high school education. Japanese and German internees supplied teachers for their schools, and the teachers designed their own curriculum, which included teaching students about their ancestral cultures and languages. In truth, however, the camp was hardly an ideal place for children. The U.S. government assumed responsibility for providing a primary and secondary school education, in accordance with the Texas state curriculum, but provided little or no funds for textbooks or teachers. While the children of internees could reasonably expect to keep up with their grade-level peers, they lacked the resources necessary to succeed.

The INS furnished internees with "camp money" and "ration points" that were used to purchase items from the canteen. Although the camp's Supply Division procured and distributed outside supplies, materials, and equipment, the camp also produced goods from within, utilizing the manpower of its captive population. The Japanese bought seeds and fertilizer from the canteen and cultivated small gardens, where they grew leafy greens, peppers, tomatoes, eggplants, beets, and radishes. There was also a 4.2 acres citrus orchard with beehives throughout the orchard.

At times, the INS relied on internees to manufacture the goods that it could not obtain due to wartime shortages. After May 1943, for example, internees engaged in a "sewing project" that yielded more than 20,000 articles of clothing and other linens, including shirts, blouses, pants, suits, dresses, coats, shower curtains, mattress covers, sheets, and pillow cases. The internees also produced uniforms for nurse's aides, aprons for assistants in the hospital clinic, and sanitary face masks.

This information was obtained from the Texas Historical Commission. The internment camp was officially closed on February 11, 1948, 3 years after the end of WWII. There were no reported escape attempts.

PIEDRAS NEGRAS

On July 20, 1942, 73 Japanese families living in Piedras Negras, Sabinas, Nava and Nueva Rosita, Coahuila, were deported to Mexico City for internment. Authorities in Piedras Negras pointed out that the move was merely precautionary and no charges were filed against the deportees. Many of the deportees were long-time residents of the border and had Mexican spouses. Special permission was granted to four Japanese businessmen that stipulated that, as long as they did not live near the border of United States and Mexico, they did not have to move to an Internment Camp. (The Guide July 30, 1942)

In 1988, in an attempt to apologize for the internment of innocent citizens, surviving internees were given $20,000 in reparations. While American concentration camps never reached the levels of evil as those of Nazi death camps, they remain a dark mark on the nation's record of respecting civil liberties and cultural differences.

PRISONER OF WAR CAMPS

FORT CLARK POW CAMP
(30 Miles from Eagle Pass)

After the United States entered World War II in 1941, the Government of the United Kingdom requested American help with housing prisoners-of-war due to a housing shortage in Great Britain. The United States agreed to house them, even though the United States was not prepared to do so. Liberty Ships returning home, that would otherwise be empty, contained as many as 30,000 prisoners arriving monthly. The Office of the Provost Marshal General (OPMG) supervised 425,000 German prisoners. They were housed in over 700 camps in 46 states.

Texas had twice as many prisoner-of-war camps as any other state. Twenty-one permanent prisoner base camps were located on military installations. Over twenty temporary branch camps were constructed throughout the state. More than 45,000 German, Italian, and Japanese prisoners were interned in Texas from 1942 to 1945. As the war continued, a policy of maximum utilization replaced a policy of maximum security of the prisoners, which resulted in the use of over 27,000 prisoners in numerous agricultural tasks, such as picking cotton, pulling corn, and harvesting rice. The prisoners were well treated, and very few escape attempts occurred from the Texas camps. After the war almost all prisoners were returned to their native countries, and many expressed their desire to return to Texas. A German POW sub-camp was located at Fort Clark in Brackettville, Texas.

EAGLE PASS AND POWS

Many times my Grandmother, Ellen K. Schwartz told me that during the war a man came to her back door at her house on Second Street (and Ceylon) in Eagle Pass begging for food. My Grandmother felt sorry for this man and was shocked when this man started speaking German to her. My Grandmother was from Austria/Hungary and spoke fluent German. She fed the man and then he went on his way. I never gave this story much thought as to the truth of it, but while researching this book, I came across an article from the Eagle Pass News Guide that described how an escaped German prisoner-of-war from an Oklahoma POW camp was caught in Eagle Pass trying to make his way to Mexico.

Could this be the same German POW in my Grandmother story? The irony of this story is that my Grandmother was Jewish and many of her family were killed in the Holocaust.

GERMAN SPIES

Mrs. Rosalie Shannon said that during WWII she knew a German family that lived in northern Mexico and owned a large ranch. The family socialized with people in Eagle Pass and Piedras Negras. One day the FBI came and arrested the whole family as German spies.

Escaped German Prisoner Captured Here

Edward Tillman Henrich Kiefer, 29, escaped German prisoner from Alba, Oklahoma Camp, was captured Friday at nine o'clock A. M. by John Chamberlain, Senior Patrol Inspector.

The German prisoner was captured near the International Bridge.

News clipping from The Guide dated 8/24/1944

THE HOLOCAUST AND MAVERICK COUNTY

*"In Germany, they came first for the Communists
And I didn't speak up because I wasn't a Communist.
And then they came for the trade unionists
And I didn't speak up because I wasn't a trade unionist.
And then they came for the Jews
And I didn't speak up because I wasn't a Jew.
And then they came for me...
And by that time there was no one left to speak up."*

—Paster Martin Niemoller, a German Christian (1946)

BACKGROUND

Many events of the 1920's and 1930's collided together to form a "perfect storm" that would greatly affect the entire world. The world-wide depression, the perception of many countries that the Versailles Treaty was unfair, German Nationalism, the underlying anti-Semitism of Europeans and their need for scapegoats, led to one of the greatest human injustices the world has ever known commonly referred to as The Holocaust.

The Holocaust was perpetrated by the Nazis and their collaborators between 1933 and 1945. It was a state-sponsored, systematic murder of over six million Jews. In addition, approximately five million Slavs, Gypsys, Jehovah's Witnesses, homosexuals, political and religious dissidents, as well as disabled individuals, were also intentionally exterminated by the Nazis. This systematic annihilation of human life, which we now refer to as "genocide," was coined by Raphael Lemkin, a Polish-Jewish lawyer, seeking to describe the Nazi's policies. By combining "geno," from the Greek word for "race" or "tribe," and "cide," derived from the Latin word "killing," Lemkin created this term that is widely understand today.

Adolph Hitler, along with his Nazi Party followers, did not care to look for solutions to their problems within Germany, but instead sought outside groups to blame for their social and economic problems. They felt that the extermination of Jews was justified because Jews were not only a 'low' and 'evil' race, but also had a negative impact on the social fabric of German society. They believed that as the "pure race," it was their right and obligation to get rid of all Jews and other "undesirables." His agenda included plans to expel the Jewish populace, whom he declared his mortal enemy. Between 1933 and 1939, to encourage Jewish families to leave Europe, more than 1,400 anti-Jewish laws were enacted. These laws were aimed to systematically isolate Jews from society and drive them out of the country. Some of these laws removed Jews from government service, from becoming attorneys, tax consultants, or veterinarians. Laws forbade Jews from attending public schools. It also limited their attendance to universities and other places of higher education.

In 1935, the Nazi Party introduced a supplementary decree defining who was to be considered a "Jew." The Nuremberg Laws of 1935 did not define a "Jew" as someone of the Jewish religion, but anyone who had three or four Jewish grandparents, regardless of whether that individual identified himself or herself as a Jew or belonged to the Jewish religious community. Many Germans who had not practiced Judaism for years, found themselves caught in the grip of Nazi terror. Even people with Jewish grandparents who had converted to Christianity were defined as Jews. There were two laws at the annual Nuremberg Rally with the idea of "protecting German blood and honor." The Nuremberg Laws forbade marriages or extramarital intercourse between Germans and Jews and employment of German females under 45, as domestic servants. The laws also declared that only those of German blood were eligible for German citizenship, all others were forbidden to display the German flag.

The destruction of European Jewish communities was not a new concept. It actually began during World War I. The tentacles of discrimination reached beyond the borders of Nazi Germany and into other European countries. The average Jew found themselves trapped between the White and Red Armies during the Russian civil war of 1918-1920. The White Army (anti-Bolshevik Russian) perceived that communism was pro-Jewish. They ransacked, pillaged, and decimated entire Jewish villages, confiscated personal possessions, and slaughtered approximately 75,000 to 100,000 people. The Red Army (Communists Russian) eventually defeated the White Army and regained power and control over Russian society. They quickly established a bureau operated by pro-Communist loyalists called Yevsektsia. The bureau's purpose was to destroy any and all religious activity among the Jewish people. All religious practices, customs, and observances of Jewish traditions and laws were banned and synagogues closed.

In Poland, during the same period, Jews were blamed for the decaying Polish economy. The Polish government passed legislation against Jews, banning their employment in the liquor, textile, and tobacco industries. This created significant financial hardships for Jews whose livelihood depended on these industries. Jewish entrepreneurs, who traditionally closed their shops on Saturdays in observance of the Sabbath, were forbidden from re-opening on Sundays. This forced many business owners to go bankrupt. In addition, Polish government further imposed heavy taxes on all food and items considered "Jewish." For example, kosher meats were banned for consumption. These harsh sanctions against the Jewish community caused the mass unemployment of thousands of Polish Jews.

In Germany, Aryan supremacy, the mindset that German whites were the master race, refused to admit defeat in the First World War. Once again, Jews were blamed. From 1920-1933, intermarriage between Jews and non-Jews reached new heights. A large proportion of Jews defected and married non-Jews, abandoning traditional marriage laws and teachings in an attempt to blend with German society. When the Nazi Regime came into power in 1933, over nine million Jews lived in every country throughout Europe, comprising of 1.7% of the total European population. European Jews could be found in all walks of life. They were scientists, Word War I veterans, doctors, teachers, accountants, seamstresses, small business owners, etc.

Between 1901 and 1933, 38 German citizens won the Nobel Prize, more than any other nation. Eleven of the 38 Nobel Prize winners were Jewish. In 1921, one of the most notable recipients of the Nobel Prize, Albert Einstein, won the prize for his contribution in Physics. While Einstein was visiting the United States in 1933, Hitler was elected Chancellor of Germany. Due to this event and for political reasons, Einstein renounced his German citizenship, taking the position of Professor of Theoretical Physics at Princeton University. He became a citizen of the United States in 1940. After Japan bombed Pearl Harbor, he sent a letter to President Roosevelt, alerting him of the potential development of an extremely powerful, nuclear bomb in Germany. Professor Einstein recommended the U.S. begin similar research. This eventually led to the Manhattan Project and the development of the atomic bomb.

As stated in the New York Times on February 10, 2002, "Some of the best German physicists were Jewish and had been driven into exile, where many continued their work with the American or British atomic bomb programs. Nazi ideology had only scorn for "Jewish physics" and thus undervalued what theoretical physicists could contribute to the war effort." With a significant number of scientists leaving the atomic bomb program in Germany, this left the German team at a significant disadvantage.

From 1920 to 1924 almost a million Jews left Russia and Western Europe. About 60% came to the United States, 25% went to Palestine and the rest to various regions of the world. In 1926, the United States closed its doors and made it more difficult for Jews from Eastern Europe to enter. As a result, the percentages flip-flopped. From 1926 to 1929 about two out of every three Jews who emigrated went to Palestine (about 350,000, compared to 185,000 to the United States). By 1929, Jews could no longer enter Palestine. From 1933 and beyond, place of refuge were almost completely cut off. The frustrations of European Jews quickly reached a boiling point.

An agreement called the Haavara Agreement between the German Zionist Federation, the Jewish Agency, and the German Finance Ministry; allowed 60,000 German Jews to immigrate to Palestine between 1933 and 1939. Representatives from 32 countries met in 1938, to discuss the growing refugee problem of Europe's expelled Jews. Governments all over the world gave excuses as to why their countries could not allow refugees. Only the Dominican Republic offered to give refuge to over 100,000 Jews, but their relief agencies were so overwhelmed that very few actually immigrated. With virtually nowhere to go, scores of Jews remained in Europe with the hopes that the worst was behind them, clearly unaware of the horror to come.

THE FINAL SOLUTION

At the beginning of World War II, after Germany invaded Poland on September 1, 1939, Hitler's determination to find the "Final Solution" escalated. The Germans established temporary ghettos as a provisional measure to control and segregate Jews while Nazi leadership in Berlin deliberated options for their goal of removing the Jewish population. Some ghettos existed for only a few days, others for months, or even years. There were over 400 ghettos established in Europe. In the initial stages, the Nazis forced Jews into ghettos, where they were put to work for the German war industry. They also activated a policy of planned, indirect annihilation by denying them basic means of survival, such as adequate food and shelter.

Before WWII, Warsaw was a major center of Jewish life and culture in Poland. Out of the city's 1.3 million inhabitants, more than 350,000 or 30% of the city's total population, was Jewish. After Germany's invasion of Poland, German officials ordered Poland to establish a ghetto in Warsaw. German authorities required all Jewish residents of Warsaw to move into this designated area, 1.3 square miles with an average of 7.2 persons per room, which was sealed off from the rest of the city. Enclosed by a wall over 10 feet high and topped with barbed wire, the Warsaw ghetto was closely guarded to prevent access to the rest of the city. Its population grew to over 400,000, due to the forced relocation of Jews from surrounding towns. About 1% of the population died monthly from maltreatment, disease, starvation, and exhaustion.

After the German army invaded the Soviet Union on June 22, 1941, a new stage of the Holocaust began. Under the cover of war and confidence of victory, Germans turned from the forced emigration and imprisonment of Jews, to mass murder. At first, men, women, and children were rounded up and shot over mass graves by firing squads called "mobile killing unit." Because shooting by firing squads were inefficient and deemed "too personal" for the Nazi killers, special camps were constructed. By 1942, six large extermination camps had been established by the Nazis, which were built solely for the purpose of mass killing. In December of 1942, the Nazi regime introduced a new method of mass murder: gas. The camps, referred to as "concentration camps" served three purposes:

1) to incarcerate real and perceived enemies of the Nazi regime

2) to have a steady supply of forced laborers to work in the coal mines, stone quarries, fisheries, and war-related production of equipment and

3) to physically eliminate targeted groups of the population

Death was determined by the SS (an elite organization within the Nazi party that served as Hitler's personal guard and Special Forces, overseeing concentration camps). Massive deportations of Jews to concentration and death camps continued until the summer of 1944. By that time, almost all of the ghettos had been liquidated.

At these concentration camps, camp doctors would select individuals who were deemed fit to work at the slave labor camps. Prisoners selected for forced labor were registered and tattooed with identification numbers on their left arms. Those not selected were taken directly to gas chambers, where they would die within 20 minutes. Those taken to the slave labor camps would be worked to death or until physical exhaustion, then shot or gassed.

At the infamous Auschwitz-Birkenau concentration camp, SS physicians, in the name of pseudoscientific research, carried out medical experiments on infants, twins, dwarfs, and even performed forced sterilizations and castrations of many adults. The estimates of the numbers of victims at Auschwitz between 1940 and 1945 were as follows: Jews (1,095,000 deported to Auschwitz, of whom 960,000 died); Poles (147,000 deported, of whom 74,000 died); Gypsies (23,000 deported, of whom 21,000 died); Soviet prisoners of war (15,000 deported and died); and other nationalities (25,000 deported, of whom 12,000 died).

SAM SCHWARTZ STORY

Adolf Schwartz, the first person to leave Hungary from the Schwartz family, immigrated to El Paso, Texas in 1886. His entrepreneurial spirit prompted him to open a department store known as, The Popular. In the early 1900's, he sponsored the immigration of his nephews, Maurice, Nandor, Manny, and Sam, to assist him in the operation of the family business. In 1910, Sam Schwartz relocated to Eagle Pass, Texas. In 1915, he opened and operated a movie theater, known as the Aztec Theater, in downtown Eagle Pass. Soon thereafter, his brother, Manny Schwartz, followed suit and joined Sam in Eagle Pass.

In 1939, Nandor Schwartz visited family in Hungary. Nandor was appalled at the anti-Semitic political storm that was brewing in Hungary and alerted his family in the United States. Nandor recommended that immediate action be taken to remove the family from Europe. At this time there were 117 family members still residing in Europe.

The United States passed The National Origins Act of 1924, which severely limited the number of visas for Eastern European immigrants. The family from Europe, Eagle Pass and El Paso decided on a plan to determine who would be the first to leave Europe for the United States. Due to the restrictive immigration laws, only a few of the 117 could immigrate. The decision was made to send for the children first. In retrospect, this fateful decision determined who would live and who would die.

Two of Sam's nephews, Nandor and Marcus Neuman, who were sons of Sam's sister, Hannah, came to the United States relatively easily. They lived with Sam and Manny in Eagle Pass. Marcus Neuman, subsequently served in the United States Army during WWII.

Mayer, Max, Leo, and Sam (sons of Sam's brother, Herman Schwartz) and Laszlo Schwartz (son of Sam's brother, Salomon) came next. But, it was impossible to bring them to the United States because of the restriction of the number of European visas issued. A decision was made by the family to bring the boys to Ciudad Juarez, Mexico, the city across the border from El Paso, Texas. Through the political influence of a local Congressman, the help of two U.S. Senators of

Texas, and Mexican lawyers, the boys finally obtained transit visas at the American Consulate in Genoa, Italy. They were allowed passage on an Italian ocean liner to New York City, then rode a train to Juarez, Mexico via Chicago and El Paso. A letter dated March 6, 1940 from Nandor Schwartz in El Paso, Texas to his brother, Emanuel "Manny" Schwartz in Eagle Pass, Texas described the trouble of obtaining the transit visas: "We had a cable from Miskolc, Monday, in which they advise that the American Consul had refused transit visas for all boys and that only small freighters go from Italy to Mexico… We got in touch with the State Department through Congressman R. E. Thomason. Maurice (Schwartz) cabled the American Consul of Genoa, Italy, stating that he was willing to put up any class and amount of bond the boys might require, to insure the boys won't remain in the United States, but will leave for Mexico in due time." After this letter, the American Consulate issued transit visas in April 1940. The Hungarian visa quota was filled, however; since their parents were born in Czechoslovakia, they were granted visas under the Czechoslovakia quota. The Schwartz family rented a house in Ciudad Juarez, Mexico. "Uncle" Nandor Schwartz moved to Mexico to take care of the five boys. Every day, "Uncle" Nandor drove the boys to school across the river into El Paso, Texas so that they could attend school in the United States. After the war, the boys finally immigrated to the United States.

THE SCHWARTZ FAMILY

When the Nazis invaded Hungary in April 1944, the fate of the Schwartz family in Europe was sealed. Between late April and early July 1944, approximately 440,000 Hungarian Jews were deported and around 426,000 of them were sent to the Auschwitz-Birkenau concentration camps. Of these 426,000, approximately 110,000 were sent to the forced labor section of Auschwitz with the remaining 320,000 of them sent directly to the gas chambers, to include almost all remaining members of the Schwartz family.

Two of the family members, Frank and Otto Klein, twin sons of Sam's sister, Lili and her husband, Salomon became "experiments" of the infamous Dr. Joseph Mengele, a SS physician. On November 19, 1984, the El Paso Times wrote an article about the survivors in El Paso of the Holocaust and interviewed Frank Klein. Frank said in the interview "*My whole life was changed that morning of June 24, 1944, when my mother, sister, aunt, twin brother, Otto, and I were put in the cattle car to Auschwitz. I was 12 years old and didn't understand what the barbed wire and the smoking chimneys were all about when we arrived.*" Frank said, when asked to recall the experiments practiced on Jewish children, "*I have tried to blot all of that out. All I remember are the constant needles and drawing of blood from head to toe, the nights of fever and pain.*" He said that he had been scarred permanently— physically and emotionally—by the experience. He continued to suffer from the nightmares and depression that brought on an emotional breakdown until his death.

After the war, sponsored by his uncle, Maurice Schwartz from El Paso, Frank immigrated to the United States. He subsequently served in the U.S. Army during the Korean War. Otto was not permitted into the U.S. because he had contracted tuberculosis in Auschwitz. Otto settled in Geneva, Switzerland. Agnes, their sister, also survived and settled in El Paso. Their mother was a victim of Auschwitz's horrific gas chambers. Their father was liberated by the British from a labor camp, but died shortly afterwards.

DO YOU HAVE AN UNCLE SAM?

Five other Schwartz family members, the Preisz sisters, (daughters of Sam Schwartz's sister Erzebet and her husband Adolf), were selected to work in the labor camp near Neidergrenzebach, Germany.

Rabbi Floyd S. Fierman described in his book "Schwartz Family of El Paso" how the Preisz sisters survived the Holocaust. "The five of them protected each other throughout the whole sordid experience. When one of them was sick, the others would work her shift. When one was ill and needed sustenance (what little they got was mostly water, soup with a piece of potato once in a while), they would give the sick sister their share. They courageously clung together and helped each other survive."

After the concentration camps were liberated in 1945, thousands of people who had been starved, beaten, and worked to exhaustion, died within their first week of freedom. In Dachau, the daily death toll following liberation was 200, in Bergen-Belsen it was 300. Some who were liberated from concentration camps died from overeating sweets and chocolate provided by friendly soldiers.

The labor camp near Neidergrenzebach, Germany was liberated in early April 1945. The Preisz sisters asked a U.S. Army sergeant if he knew their Uncle Maurice in El Paso, Texas. The sergeant wrote a cable gram to Maurice Schwartz, who in turn sent a cable gram to his son, Captain Albert Schwartz, who was a Company Commander with the 104th Timberwolf Infantry Division headquartered near the town Delizsch, Germany. Maurice told his son of his cousins' situation and whereabouts. The U.S. Army was at a halt. For political reasons, it was determined that the Russian army was allowed to take over Berlin. During this halt, Albert requested a three day leave, a jeep, an interpreter who spoke German, and a trailer with supplies of soap, K-rations, toilet paper, toothbrushes, toothpaste, etc. from Major General Terry de la Mesa Allen, Division Commander, to rescue his cousins. The leave was granted. Albert went to Neidergrenzebach and found that the military set up a kitchen to feed the survivors from the camp twice daily.

In the *"Schwartz Family of El Paso"* by Floyd S. Fierman, Southwestern Studies Monograph No. 61 1980, Albert said *"We pulled alongside this girl and asked where the inmates of the camp were, and she explained to us they were scattered in all directions. I told her I was looking for some Hungarian girls and asked if she knew the Preisz sisters, and she turned as white as a tablecloth and asked why I wanted to know. Being a hard-nosed GI in battle fatigues and under arms, I curtly suggested to her it was none of her business, it was enough that I just wanted to know. Obviously frightened, she told me she was one of the Preisz sisters, Alice. I told her I was her cousin, but, understandably, she did not believe me. It took me a long time to convince her. After asking if she had an Uncle Maurice in El Paso, Texas, she said "Yes," I asked if she had an Uncle Nandor. "Yes." "Do you have an Uncle Sam? "Yes" and on and on. Albert, then showed a photo of his father Maurice, with his son, Skipper, on his shoulders. Do you recognize this man? She burst into tears, and asked that I come with her to see her sisters.*

Alice took me to a stable behind a farm house. We climbed up a ladder, and on some clean hay and straw were her four sisters. They thought their living conditions were marvelous. To them, the hayloft was like heaven, soft, comfortable, and clean. It was late April, 1945, just before the end of hostilities. We talked for a long time, with the help of my interpreter. We spoke no Hungarian, so we spoke German and some Yiddish, and he knew some Polish and Czech; so, we were able to communicate fairly well. I was afraid Olga, the youngest, was pregnant, because her stomach was distended. All of their heads were shaven, but the hair was beginning to grow out, so they looked very boyish. It turned out that Olga wasn't pregnant. Their appearance may have kept them from being molested – it was near starvation that caused her stomach to distend... I didn't like where they were staying and told them I wanted to get them a more comfortable place... I evicted the Germans who were living in the (farm) house. They were moved to their barn, and "my" girls moved into the house."

The girls were eventually turned over to the Joint Distribution Committee in Paris, France. Under the sponsorship of their uncle, Maurice Schwartz, they came to the United States. The sisters moved to New York and Los Angeles with the help of their American family. Albert and the Preisz sisters became very close during their lifetimes and remained in constant contact with one another.

Their mother and three brothers perished at the concentration camp. Their father, imprisoned in the labor camp, decided to go back to Hungary after he was liberated.

After the war, the American Schwartz family received money under the Hungarian Reparation Act. The family set up a Schwartz Family Fund that included this money to help the survivors of the Holocaust with living expenses. This Fund remained active for many years after the war.

THE LIBERATORS

The following are stories of men from Maverick County who helped in the Liberation effort of the different concentration camps.

Tec5 Jesus Yzquierdo Story:

Tec5 Jesus Yzquierdo was a combat engineer in Company B, 271st, Engineer Combat Battalion, 71st Infantry Division, 3rd Army (commanded by General George S. Patton). His division crossed into Germany at the Siegfried Line and shortly thereafter, liberated the Sien labor concentration camp. He vividly remembers giving food and medical help to victims and burying the dead. After he returned to Eagle Pass, he suffered nightmares and flashbacks from the horrible scenes. He consulted Dr. Kaback to help him with the anxiety.

PFC Alejandro Herrera Story:

PFC Alejandro Herrera served in the Headquarters Company, 876th Aviation Engineer Battalion, 28th Infantry Division. He fought in the battles of Normandy, Northern France, Rhineland, and Central Europe. Herrera's nephew, Chief Tony Castaneda of the Eagle Pass Police Department, said, "My Uncle (Alejandro Herrera) developed a large lump around his neck. I took him to several doctors in San Antonio for treatment. We finally found a doctor who happened to be Jewish. During his first initial visit, the doctor saw a tattoo on my Uncle's upper torso. He inquired about it. My uncle, for the first time, started telling of his involvement in the war. My Uncle also mentioned that several members of his unit agreed to tattoo themselves as a reminder of what they had experienced and how lucky they had been to have survived the years of fighting. My Uncle mentioned that his unit liberated thousands of people from one death camp, mainly Jewish people. They remained there burying the dead, feeding the hungry and providing medical attention to almost all of them (children and adults). The doctor and I were so overcome with the tattoo experience that his doctor called another Jewish doctor and both doctors decided to operate on my Uncle at no cost. My Uncle was a gentleman and I could never muster enough strength for more information."

IN CONCLUSION

Of the nine millions Jews who lived in Europe before the Holocaust, an estimated 2/3 or 6 million were murdered. Another 5 million of "undesirables" were exterminated. This brought the Holocaust death toll to a staggering 11 million.

"Just because the Holocaust happened, does not mean it was inevitable. The Holocaust took place because individuals and nations made choices or decisions to act or not to act." *(Saho South African History Online. How and Why did the Holocaust happen?)*

THE SCHWARTZ FAMILY FROM HUNGARY

Schwartz Family before the war

Sam, Laszlo, Leo, Max Schwartz, along with Mitsu Preisz, a brother of the Preisz girls.
Mitsu, his two brothers, and his parents all were victims of the Nazi regime. The Picture was taken in Miskolc, Hungary about 1939.

The Klein Family

The Preisz sisters in Germany in 1945: Irene, Judith, Olga, Edit, Alice in a picture taken by Albert J. Schwartz after American liberation.

Captain Albert Schwartz in Cologne, Germany

List of missing persons in Europe relatives of the Schwartz Family in El Paso, Tex., U.S.

Family #1
My brother, Izidor Schwartz, about 70 years of age, pensioned teacher born in Czechoslovakia, his wife, Julia Markovics Schwartz about 54 years of age born in Czechoslovakia. Their last address was Levoska u 54, Presov, Czech. According to information received both of them were deported to Auschwitz, Silesia about 2½ years ago.

Family #2.
My brother Herman(Herschel) Schwarcz about 58 years of age, born in Czechoslovakia, his wife, Szeren Friedman Schwarcz about 48 years of age born in Czechoslovakia Hungary and their two children, Vera (girl) 18 years old and Isidor (boy) 15 years old. Both children were born in Miskolc, Hungary. All four of them were deported from Miskolc, Hungary to Auschwitz, Silesia in June 1944. Their last address was Hunyadi u 54, Miskolc Hungary.

Family #3
My sister,-in-law, Mrs. Salamon Schwarcz, whose maiden name was Saralta Reichman about 48 years of age, born in Hungary and two children, a boy, Sandor Elek (nicknamed Sanyi) 14 years of age and a girl Eva Magdolne (nicknamed Evike) 10 years old. Both children were born in Miskolc, Hungary. Their last address was Lichtenstein, Jozsef u 26, Miskolc Hungary. All three of them were deported from Miskolc, to Auschwitz in June 1944 and not heard from since. (The other members of this family my brother, Salamon Schwarcz and three children, Edith, Ervin and Imre are located and back in Miskolc)

Family #4
My sister, Mrs. Adolf Preisz, her maiden name, Elizabeth (Erzsi) Schwarcz about 43 years of age, born in Czechoslovakia and her three boys, Mayer (nicknamed Micu) 18, Lazar 14, and Martor (nicknamed Matyu) 11 years of age. My sister, Mrs Preisz, and the two younger boys were deported from Miskolc to Auschwitz in June 1944 and not heard from since. The oldest boy, Mayer remained in Hungary with a labor batalion at that time and was not heard from since. (The other members of this family, Mr. Adolf Preisz and five daughters, Iren, Alice, Judith, Edith and Olga are located. Mr. Preisz is back in Miskolc and the five girls in St. Maur France.

Family #5
My brother-in-law, Salamon Klein about 53 years of age, born in Hungary and his wife Lilly (maiden name Schwarcz) about 43 years of age, born in Czechoslovakia. Their last address was Hajduboszormeny, Hungary. According to information received Salamon Klein was taken away from Hajduboszormeny by the Germans and a letter was received from him from Vienna in November 1944. No further information about him since. His wife, my sister, Lilly, was deported with the Ghetto of Debrecen, Hungary to Auschwitz with three children in June 1944. The three children are located and are at presnet in Miskolc, Hungary with my brothers, but we have no information about my sister, Lilly.

Family #6
My brother-in-law, Dr. Miksa Silberman, about 47 years of age, born in Miskolc, Hungary his wife, my sister, Adel (maiden name Schwarcz) about 40 years of age born in Czechoslovakia and their little daughter Edith 13 years of age, born in Miskolc, Hungary Their last address was Szentpal ucca, Miskolc, Hungary. All three of them were deported to Auschwitz in June 1944 and not heard from since.

A document of Leo Schwartz discovered in his estate papers by his daughter, Annie. This was written by one of the Schwartz brothers.

END OF THE WAR AND BEYOND

END OF THE WAR

On August 14, 1945, Japan surrendered and the war was over. Vicki Maldonado, an 11 year-old girl, whose family lived across the street from San Juan Plaza, vividly remembers the end of the war. At that time, air conditioning wasn't available and all of the windows were open because of the August heat. Every radio on her block was blaring that the war was over. San Juan Plaza was soon crowded with what she thought was the whole town. Everyone cried for joy and was celebrating. It was a celebration like no other.

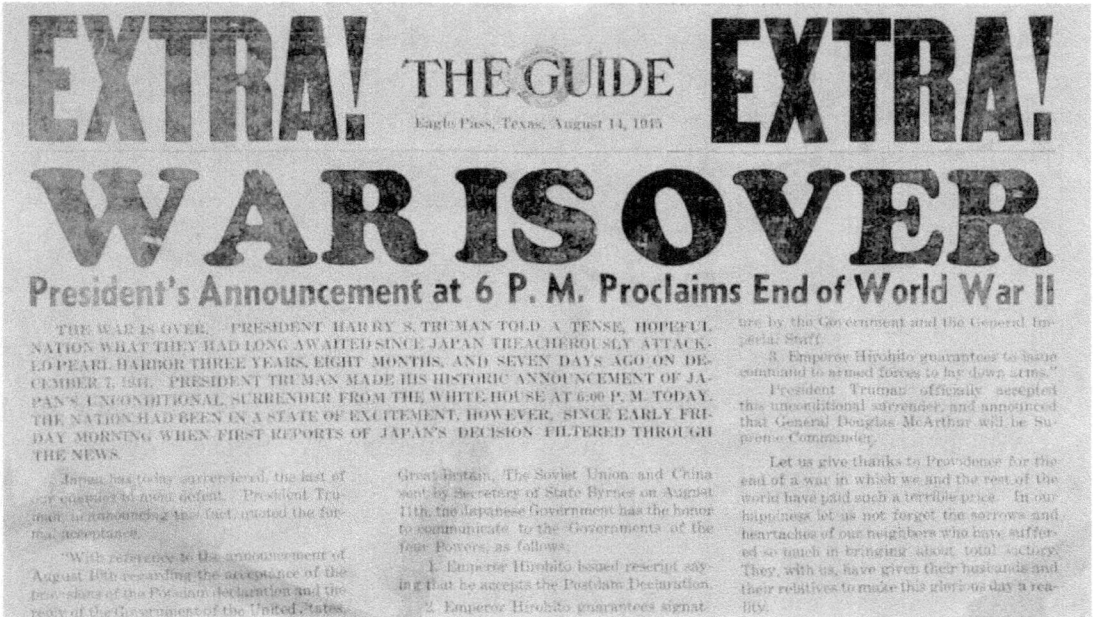

After the war, the economic, social, and political landscape of Maverick County changed forever. Economically, the city of Eagle Pass grew dramatically. The Great Depression had ended by the influx of spending during WWII. The employment rate rose in all areas. With the completion of Highway 57, Eagle Pass became a major gateway to Mexico, developing tourist trade, retail, international trade, and state and federal government jobs. By 1987, there were five industrial plants located in Eagle Pass and 19 in Piedras Negras, Southwest Texas Junior College from Uvalde and Sul Ross State University from Alpine opened up campuses in Eagle Pass.

There were many soldiers who married local Maverick county women and stayed in the Maverick County area such as my father Lloyd Munter. Many other soldiers married women from around the country and relocated to their hometowns. According to General Homer I. Lewis, soldiers would usually settle in their wives hometowns. Rodolfo Reyes, former sergeant, met his wife in a staging area in upstate New York before being transferred to the 8th Air Force in

England. After his tour in Europe, Reyes moved back to New York, where he married and lived the remainder of his adult life.

Soldiers came home to Eagle Pass with a new view of life-economically, culturally and politically. Since these veterans traveled to different parts of the world, they saw how different people lived and thought. In many letters that we have read of the soldiers who were stationed overseas, there was a new appreciation of home. This also explained their hopes and expectations. Many soldiers took advantage of the G.I. bill to further their education by going to college. Other veterans bought houses with the Veterans Administration Loans. Medical care was provided by the Veterans Administration.

Many WWII vets became politically involved. Pete Rossi, Jr., former Sergeant of WWII became the first Hispanic mayor, Raul Rodriguez became County Commissioner, and Dan McDuff became County Judge. Rick Harper, a son of WWII veteran Richmond Harper wrote in a book Rodriquez . . . Texas Ranger about the political changes after WWII. For the further analysis of this political shift in Maverick County, we suggest Rick Harpers book. This book stated that after WWII no politician could not be elected without the Hispanic vote in Maverick County and in south Texas.

Some soldiers came home wounded and sick, physically and psychologically. After WWII, Post-Traumatic Stress Disorder (PTSD) was not a psychological term, but many veterans came home with all the symptoms – nightmares, anxiety, insomnia, and depression. Lone Star Beer was the antidepressant of the time, bartenders and fellow veterans became counselors. Sgt. Manuel Sanchez, who came home from the war without a foot, opened a bar called "The Sunset" on Main Street. It was undoubtedly named after the beautiful sunsets that appear every evening at the far end of Main Street and trails off into the Rio Grande River. Soon it became a place where many WWII vets would come to relax and have a few beers. Rick "Bobo" Castro, son of Pvt. Enrique Castro told me those veterans who went through combat related with other veterans with similar experiences. It is ironic that another WWII veteran, Major William Shannon and Sgt. Sanchez were both part of the 15th Army air Force. They never met each other during the war, but their paths crossed in Eagle Pass.

The greatest tragedy of course was the sons of Maverick County that did not come home. In reading the letters of these soldiers before they died, we shed many tears because we knew that they gave the ultimate sacrifice and never made it home. These letters contained their dreams of the future and their concerns about their families.

ADVANCES FROM THE WAR

WWII affected the vets and their families, but also affects our lives today. Technology blossomed during WWII out of necessity. One necessity was called Operations Research (OR), a method using statistics and probability to help organize any organization, such as the logistic and deployment of soldiers. This technology also helped the Allies hunt German U-boats in the Atlantic. These methods are used today from booking air travel to scheduling the delivery of goods to retail stores. Radar was developed to track attacking bombers and to guide bombers to their targets. This technology was critical in development in digital computers, satellite communication and television. Electronic components, batteries and new plastics allowed soldiers on the front line to communicate with headquarters. This helped develop cell phones. The Colossus was the first electric programmable computer, developed by Tommy Flowers, to help the British code breakers read encrypted German messages in December 1943. During WWII, there were more deaths from diseases than weapons. Penicillin was developed during WWII and has helped people around the world fight bacterial infections. The Germans developed the first jet aircraft in July 1944 and in September 1944, German V-2 rockets began to attack London. This technology was the predecessor of the satellites and the rocket that landed on the moon. Semi-automatic rifles were first introduced. The nuclear bomb discovery changed how wars will be fought in the future.

The United States was changed forever by WWII. This war became a struggle for freedom and justice at home and abroad. Because of the veteran's bravery, the determination of the citizens of the United States to make the necessary sacrifices and fight for a goal to make this world a better place for their future generations, we salute this generation for our life, liberty and pursuit of happiness.

APPENDIX

ACKNOWLEDGMENTS

Six years ago, I had an idea to compile stories the World War II heroes of Maverick County, but I knew I couldn't do it alone and enlisted the help of my wife, Judy, who has taken my passion for this project and made it her own. During the process of writing this book many friends and individuals from Maverick County and other communities, have taken the time to help us with this venture. We would like to take this opportunity to give thanks to everyone who shared their knowledge, stories, time, support, and most of all, encouragement and belief in our ability to complete this project. This book would not have come to fruition without their support.

A special thank you goes out to my lifelong friend, Dan Riskind. Dan served as our audio visual engineer, who enthusiastically filmed hours of interviews and took countless numbers of photographs. He was instrumental in compiling these sources of media, despite various barriers and difficulties in doing so.

A special thank you goes to our friend and mentor, John Stockley. John's invaluable knowledge of Maverick County history and World War II made him our technical advisor who ensured that we accurately portrayed each story told.

A special thank-you also goes to Maxine Payne-Kennedy for the long hours of transcribing and summarizing the oral histories.

A special thank-you goes out to another life-long friend, Linda Moreno for her creative advice on graphic design and social media.

Thank you to the Maverick County Clerk, Sara Montemayor, and her staff for assisting us while researching the hundreds of discharge documents of the veterans featured in our book.

Thank you to Rex McBeth and C. Escontrias for allowing us to photocopy hundreds of news clippings from the Eagle Pass newspaper, "The Guide" (1941-1944).

A very special thank you to our daughters, Ellen Munter Schwabe and Lisa Munter, for all of their help and support during this lengthy project. We love you very much!!

We would humbly like to extend our sincere thanks to the following individuals and organizations:

Tere Abascal-Ramírez; Ginny Adair; Kay Adams; Ritchie Avants; Alfred Baron; Irma Barrientos; Bobby Barrientos; Leslie Beattie; Brenda Benavides; Francis Blumenthal; Margo Campos; Margarito Carbajal; Minerva Carroll; Tony Castaneda; Bobo Castro; Liliana Ceniceros; Glen Claybrook; Faye Copland; Michael Copland; Kay Cunningham; Rick Cunningham; Albert Daniel; Bradley Davis; Jesus De la Garza; Phillip De la Peña; Danny Farhat; Sandra Farhat; Marcie Fenster; Guillermo Flores; Sherrie Foster; Petra Gil; Henry Gonzales; Pat Goodson; Concepción Harper; Ricky Harper; A.J. Hausman; Orbilia Hayes; Robert Helms; Ed Hernández; Donald Jackson; Robert Jackson; Sandra Jackson; Sammy Juve; Casey Lang; Melissa Lara-Cruz; Elby Leighton; Larry Levine; General Homer I. Lewis; Anna López; Vickie Maldonado; Brandon Maldonado; Alicia Moncada; Pipa Maurer; Roberto Mireles; Betsy Morgan; Mark Munter; Catherine Munter; Maurice Munter; Rosa O'Donnell; Maxine Payne-Kennedy; Mario Ramírez; Vangie Reza (Yzaguirre); Jerry Rhodes; David Riskind; Miriam Riskind; Corky Rubio; Helen Rubio; Hugo Sánchez; Manuel Sánchez; Sylvia Sánchez; Julio Santos-Coy (deceased); Tibor Schecter; Albert Schwartz (deceased); Joseph M. "Pepe" Schwartz; Terri Schwartz; Julie Schwartz; Nancy Schwartz; Annie Schwartz-Simansky; Rosalie Shannon; Sonia Shannon; Reba Shofner; Sammye Smallwood; Jeff Taylor; Greg Torres; Dawn Valdez; Nancy Vela; Cecilia Wittels (deceased); Ernie Wueste; Ward Wueste; Michael Yeager; The Briscoe History Center, University of Texas; and The National World War II Museum, New Orleans

APPENDIX

GLOSSARY OF TERMS

•Airborne Forces:
Airborne forces are military units, usually light infantry, set up to be moved by aircraft and "dropped" into battle, usually by parachute.

•Ardennes:
The Ardennes or also known as the Ardennes Forest is a mountainous region primarily in Belgium and Luxembourg but stretches into Germany and France. Germany attacked the Allies through this region on May 1940 to begin the war in the West; and again in December 1944 (the Battle of the Bulge).

•Army Air Corps:
The Air Corps became the branch for Army aviation in 1926. A few years later, in 1935, General Headquarters (GHQ) Air Force was created for centralized control of aviation combat units within the continental United States. They were separate but coordinated with the Air Corps. This arrangement existed in the period leading up to United States entry into WWII. There were two aviation organizations: the Air Corps managed supplies and equipment and training while the GHQ Airforce had operational units.

•Army Air Forces:
The Army Air Forces (AAF) came into being on June 20, 1941, six months before Pearl Harbor. As war approached, Secretary of War Henry L. Stimson and Army Chief of Staff George C. Marshall saw the need for a stronger role for Army aviation. Consequently they created the Army Air Forces with General H. H. (Hap) Arnold as its head. Army Air Forces attained quasi autonomy in March 1942, a few months after they entered the war. Acting under authority of the War Powers Act, Secretary Stimson approved a major War Department reorganization. By executive order the Army Air Force was divided into 3 forces: Army Air Forces, Army Ground Forces, and the Services of Supply (which in 1943 became the Army Service Forces). Significantly, as Commanding General of the AAF, General Hap Arnold became a member of the WWII Joint Chiefs of Staff along with the Army Chief of Staff (General Marshall), the Chief of Naval Operations (Admiral Ernest J. King), and President Roosevelt's principal military adviser (Admiral William D. Leahy).

•Bataan Death March:
Bataan Death March was the infamous forced march of of 75,000 U.S. and Filipino prisoners of war captured by the Japanese on the Bataan Peninsula following the fall of the Philippines. As many as 18,000 POWs died from dehydration, mistreatment or outright murder during the week-long, 60-mile ordeal.

- **Battle of the Bulge:**
Battle of the Bulge is the last major offensive by the Germans in WWII launched against the Allies in the West through the Ardennes region of Belgium on December 16, 1944. The unattained goal was to reach the port of Antwerp, thereby cutting the Allied armies in two.

- **Battalion:**
The battalion is a military unit which is divided into a number of companies. It is typically commanded by a lieutenant colonel.

- **Company:**
The company is a military unit, consisting of 80-250 soldiers which usually consists of a two or more platoons with a company headquarters. It is most often commanded by a captain or major.

- **Corpsman:**
Enlisted medical specialist who serves in the U.S. Navy and Marine Corps.

- **Division:**
A division is a large military unit, usually consisting of between 10,000 to 20,000 soldiers. The division is composed of several regiments. It is most often commanded by a general.

- **Gold Star Mother Flag:**
A service flag with a gold star is issued to every mother who lost a child in WWII. The flag was displayed in the window in the home to designate that a member of the family has died in the war.

- **Guadalcanal:**
The Battle of Guadalcanal was the first major offensive and a decisive victory for the Allies in the Pacific Theater. The U.S. Marines launched a surprise attack in August 1942 and took control of the air base under construction in the Solomon Islands. This was important to control the sea lines of commununication between U.S. and Australia.

- **Iwo Jima:**
Battle of Iwo Jima from February 19 to March 26, 1945 was a major battle in which the U.S. Marines landed on and eventually captured the Island. Iwo Jima is located 650 miles from Japan, midway between Japan and American bomber bases based in the Marianas Islands. More Medals of Honor were awarded for actions on Iwo Jima than in any other Marine Corps battle. As one of the bloodiest battle in the Pacific, the Japanese fought the entire battle underground with 16 miles of tunnels and 1,500 rooms. The Navy Seabees rebuilt the landing strips which were used as emergency landing strips for USAAF B-29s.

- **KIA:**
Military abbreviation for "killed in action."

APPENDIX

•Leyte Gulf:
The Leyte Gulf was the site of the Pacific battle on October 22 - October 27, 1944, that put an end to the Japanese fleet as an offensive force.

•Leyte Island:
The first Philippine island retaken by the United States (October 1944-March 1945) from the Japanese. 'Better Leyte than never".

•Marshall Islands:
Marshall Islands is the Pacific island group east of Micronesia that includes Eniwetok, Kwajelein and other atolls U.S. forces retook from Japanese military occupation in early 1944, as part of their island-hopping campaign, after the Gilbert Islands and before the Mariana Islands.

•MIA:
Military abbreviation for "missing in action."

•Normandy:
Normandy is a region of northwest France and location of the June 6, 1944, Allied invasion of Western Europe (operation Overlord) which involved more than 150,000 men and 5,000 ships. This was also called the D-Day invasion.

•Okinawa:
Japanese-occupied island halfway between southern Japan and Taiwan and site of the largest amphibious assault of WWII, starting April 1, 1945. The almost two-month long battle cost 12,500 U.S., more than 60,000 Japanese, and between 75,000-140,000 civilian lives.

•Omaha Beach:
D-Day beach assaulted by the U.S. 1st and 29th Infantry Divisions on June 6, 1944. Known as "Bloody Omaha" due to the large number of American deaths that day.

•Pearl Harbor:
A sneak attack on the naval base at Pearl Harbor in the Hawaiian Islands on December 7, 1941 by more than 350 Japanese aircraft.

•Platoon:
A platoon is a subdivision of a company-sized military unit, normally consisting of 2 or more squads. It is usually commanded by a lieutenant. A typical platoon consists of around 15 to 30 soldiers.

•Ploesti:
Ploesti was a vast complex of oil refinery facilities located 30 miles north of Bucharest, Romania. It supplied 60% of refined oil to keep the German war machine running during WWII. The Allies conducted air raids over the city on August 1, 1943, and again in April 1944, to destroy these facilities.

•Quartermaster Corps:
The Army's Quartermaster Corps was responsible for providing various supplies to the Army in all theaters.

•Regiment:
A regiment usually consists of 2 or more battalions and is usually commanded by a colonel.

•Seabees:
The Seabees is a construction battalion where U.S. Navy engineering units were assigned to clear jungles, to build roads and airfields and to construct ports and bases.

•Squad:
The squad is smallest unit of an organization in the U.S. Army. Number of men varies from 5 to 16.

•U.S.S. Arizona:
U.S.S. Arizona was a battleship sunk by Japanese during their attack on Pearl Harbor. 1,177, more than half of the American deaths on December 7, 1941, resulted from this ship's sinking.

•Utah Beach
Utah Beach was a code name for one of the 5 sectors of the Allied invasion of German occupied France in Normandy on D- Day June 6, 1944. The assault primarily by the U.S. 4th Infantry Division and the 70th Tank Battalion, was supported by the 82nd and 101st Airborne Division.

•Victory Mail:
Victory Mail operated during WWII to expedite mail service for American armed forces overseas. Moving a large volume of wartime mail posed a huge problem for the Post Office and the armed forces. Officials sought to reduce the bulk and weight of letters. "V-Mail" used standard stationery and microfilmed the letters to produce a lighter, smaller cargo. The letters could reach military personnel faster, making space for other war supplies.

SOURCE: http://www.aafha.org/

APPENDIX

MEDALS OF WORLD WAR II

Air Medal
The Air Medal (AM) is given to military personnel for meritorious achievement while participating in aerial flight; awards may also be given to acknowledge single acts of merit or heroism. The AM is mainly intended to recognize those personnel who are on current crew member or non-crew member flying status which requires them to engage in aerial flight on a regular and frequent basis in the pursuit of their primary duties. However, the AM may also be granted to other particular individuals whose combat obligations require regular and frequent flying in other than a passenger status, or individuals who complete a specifically noteworthy act while performing the function of a crew member but who are not on flying status. These individuals must accomplish a distinct contribution to the operational land combat mission or to the mission of the aircraft in flight. The AM was established on May 11, 1942 and was awarded retroactive to September 8, 1939.

Army Good Conduct Medal
The Good Conduct Medal is awarded to any active-duty enlisted member of the United States military who completes three consecutive years of "honorable and faithful service". Such service implies that a standard enlistment was completed without any non-judicial punishments, disciplinary infractions, or court martial offenses. During times of war, the Good Conduct Medal may be awarded for one year of faithful service.

American Campaign Medal
To be awarded the American Campaign Medal, a service member was required to either perform one year of duty within the continental borders of the United States, or perform 30 days consecutive/60 non-consecutive days of duty outside the borders of the United States but within the American Theater of Operations. The eligibility dates of the American Campaign Medal were from December 7, 1941 to March 2, 1946.

Branch Insignia Collar Device
U.S. Army branch insignia badges represent each individual service member's specific field of service. Each soldier – both enlisted personnel and officers – wear their branch insignia badge on his or her formal uniform (Class A or Army dress blues) denoting their particular skill set. The U.S. enlisted disk is worn on the right collar and the branch insignia on the left. The bomb insignia shown here is for Ordnance personnel.

Bronze Star Medal
The Bronze Star Medal (BSM or BSV) is an award presented to United States Armed Forces personnel for bravery, acts of merit or meritorious service. When awarded for combat heroism it is awarded with a V device for Valor. It is the fourth highest combat award of the Armed Forces. Originally created in February of 1944, this medal was retroactively awarded to many WWII veterans. During 1947, policy was put into place that authorized the retroactive award of the Bronze Star Medal to any serviceman who had received the Combat Infantryman Badge or the Combat Medical Badge. Both of

these badges required the recommendation of a commander and had to be accompanied with a citation. Additional awards of the Bronze Star Medal are represented by Oak Leaf Clusters in the Army and Air Force while 5/16th inch Gold Stars are used by the Navy, Marine Corps and Coast Guard. Foreign Service Personnel are eligible for the award if they are serving with US Armed Forces.

Combat Infantry Badge

The Combat Infantry Badge (CIB) is awarded to Army enlisted infantry, infantry officers in the grade of Colonel or below, as well as warrant officers with an infantry. Subsequent to December 6, 1941, recipients must have satisfactorily performed duty while assigned as a member of an infantry during any period in which such unit was engaged in active ground combat. The recipient must be personally present and under hostile fire while in a unit actively engaged in ground combat with the enemy. The CIB and the Expert Infantry Badge were created primarily as a means of recognizing the sacrifices of the infantrymen who were disproportionately likely to be killed or wounded during World War II.

European-African-Middle Eastern Campaign Medal

The European-African-Middle Eastern Campaign Medal is awarded for any service performed between December 7, 1941 and March 2, 1946 provided such service was performed in the geographical theater areas of Europe, North Africa, or the Middle East. For those service members who participated in multiple battle campaigns, service stars are authorized to the decoration.

Silver Star Medal

The Silver Star (SS) Medal is a decoration presented by the U.S. military to recognize gallantry in battle. It is the third highest ranking award that can be received for valiant actions and may be awarded to any service member of the Armed Forces who is recognized for heroism in one of the following situations: Action against an enemy of the United States, Action while serving in military operations involving conflict with a foreign foe or action while serving with allied forces in armed combat against an opposing force where the United States in not the aggressor.

Purple Heart Medal

The Purple Heart Medal (PH) is a decoration presented in the name of the President of the United States to recognize members of the U.S. military who have been wounded or killed in battle. It differs from other military decorations in that a "recommendation" from a superior is not required, but rather individuals are entitled based on meeting certain criteria found in AR 600-8-22. Personnel wounded or killed by friendly fire are also eligible for this award as long as the injuries were received in combat and with the intention of inflicting harm on the opposing forces. The Purple Heart Medal is not awarded for non-combat injuries and commanders must take into account the extent of enemy involvement in the wound.

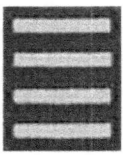

Overseas Service Bar

Army Overseas Service Bars are worn on an Army uniform to represent the cumulative amount of time spent overseas, meaning one bar could be earned for each 6 month deployment. A service member may be presented multiple Overseas Service Bars in cases where several years were spent in an overseas combat zone. Multiple Overseas Service Bars are worn simultaneously, extending vertically on the sleeve of the uniform.

Service Stripe
A service stripe, commonly called a hash mark, is a decoration of the United States military which is presented to members of the U.S. military to denote length of service. The United States Army awards each stripe for three years of service. These particular service stripes are intended for the old Army Dress Blue uniform.

The Distinguished Flying Cross
The Distinguished Flying Cross Medal (DFC) is an award that is bestowed upon any officer or enlisted personnel of the United States Armed Forces who distinguishes themselves in support of operations by "heroism or extraordinary achievement while participating in aerial flight." The medal was created on July 2nd, 1926 and the first awards were bestowed by President Calvin Coolidge on December 21st, 1927 to ten Army Air Corps aviators who participated in the US Army Pan-American Flight. Two of those awards were bestowed posthumously as they had died in a mid-air collision during that flight. The first person to actually be presented with the medal was Charles Lindbergh after returning from his trans-Atlantic Flight.

While it has been used to honor both civilian and military achievement, it is now almost exclusively a military award. Also, due to the advancements in aerial technology, the requirements for the award have varied from conflict to conflict, theater to theater.

World War II Victory Medal
This medal commemorates military service during World War II and is awarded to any member of the United States military, including members of the armed forces of the Government of the Philippine Islands, who served on active duty, or as a reservist, between December 7, 1941 and December 31, 1946.

Army of Occupation Medal
To be awarded the Army of Occupation Medal, a service member was required to have performed at least thirty consecutive days of military duty within a designated geographical area of military occupation. The Army of Occupation Medal was presented with a campaign clasp, denoting either European or Asian service, depending on the region in which occupation service had been performed.

BIBLIOGRAPHY

PRIMARY SOURCES

Department of the Army, Death Records, DCS Personnel & Logistics. 200 Stovall Street, Alexandria, VA 22331.

Farhat, Danny. Sent letter on behalf of George Farhat

Maverick County Clerk Office Discharge Documents

Oral Histories:

> Adan, Jose. Eagle Pass, TX 2013
> Beard, Elby. Telephonic interview
> Beattie, Leslie, Manager of Maverick County International Airport, 2015
> Benavides, Raul. Eagle Pass, TX
> Blake, Ray (Major). Telephonic interview 2011
> Cunningham, Kay. Quemado, TX on behalf of Scottie Carver, 2013
> Cunningham, Rick, Telephonic interview 2014
> Frisch, Judith. Los Angeles, CA, Holocaust survivor & niece of Sam Schwartz
> Garcia, Arturo, Eagle Pass, TX 2012
> Garcia, Rodrigo. Eagle Pass, TX, 2011
> Gil, Petra. Eagle Pass, TX, 2015 on behalf of Alberto Gil
> Hausman, AJ. San Antonio, TX on behalf of Harold Hausman
> Mezey, Edith. Los Angeles, CA, Holocaust survivor & niece of Sam Schwartz
> Michaels, Sam. Telephonic interview 2015
> Perry, Billy, Quemado, Texas 2014.
> Ramirez, Rogelio. Eagle Pass, TX 2010 interview on behalf of Gerardo Ramirez "Calulo"
> Reyes, Rodolfo. Del Rio, TX, 2012
> Riskind, Rueben. Jewish War Veterans Project, Jewish Community Center, San Antonio, TX
> Rubio, Jesus Ramiro. San Antonio, TX, 2013
> Schofner, Betty. Quemado, TX interviewed on behalf of the Adams and Schofner Family.
> Shannon, Rosalie. Eagle Pass, TX on behalf of William Shannon
> Yzquierdo, Jesus. Eagle Pass, TX 2010

SECONDARY SOURCES

"Albert Einstein –Biographical." Nobelprize.org. Nobel Media AB 2014. Web. 11 Oct 2015 http://www.nobelprize.org/nobel_prizes/physics/laureates/1921/einstein-bio.html

American Heritage Center Foundation. "Supporting the Nation: The Women's Army Auxiliary Corps & Women's Army Corps" https://www.armyheritage.org/images/stories/Education_Content/Anna_Mae_Hays/WAC-WWII_Sidebar.pdf

Anonymous. *A Woman in Berlin. New York*: Picador, 2000.

Atkinson, Rick, *The Guns at Last Light*. New York: Henry Holt and Company, 2013.

Berebaum, Michael. "Nurnberg Laws- German History," Encyclopaedia Britannica

http://www.britannica.com/topic/Nurnberg-Laws

Boffey, Phillip M. New York Times February 10, 2002 Still a Mystery: Nazi Germany's Atomic Bomb Failure http://www.fpp.co.uk/History/General/atombomb/OOF100202.htm

Brosveen, Emily. "World War II Internment Camps," *Handbook of Texas Online* (http://www.tshaonline.org/handbook/online/articles/quwby), accessed October 07, 2015. Uploaded on June 15, 2010. Published by the Texas State Historical Association

Central Identification Command, Joint POW/MIA Accounting Command 310 Worchester Ave, Hickam AFB, HI 96853.

Chambers, John Whiteclay "National Defense Acts" The Oxford Companion to American Military History. 2000. Encyclopedia.com. 3 Oct. 2015. <http://www.encyclopedia.com>.

Cowen, Tyler, "How did America pay for World War II Marginal Revolution Small Steps toward a much better world" http://marginalrevolution.com/marginalrevolution/2010/09/how-did-american-pay-for-world-war-ii.htm

Discovering the Secrets of Mexico. "International Nacho Festival at Piedras Negras," http://mexicolesstraveled.com/nachofest.htm

Dower, John W. *War Without Mercy, Race & Power In the Pacific War.* New York: Pantheon Books, 1986.

Eagle Eye Base Newspaper, various articles, Dolph Briscoe Center for American History, Micro film collection of University of Texas

The Eagle Pass News Guide, various articles 1941-1944.

Fierman, Floyd S. *The Schwartz Family of El Paso*, University of Texas at El Paso: Texas Western Press, 1980

Fleming, Thomas. *The New Dealers War.* New York: Basic Books, 2001.

Gateway to Women's History. Ola Rexroat Oral History Interview, September 8, 2006

Gill, Anton. *A Dance between Flames Berlin between the Wars*, New York: Carroll & Graf Publishers, Inc., 1993.

Harper, Rick. *Rodriquez...Texas Ranger.* Bloomington: iUniverse LLC, 2013.

Hastings, Max. *Catastrophe 1914 Europe Goes to War.* New York: Alfred A Knopf, 2013.

Hastings, Max. *Inferno the World at War 1939-1945.* New York: Vintage Books, 2011.

Kennedy, David. Freedom from Fear the American People in Depression and War, 1929-1945. New York: Oxford University Press, 1999.

Kessler-Harris, Alice. *Out of Work: A History of Wage-Earning Women in the United States,* New York: Oxford University Press, 1982

Kinsal, Al. *Graveyard of the Confederacy.* Fort Duncan Restoration Association by Border Studies Center, 1996.

Library of Congress, *World War II Companion*. New York: Simon & Schuster, 2007.

Lowder, Hughston E., *Batfish The Champion "Submarine-Killer"* New Jersey: Prentice Hall, 1980.

Munter, Billy. "Texas Biggest Gravity Canal" Junior Historian, 1968.

Nagorski, Andrew. *Hitlerland*. New York: Simon & Schuster, 2012.

National WASP World War II Musuem, "Jackie Cochran Biography" https://www.google.com/?gws_rd=ssl#q=Jackie+Cochran

Nicholls, William. *Christian Antisemitism A History of Hate*. New Jersey: Jason Aronson Inc., 1995.

Ochoa, Ruben E. "Maverick County" Texas State Historical Association. June 15, 2010, Modified on November 25, 2013 http://www.tshsonline.org/handbook/online/artiles/hem06.

PBS "American Experience- The WASP and the B-29 " www.pbs.org/wgbh/amex/flygirls/sfeature/waspsb29.html

Paz, Maria Emilia. *Strategy, Security, and Spies Mexico and the U.S. as Allies in World War II.*, University Park, Pennsylvania: The Pennsylvania State University Press, 1997.

Peters, Gerhard and Woolley, John T. "Franklin D. Roosevelt: Fireside Chat *The American Presidency Project*. http://www.presidency.ucsb.edu/ws/?pid=16056.

Rosie the Riveter- United States History. http://www.u-s-history.com/pages/h1656.html

Shaw, Anthony. *World War II Day by Day*. New York: Chartwell Books, Inc., 2012.

Schwartz, Albert.Terry Allen de La Mesa Collection at University of Texas, El Paso TX, 1976.

Shirer, William. *The Rise and Fall of the Third Reich, A History of Nazi Germany*, New York: Simon and Schuster. 1960

Smith, Jean Edward. *Eisenhower in War and Peace*. New York: Random House, 2012.

Smithsonian Center for Education and Museum Studies. " Wartime Shortages" http://www.smithsonianeducation.org/idealabs/wwii/

Taylor, A.J.P. *The Origins of the Second World War*. New York: Simon & Schuster Paperbacks, 2005.

The Eagle Pass News Guide, various articles 1941-1944

"The Triumph of Hitler--- The Nuremberg Laws." The History Place 2001 http://www.historyplace.com/worldwar2/triumph/tr-will.htm

Texas Historical Commision Crystal City (Family) Internment Camp http://www.thc.state.tx.us/preserve/projects-and-programs/military-history/texas-world-war-ii/world-war-ii-japanese-american-2

Texas Woman's University. " History of the WASP" http://www.twu.edu/library/wasp-history.asp

Texas Woman's University. " WASP Training" http://www.twu.edu/library/wasp-training.asp

Tuchman, Barbara W. *Stilwell and the American Experience in China, 1911-45*.New York: Grove Press, 1970.

United to End Genocide "Past Genocides and Mass Atrocities" http://endgenocide.org/learn/past-genocides/?id=gad&gclid=CMSPu8ztt8gCFYM-aQodacgD1A

United States Holocaust Memorial Museum, Washington, D.C. "Holocaust Encyclopedia – Aushwitz http://www.ushmm.org/wlc/en/article.php?ModuleId=10007710

United States Holocaust Memorial Museum, Washington, D.C. "Holocaust Encyclopedia – Mobil Killing Squads http://www.ushmm.org/wlc/en/article.php?ModuleId=10005189

United States Holocaust Memorial Museum, Washington, D.C. "Holocaust Encyclopedia - Warsas http://www.ushmm.org/wlc/en/article.php?ModuleId=1000506

United States Holocaust Memorial Museum, Washington, D.C. "Holocaust Encyclopedia - What is Genocide?" http://www.ushmm.org/wlc/en/article.php?ModuleId=10007043

United States Holocaust Memorial Museum, Washington, D.C. "Holocaust Encyclopedia - Jewish Population of Europe in 1933: Population Data by Country" http://www.ushmm.org/wlc/en/article.php?ModuleId=10005161

Ware, Susan. "Women and the Great Depression" The Gilder Lehrman Institute of American History. https://www.gilderlehrman.org/history-by-era/great-depression/essays/women-and-great-depression

Ware, Susan. *Holding Their Own: American Women in the 1930*, Boston: Twayne Publishers, 1982.

Wein, Berel adapted by Yaakov Aster, "Free Crash Course in Jewish History Jewish Europe Between the Wars" Jewish History.org, http://www.jewishhistory.org/jewish-europe-between-the-wars/

Wendorff, Andrew March 24,2014 German Nuclear Program Before and During World War II http://large.stanford.edu/courses/2014/ph241/wendorff2

Wessels, " Farming In The 1940s- Victory Gardens" Living History Farm http://www.livinghistoryfarm.org/farminginthe40s/crops_02.html

Wilkes, William C. and Standifer, Mary M., "Texas State Guard," *Handbook of Texas Online* (http://www.tshaonline.org/handbook/online/articles/qqt01), accessed October 07, 2015. Uploaded on June 15, 2010. Published by the Texas State Historical Association.

Women in the US Army "WAAC/WAC" http://www.army.mil/women/wac.html.

Yergin, Daniel. *The Prize The Epic Quest for Oil, Money & Power,* New York: Free Press, 2010.

About the Authors:

William J. Munter is an accomplished Immigration Attorney who was raised in Eagle Pass, Maverick County, Texas. He is an avid history aficionado and has immeasurable love & passion for his community of Eagle Pass, Texas and Maverick County. He has written several articles to include "Biggest Gravity Canal in Texas," "Sam Schwartz and the Aztec Theater" and "The Jewish History of the Texas Middle Corridor.", authored at the age of 15. Munter is a graduate of The University of Texas and South Texas College of Law.

Judy Munter, CPA is a charter member of the WWII Museum in New Orleans and the Texas Jewish Historical Society, along with her husband, William J. Munter, Judy is a graduate of The University of Houston.

Jolene Garcia, United States Air Force, retired.

Please email any additional information, comments or questions to Warriorsoftheriogrande@gmail.com